D0450604

FIRST AMONG EQUALS

FIRST AMONG EQUALS

The Role of the Chief Academic Officer

James Martin, James E. Samels & Associates

The Johns Hopkins University Press   *Baltimore & London*

© 1997 The Johns Hopkins University Press
All rights reserved. Published 1997
Printed in the United States of America on acid-free recycled paper
06 05 04 03 02 01 00 99 98 97   5 4 3 2 1

The Johns Hopkins University Press
2715 North Charles Street
Baltimore, Maryland 21218-4319
The Johns Hopkins Press Ltd., London

Library of Congress Cataloging-in-Publication Data will be found at the end
of this book.

A catalog record for this book is available from the British Library.
ISBN 0-8018-6673-1

Contents

Preface

Traditionally, the chief academic officer of an American college has been its academic dean. However, in recent years a new position, vice president for academic affairs, or academic vice president, has emerged, and the person in this position has become the principal formulator of academic policies. This new title is accompanied by an extensive set of new responsibilities, many of them more management oriented than those fulfilled by traditional deans. In fact, the vice president for academic affairs or, on a university campus, the provost now serves as the principal connection between individual student progress and the overall implementation of new academic programs. He or she oversees the development of explosive new information technologies while also shaping traditional curricula and standards for teaching effectiveness. Finally, the complex organizational linkages among budget management, strategic planning, alumni cultivation, grant writing, capital campaign participation, government relations, and the institution's most complex legal questions are also often in his or her purview. To compound these challenges, many campuses have failed to keep pace with the significant changes taking place in the lives of their students. One Boston academic vice president remarks that "trustees, alumni, and even students do not realize how we are forced to build 1990s policies with 1950s resources."

This is a handbook of best practices for college and university chief academic officers. Each chapter looks beyond the policies of the 1990s to envision the campus in the year 2000 and to articulate the restructuring necessary to achieve educational excellence as traditional "communities of scholars" are transformed into "learning organizations."

Between 1975 and 1985, the number of nonfaculty professionals on American campuses grew by 60 percent and faculty members by only 6 percent, according to the U.S. Department of Education. Between 1985 and 1990, those same figures were 28 percent for nonfaculty and 9 percent for faculty. Significantly, the majority of individuals in *both* categories are now supervised by a vice president for academic affairs or a provost. In the past, the dean of curriculum, the director of academic advising, the director of continuing education, and others reported to the academic dean. Today, those in positions such as chief financial officer, business officer, college counsel, even the staff psychiatrist, typically report to the chief academic officer.

Our goal is to address the full scope of roles and responsibilities of those in this position as no previous study has done and yet also preserve the practical qualities of a resource guide for working professionals. In each of the following chapters, a chief academic officer (CAO), sometimes in collaboration with a senior administrator from that particular area of academic operations, articulates current best practices for that aspect of institutional leadership. Each contributor projects this model to the year 2000 and outlines specific advances that must occur in this area of higher education management and policy development. The volume also includes numerous boxed checklists for easy reference in areas such as models for effective governance, budget planning, faculty professional development, curriculum revision, accreditation, and legal audits.

The overall text has been divided into three sections. Part I addresses broader issues connecting the chief academic officer to the educational mission of the institution. In the opening chapter, Martin and Samels outline the current status of chief academic officers at U.S. colleges and universities. They provide a historical context for the position, a review of its current roles and responsibilities, a discussion of five critical questions confronting every CAO, a list of ten characteristics that distinguish the "new" chief academic officer, and an introduction to the book's broader concerns. Chapters 2, 3, and 4 focus on the core of the vice president's responsibilities for the faculty and curriculum. Chapter 2, by Roy A. Austensen, provost and vice president for academic affairs at Valparaiso University, examines the spectrum of responsibilities the chief academic officer holds in relation to the faculty, including faculty relations, recruitment, and professional development, as well as the challenge to shape institutional faculty culture, often while holding faculty status in the process. Chapter 3, by James R. Coffman, provost at Kansas State University, addresses the fundamental responsibility each chief academic officer holds for the ongoing campus curriculum review process. This chapter also assesses the impact of such new technologies as computer-assisted curriculum, distance learning, and telecommunications on

traditional curricular models and student learning styles. Mark G. Edelstein, president of Diablo Valley College, and former vice president for
academic affairs at College of the Redwoods, focuses in chapter 4 on the
critical roles a chief academic officer plays within a college or university
governance system while also detailing a blueprint for productive gov-
ernance-based relationships across the institution.

Part II of the narrative focuses on specific relationships with the principal members of the campus's leadership team. Chapter 5 outlines the
best model for an effective relationship between the vice president for
academic affairs and her or his supervisor, the president. Alice Bourke
Hayes, president of the University of San Diego, and formerly executive
vice president and provost at St. Louis University, also clarifies the major
responsibilities each chief academic officer holds in relation to the chair
and members of the board of trustees. Chapter 6, by Paula Hooper Mayhew, vice president for academic affairs and dean of the faculty at Marymount Manhattan College, outlines the responsibilities a vice president
for academic affairs holds for the quality of student life—resident and
commuter, graduate and postgraduate—and for institutional diversity
and affirmative action. In chapter 7, Michael A. Baer, provost at Northeastern University, and Peter A. Stace, vice president for enrollment at
Fordham University, explore an area new to many senior academic officers: the role and responsibilities of the CAO in the admissions and
enrollment management processes. In chapter 8, the complexities of integrating financial management and budget planning with academic leadership are addressed by Michael C. Gallagher, president of Mesa State
College, and former vice president for academic affairs at Idaho State
University.

Part III articulates the responsibilities of the chief academic officer to
the larger, external community. Chapter 9, by Jon M. Strolle, associate
provost, and Ruth Larimer, dean, of the Graduate School of Language
and Educational Linguistics at the Monterey Institute of International
Studies focuses on the expanding area of government relations, contract
and grant administration, and patents. They outline the complex responsibilities a chief academic officer must now manage regarding the
academic, financial, and governmental implications of faculty research.
In chapter 10, Georgia E. Lesh-Laurie, interim chancellor and former
vice chancellor of academic and student affairs at the University of Colorado at Denver, examines a relatively new set of external responsibilities for many chief academic officers, including institutional advancement, fund-raising, and the cultivation of alumni networks. Chapter 11,
by Samels and Martin, provides a proactive set of guidelines for chief
academic officers concerning legal issues and liability, collective bargain-

ing, and accreditation. In the concluding chapter, Martin and Samels consider the role of the chief academic officer in the year 2000 and link its vitality and success to initiatives in such areas as leadership development and entrepreneurship now emerging on many campuses. The book closes with a bibliography of pertinent readings on the position of chief academic officer.

We thank four individuals in particular for their contributions to this volume. Jacqueline Wehmueller, our editor at the Johns Hopkins University Press, once again challenged and guided us with skill, patience, and ingenuity. Carol Chauncey, our word-processing assistant, swiftly and precisely transformed hundreds of drafts into a coherent final document. Arlene Lieberman provided helpful research for the chapter on legal issues. Finally, Sheila Murphy deserves thanks for providing the book's title, noting that "first among equals" is both symbol and reality for chief academic officers.

J. M.
J. E. S.

I

The Academic Mission

First among Equals: The Current Roles of the Chief Academic Officer

James Martin and James E. Samels

The turn of the century promises to be one of the most challenging periods in the history of American higher education. Chief academic officers at institutions in every category will be asked to provide leadership, accountability, and innovation for their campuses and for higher education as a whole. Nevertheless, as faculty rights and responsibilities and presidential prerogatives have become increasingly clarified over the past two decades, the role and status of the chief academic officer has remained a blur at many colleges and universities. In order to shape academic policy and implement even basic operational decisions, provosts and academic vice presidents will find it advantageous to understand and define their place in the institution.

The Chief Academic Officer: Dean, Provost, or Vice President?

At almost every American college or university founded prior to 1950, the first chief academic officer was the president. Research on the early years of American higher education depicts a benevolent chief executive, able to serve all institutional constituencies with equal amounts of patience, passion, wit, and imagination. That the campus's primary "academic" officer, and moral force, was the president was never questioned, nor should this historic figure be confused with today's "chief executive officer."

In 1870, Charles W. Eliot, president of Harvard, appointed the institution's—and American higher education's—first dean to relieve him of some portion of the college's "administration." As initial deans on other campuses were installed as "secretaries" to their faculty colleagues, Eliot described the position as work performed "in conformity with rules laid down by a faculty. . . . In most cases [the dean] is also a professor and an active teacher, who gives part of his time to administrative work."[1] More than a century later, Eliot's observations on the attributes of a worthy dean provide a nostalgic backdrop. "The men who are most successful in the work of a dean are neither dry nor gushing, neither rude nor soft; they are alert, attentive, sympathetic and hopeful. . . . the work of a dean makes a serious demand upon a conscientious man whose feelings are quick; so that deans are often compelled to retire from service in consequence of the incessant drain on their sympathies."[2]

American campuses grew in size and complexity from the 1880s onward, and as larger universities began to divide themselves into various schools and colleges, "dean of the college" became the most common appointment to head these new, inter-related subdivisions. The title "academic dean" appears gradually to have gained prominence as the overall academic governance of an institution eventually transcended the narrow, original focus on one of its colleges. Over the course of the first half of the twentieth century, academic deans gradually came to function as second in command to the president, assuming authority for all areas of institutional operation in his or her absence. This period produced its own literature reflecting an emerging lore of the deanship and elevating particular individuals to an unprecedented, mythical status, often aided by popular opinion and what William DeVane termed in 1964, "the Hollywood conception of a college."[3]

During these same decades, the title "provost" became associated with the chief academic officer at research universities, while at many state-supported colleges and universities and midsized private institutions, the new titles "vice president for academic affairs," or "academic vice president," were commonly used. In fact, by 1962, one author noted that the terms academic vice president, provost, and dean of faculties were interchangeable.[4] Since the 1970s, the position of academic dean has been transformed, on a growing number of campuses, from that of the overall chief academic officer to head of one or more units within the institution.

The responsibilities within each of these positions have also changed significantly since midcentury, with the provost and vice president for academic affairs exercising an ever widening scope of authority on the campus, far from the model Charles Eliot outlined a century ago. Whereas in 1961, only 621 higher education institutions offered master degrees, by 1985, the number had risen to 1,192 colleges and universities. Nationally, this degree elevation movement exerted steady pressure on participating institutions to "elevate" the institutional deanship to a more comprehensive academic vice presidency. Over this same period, the nation's more than one thousand public community colleges devised their own model for the chief academic officer's position creating the title dean of instruction," which had most probably been drawn from a combination of director of instruction in a public school and a generic higher education "dean."[5]

Well before the 1980s, however, most American campuses had experienced a permanent change in the range of authority ascribed to the traditional dean, with a vice president for academic affairs often assuming the daily managerial responsibility for the entire campus, or system, formerly exercised by the president. As Jonathan Fife and Eric Goodchild note in *Administration as a Profession*, academic administration has irreversibly evolved into its own "profession,"[6] with chief academic officers forced to choose between the familiarity of the classroom and the unpredictabilities of institutional budget planning and federal aid requirements, with no training and little preparation for the challenges involved.

The Context for Leadership: A National Profile of the Chief Academic Officer

John W. Gould surveyed 166 deans in the early 1960s. He found that only one-third of the deans rated formal training in administration "desirable," 36 percent had stopped teaching, and 71 percent had no experience when they were appointed. For these deans, from institutions ranging in size from four hundred students to more than twenty-two thousand, the responsibilities most demanding their time and skill, in order of descending importance, were as follows:

1. faculty relations and morale

2. recruitment of faculty

3. curriculum work

4. budget, promotions, personnel evaluation

5. committee work

6. routine administration

7. student counseling

In 1964, academic deans served on an average of seven committees, and they chaired an average of two. The deans had served an average of 6.6 years in their positions, and 18 percent spent an hour per day in conference with the president. Overall, a majority of those surveyed agreed that the faculty still should make the majority of educational decisions, with the dean "merely a more central participant in the process of discerning and adopting appropriate courses of action."[7]

By the time Richard Miller surveyed chief academic officers twenty-five years later, many aspects of the position, including its title, had changed noticeably. Miller polled 451 chief academic officers from a random, stratified group of institutions. The 73 percent response rate was weighted appropriately to reflect the span of all colleges and universities. Miller noted that "dean of the college" was "the traditional small college title"; "provost" and "vice president for academic affairs" were terms employed at larger institutions and universities. Eighty-one percent of those responding were male, with "significantly more" chief academic officers of two-year colleges being women.[8] By the late 1980s, the median for tenure in the position had dropped to 3.9 years, with almost one-quarter of those surveyed (22 percent) having been in the position for less than one year. Fewer than 14 percent had held their position for more than ten years. The typical chief academic officer in Miller's survey was a man, slightly younger than fifty years of age, who had held the position for fewer than four years.

In 1988, the proportion of chief academic officers surveyed who still taught had dropped to 42 percent from the 64 percent in Gould's survey, with only 26 percent pursuing research or publishing, the majority of which was now in higher education. On the issue of professional credentials, in an unrelated 1989 survey of 1,100 senior administrators at all categories of colleges and universities, Barbara K. Townsend and Michael D. Wiese asked respondents to compare a doctorate in higher education to a doctorate in an academic discipline as a qualifying degree for candidates for three types of positions: college presidency, student affairs management, and academic affairs. Sixty-two percent viewed a doctorate in higher education as "less preferable" than the traditional doctorate in an academic discipline for the academic affairs position.[9]

Miller notes a shift in the responsibilities for daily management of the campus. In the following list, percentages indicate on what proportion of campuses surveyed this area reported to the chief academic officer:

—academic units   85%

—library and learning resources   81%

—registrar   55%

—admissions   31%

—institutional research   23%

—institutional planning   19%

—student affairs   18%

—financial aid   11%

A New Kind of Higher Education Professional

In contrast with Gould's 1964 survey, Miller discerned a somewhat different pattern of activities requiring the most time each week. The new order was as follows:

—individual and small group meetings   32 hours each week

—mail and correspondence   7 hours

—social and ceremonial functions   6 hours

—planning and reading   2.5 hours [10]

The *1995 Higher Education Directory* identified approximately 29 percent of chief academic officers as female, after accounting for positions currently vacant, institutions that did not report a chief academic officer, and entries that did not indicate gender due to name similarity. Of the 3,277 institutions that did report a chief academic officer in that edition, 1,270 used a title such as "vice president for academic affairs" or "academic vice president." While the word "dean" appeared in the title at roughly the same number of colleges and universities, fewer than 700 schools in that group designated the individual specifically as "academic dean" or "dean of academic affairs," as opposed to "dean of the college" or "dean of faculty," as examples. The title "provost" was used at 512 institutions.

With these national and historical profiles as background, we now consider five of the most pressing questions confronting contemporary chief academic officers.

What Is the Nature and Scope of "Academic" Leadership?

The most critical question now confronting provosts, academic vice presidents, and deans concerns the nature and scope of "academic" leadership. In this instance, a distinction has been drawn between academic and administrative leadership. Based on interviews and discussions with more than two dozen chief academic officers, as well as participation for a decade in the Chief Academic Officers Think Tank sponsored by the New England Resource Center for Higher Education at the University of Massachusetts, Boston,[11] we note that the central challenge for those now holding a provostship or deanship is to understand how to define and then implement academic leadership on campus in a climate of changing faculty priorities, declining institutional resources, fickle student consumer preferences, and eroding public confidence.

On campuses where new "knowledge workers" are highly trained, highly specialized faculty members, a pivotal leadership challenge for the chief academic officer is to shape calls for faculty autonomy into authentic consensus while balancing this against the prerogatives of the president and trustees. Successful vice presidents for academic affairs learn how to control the symbolic framework of the campus, incorporating within it the student body, both part- and full-time faculty, and even the chair of the board.

There are new ways to think about the roles and functions of chief academic officers in exercising academic leadership. Estela M. Bensimon, Anna Neumann, and Robert Birnbaum describe academic leaders as, simultaneously, heads of a bureaucratic organization, a peer group, a political structure, and, finally, a system of myth and metaphor.[12] More than at any point in the past, it is the chief academic officer who now must draw each campus's competing, conflicting constituencies together to implement new forms of partnership and productivity, moving beyond traditional tensions in order to construct an effective, supportive framework for both teaching and learning.

Future provosts will be expected to combine passion, integrity, and intellectual coherence with the managerial competence of corporate executives into an unprecedented set of campus skills. In this process, academic managers will be required to master not only a traditional group of primary roles, including faculty advocacy, campus consensus building, academic policy formation, executive decision making, curricular innovation, and student counseling, but also one that is far less common: educational entrepreneurship. In short, academic leadership has come to include the responsibility, and liability, for new areas such as budget oversight, government relations, fund-raising, marketing, and legal affairs.

How Have External Forces Reshaped the Position of Chief Academic Officer?

In 1992, for the first time in more than twenty years, total state support for higher education declined over the previous year. During the period from 1992 to 1994, the rate of corporate philanthropic support to higher education came to a sudden halt as grants increasingly went to elementary and secondary school systems and special interest groups for the environment, health care, and social concerns. Simultaneous with this eroding financial support for higher education, national demographic trends have been changing dramatically. Between 1990 and 2010, the nonwhite youth population will increase in America by 4.4 million people, and the white youth population will decrease by 3.8 million. Minority students will constitute 40 percent of America's public school population in 2010, and over this same period, twenty states will become "youth poor," necessitating cutbacks in support for education.[13]

The authors of the Pew Higher Education Roundtable series, commenting on these recent developments, have stated that the changes most important to higher education are now external to it, including the ways in which "market forces" are shaping the academy. "Some institutions have understood well just how much and how fast their world is changing; others are only now feeling the shock of diminished resources and the rising demand for alternate services. . . . Our argument is simple and to the point: no institution will emerge unscathed from its confrontation with an external environment that is substantially altered and in many ways more hostile to colleges and universities.[14]

Many of the external forces that have reshaped our higher education system since the late 1960s, and the careers of most chief academic officers in the process, are now clear. Factors such as precipitous declines in federal and corporate support, an aging professoriate, expanding trustee involvement, shifting demographics, and changes in teaching and learning produced by telecommunications have become somewhat old business for the management of higher education. The more significant question for this study is how the next generation of provosts and academic vice presidents will respond to a newer, more formidable set of external challenges.

While it is fashionable to claim that "Americans experience more technological change in a single year than their grandparents witnessed in a lifetime,"[15] how many aspiring deans realize that the initial statements submitted by twenty-four hundred colleges and universities in compliance with the Federal Student Right-to-Know and Campus Security Act in 1990 revealed thirty murders, almost one thousand rapes, and more than thirty-two thousand burglaries on American campuses?[16] Unprecedented criminal behaviors form just one example of the forces that have caused many university administrators to rethink the ways they accomplish their agendas. Statistics such as these also reflect deeper trends now shaping future faculty and student expectations, yet they are rarely, if ever, incorporated into the orientation of a new chief academic officer.

Many higher education professionals are beginning to voice fears that the core experiences of academic life have begun to erode and disappear. Government statistics in 1994 confirm that the proportion of money used by all colleges for instruction and libraries is shrinking, while the amount spent on public relations, marketing, and fund-raising has steadily increased.[17] At the same time, some researchers speculate that students will soon be able to tap into any classroom or educational course in the world using their home "teleputer," leaving many institutions, and provosts, simply as "certifiers" of educational progress accomplished elsewhere.[18]

In the midst of, and in response to, this upheaval, many faculty members have gradually pulled away from their institutions, divisions, even their departments, and have chosen to focus on individual work in classrooms and the laboratories, offering loyalty not to their college or university but rather to a new definition of the "profession." As these teachers build their careers, they demonstrate fewer of the traditional allegiances to committees, governance, and faculty culture.

Little wonder that, in concert with their faculty colleagues, many chief academic officers wistfully recall the coherence and collegiality of the 1950s and 1960s, a time in which academic leadership seemed to flow more easily and naturally from the shared understandings that defined most campuses. However, with both large and small institutions ferociously committed to raising their positions in the annual college and university rankings in *U.S. News and World Report*, and collectively devastated if their school slips a single notch, chief academic officers now acknowledge, publicly as well as privately, that external forces have permanently reshaped the nature of their responsibilities.

What Role Should the Chief Academic Officer Play in Restructuring the Institution?

Zelda Gamson has characterized the collective life of contemporary higher education as "deeply flawed." From her perspective, "A sense of community is hard to find anywhere, even in small colleges. Collaborative projects among faculty often fail because of competitiveness, jealousy and territoriality. The gap between faculty and administration grows wider as resources shrink. . . . Pathologies in the larger society—family tragedies, substance abuse, racism, domestic violence—are overwhelming the healthy aspects of student culture."[19] To compound these difficulties, they occur during a period of increasing "massification" of higher education, as rising numbers of individuals from every age group seek a university degree not for its grounding in great books and the liberal arts and sciences but simply as the necessary credential for entry into a career. In turn, the classic baccalaureate degree has become "vocationalized," and student "consumers" now evaluate educational effectiveness through the choice of where they spend their dollars.[20]

Only one or two of these social forces would have altered how colleges and universities fulfill their missions; cumulatively, they are provoking the most serious and thorough restructuring of American higher education in this century. As the campus's ongoing connection between student success and board policy, what roles can the academic vice president play to implement more effective academic models by the year 2000?

1. *Provide support for collaborative and community service learning programs.* Gamson and others have noted how collaborative learning techniques in the classroom can have a cumulative effect across the institution by stimulating the creation of structures that are integrative and which cross traditional boundaries. In order to halt the growing fragmentation of the campus community, chief academic officers can begin a relatively quiet "restructuring" by developing initiatives in such areas as *collaborative* and *cooperative* learning in which students are encouraged to work together to achieve a common goal, sometimes beyond traditional classroom authority structures; *active* learning, in which faculty members are challenged to focus a significant portion of their syllabi on involving students in, and asking them to take more responsibility for, their own learning models; and *community-service learning*, in which students learn by working outside of the classroom and in courses that incorporate the results and meanings of the experience into a service ethic that shapes the campus culture. This is the one of the "quietest" forms of restructuring and can be achieved with even a small budget.

2. *Encourage new partnerships between academic and student affairs.* Formerly, a title such as vice president for academic and student affairs sometimes carried with it an impression of consolidation and diminished resources; now, the combining of academic and student affairs suggests a more coherent, effective way to approach institutional planning. From small community colleges to massive university structures, many leadership teams are implementing a more strategic model of academic and student development programs and staffing it through a combined office of academic and student affairs. In this model, faculty members are invited to the same leadership development workshops that students attend; similarly, student affairs professionals are appointed, with full vote, to faculty committees that focus on both the quality of student life and academic policy formulation.

3. *Create campus "institutes"*. Collaborative teaching techniques and new partnerships between academic and student affairs can accomplish significant institutional restructuring at relatively little cost. Similarly, several researchers have described innovative, informal "institutes" emerging on some campuses that have stimulated new collaborations among faculty members, students, administrators, and trustees toward making higher education structures more sensitive and accountable to the life-long learning needs of teachers as well as students. Kenneth E. Eble describes this new model as "a 'center' for university teaching and administration which would draw faculty from both the academic disciplines and the ranks of administrators. . . . Learning would not be terminal but ongoing, not from professor to student but toward the development of both."[21]

Within this new entity—called an "institute," a "center," or simply a new form of "resource collaboration"—shifting groups of project-based planners develop workshops, seminars, and training programs for teachers, administrators, and students on subjects such as leadership development and institutional accountability. These tools help prepare participants for challenges beyond those traditionally addressed within a baccalaureate curriculum.

4. *Implement institutional partnerships, affiliations, and strategic alliances*. As a final example of academic restructuring, we would note the proactive choices by hundreds of colleges and universities since the 1970s to affiliate with one or more partners in a resource-sharing enterprise that could not have been undertaken alone. A rising number of institutions from every geographic sector have designed coventures with hospitals, museums, airports, shopping malls, later lifecare facilities, farms, television stations, and health clubs to accomplish "more with less" and leverage their resources into a more flexible, resourceful organizational model. Often coordinated by networks of chief academic officers, these "strategic alliances" produce new educational resources, reduce joint-operating costs, and allow even fragile institutions to become more effective and competitive.

What Are the Chief Academic Officer's Responsibilities toward Students?

Students, no matter what their age group, have become discriminating "consumers," exercising greater authority over not only individual courses but also the way entire degree programs are designed. As a result, the shifting educational "market" has emerged as an undeniable force in the strategic plans of most chief academic officers. As one vice president for academic affairs says of provosts and presidents, "Neither embodies the reflective, scholarly model of time past, nor is that time likely to come again. Both . . . are heavily involved in marketing and the negotiation of community partnerships and alliances."[22] Clearly, students have begun to pose a set of unfamiliar questions to these institutional leaders.

The subject of tenure, for instance, is an issue at the core of most chief academic officer's responsibilities. On some campuses, students have called for its abolishment because it has come to symbolize a protection from responsiveness and accountability. Similarly, undergraduates now expect academic, career, and personal counseling of a complexity and depth far beyond the traditional model, where busy professors carved out a few minutes between lectures to discuss sophomore essays.

Students readily inform academic deans that they seek a new kind of relationship to their college or university. In Arthur Levine's words, "The relationship . . . students want with their college is like the one they already have with their banks [and] supermarkets. . . . They want easy, accessible parking, short lines, and polite and efficient personnel and services. They also want high quality products but are eager for low costs."[23] Students want less of what he calls the "extras"—entertainment, health care, varsity sports, and religious services—and they are no longer willing to pay for them either. In response to this stripped-down model for higher education, chief academic officers are often forced to choose one of two difficult paths, solidarity with the tenured faculty and an avoidance of the turbulence below the surface of their administrative activities, or a more purely managerial approach, distanced from faculty concerns and the collegium that has shaped their profession.

If either of these strategies is employed, the chief academic officer will ultimately fail in achieving her or his objectives with contemporary students. More than anything else, the provost must presume that quality of service to students encompasses both an identification with classroom colleagues *and* the ability to exercise authority as the "first among equals" to achieve excellence in teaching and advising. Maintaining and delivering quality is not a new assignment for an academic vice president. What is new, and more challenging, is the need to redesign traditional degree requirements and classroom experiences to accommodate changing student lifestyles while not reducing course substance or faculty expectations for success.

The new accountabilities of a chief academic officer to students are simpler to declare than to achieve; however, to the degree that a provost or dean of instruction views each as an opportunity for leadership through collaboration with undergraduates who hold a new set of definitions and expectations for that position, an authentic community can be formed.

How Can Struggles and Rewards Be Balanced in the Academic Workplace?

Gould's 1964 national survey of academic deans revealed that 64 percent continued to teach after assuming the position, and more than 70 percent had no experience at all in a dean's office when appointed. Approximately twenty-five years later, Miller's survey showed that the percentage of provosts and academic vice presidents who continued to teach had dropped to 42 percent with only one in four still pursuing research and publishing.[24] Remembering those first deans at Harvard a century ago as faculty members called by the president to perform a bit of part-time "administration," Edwin Lyle's examination of this question in 1963 in "Should the Dean Teach?" forms a quaint coda to earlier views on this subject. "It may help somewhat to be able to say: 'But the dean is a *member* of the faculty.' But is this slight advantage worthwhile when one of the following two results is practically inevitable if the dean teaches? First, if he chooses to teach well and devote the necessary time to it, he will have *less* time to meet with faculty in individual and group conferences. . . . Secondly, if he chooses to slight his teaching in order to keep his latch-string out to the faculty, then down goes his teaching image."[25]

Contemporary vice presidents for academic affairs remain caught between the more comfortable role of a faculty colleague temporarily called to "supervise" institutional instruction and curricular issues and that of the coldly efficient manager of a campus's academic affairs, whether financial, legal, or classroom-related. If a new generation of professionals is to succeed in shaping a leaner, more accountable campus, difficult questions must now be answered at many colleges and universities regarding the roles of their chief academic officers.

For example, what is the best career preparation for the academic vice presidency? And, once appointed, what is fair compensation? Should one hold tenure as a faculty member during and after service? What role will follow for the provost who relinquishes these responsibilities, and how can endings be made gracefully? According to Miller's findings, at least 40 percent of America's thirty-five hundred chief academic officers aspire to a presidency or chancellorship. Fifteen percent aspire to another vice presidency or provostship, and a similar number plan to return to the faculty. At least 20 percent believe they will retire from their present position.

This professional diversity begs for a new kind of formal orientation to the responsibilities of the position as well as a national initiative to clarify its roles in order to address the various lacks of leadership noted here and elsewhere. This initiative also needs to include an in-depth consideration of compensation and benefits for chief academic officers. Compensation structures for provosts and deans have undergone little systematic review nationally other than annual averages published by the *Chronicle of Higher Education* and periodic questionnaires by doctoral students. The 1995 *Almanac* issue of the *Chronicle of Higher Education* listed the median salary for all chief academic officers as $81,445, with those at two-year colleges earning the least at $68,884, and the provosts of doctoral degree–granting universities leading the profession with an average of $128,150 annually.

Beyond basic salary levels, however, the "rewards" for the deanship as an occupation need to be considered candidly by the academy. Traditionally, deans have simply been paid some degree more than faculty members, ostensibly for the longer hours and broader responsibilities they fulfill. Sometimes, although less so than in prior decades, the individual was also awarded tenure and a full professorship. Increasingly, senior academic officers are claiming this is not enough and that the benefits are not commensurate with the pressures that constrain the daily life of those with final responsibility for academic policy formulation, faculty professional development, curricular rigor, and student satisfaction. In this area as well, a national initiative is needed to create a new way to *think* about the ways an academician should be rewarded for assuming these leadership and management responsibilities.

While some argue that higher education doctoral programs hold the key to managerial success for the next generation of academic deans, as noted previously, Townsend and Wiese in surveying approximately 1,100 senior college and university administrators regarding the appropriate credentials for a position in academic affairs discovered that 62 percent of the respondents still viewed a doctorate in higher education as less preferable than one in a traditional academic discipline. However, there is a growing consensus that the position of chief academic officer can no longer be defined by a succession of skilled amateurs rotating out of their faculties for short periods of time. Individuals who make the commitment to serve as the campus's principal academic administrator should, as an administrator, hold the position without time or term limits in the same way that the chief executive of a museum, hospital, or software development company maintains the position subject to satisfactory annual evaluation. Effective chief academic officers will preserve the unique aspects of academic governance and collegial decision making with the same degrees of skill and sensitivity displayed by previous generations of traditional deans. In response to this new model of academic professionalism, colleges and universities can enhance their evaluation procedures and demand new levels of accountability among provosts and presidents alike to achieve the improvements both faculty and students expect.

Drawing on the concept of campus "institutes" or "teaching and learning centers" that are project-based and composed of changing groups of personnel, chief academic officers are now jointly coordinating conferences with chief financial officers on new models of budget accountability. Institutional advancement officers are collaborating with deans of instruction in the development of capital campaigns, while admissions officers and alumni coordinators are basing recruitment strategies on the work of provosts' councils and curriculum committees.

Across regions, academic deans are carefully constructing stronger networks in order to accomplish cooperatively developed legislative and accreditation initiatives. In Massachusetts, for example, there are formally constituted organizations for all community college deans, public college deans, and private two-year college chief academic officers, as well as separate think tanks sponsored by the New England Resource Center for Higher Education for chief academic officers, associate deans, and directors of general education. While organizations of this sort are not new, a difference in the current situation is the degree to which chief academic officers have served as catalysts for the larger enterprise.

At the close of their book, *The Academic Dean: Dove, Dragon, and Diplomat*, Allan Tucker and Robert Bryan observe, "Six years of hard work, long hours, and a reasonable amount of success normally make a dean begin to think either about greater challenges or about a return to a quieter life."[26] This comment is based on at least two assumptions that we would question. First, six years may have been the average tenure for traditional deans of faculty, but provosts and academic vice presidents are less and less bound by the desire, or need, to relinquish their position at the point when their counterparts in nonprofit and corporate sectors are just beginning to achieve a mature vision of strategy and authority. Second, some "new" chief academic officers, outlined more fully in the following section, are gradually redefining the position as a career objective rather than as a stepping-stone to a presidency or shelter from a failed professorship.[27]

The "New" Chief Academic Officer: Ten Characteristics

The following characteristics reflect the challenges, and in many cases mandates, facing chief academic officers as they approach the close of the twentieth century.

1. *An expert with ambiguity.* The foremost ability of future chief academic officers will be to identify and accomplish the institution's educational, political, cultural, and fiscal goals in the light of changing community standards and expectations. In the process, each individual will need to develop, within a context of increasing complexity and unpredictability, an effective answer to the first question of this chapter, "What is the nature and scope of academic leadership?"

The demands of the academic workplace now involve government regulations, financial exigencies, and student preferences to unprecedented degrees, all factors distinctly foreign to the traditional faculty- and curriculum-related responsibilities of traditional deans. More than in prior decades, future chief academic officers will need to tolerate ambiguities of role and expectation while shaping them into new forms of moral authority for multiple campus constituencies.

2. *A champion of new technologies.* Relentless technological advances in teaching and learning styles have forced many campuses closer to virtual reality in the classroom. Within this tension, the chief academic officer must act as an experienced shaper of policies governing new technologies, particularly those related to distance education and the hardware necessary for the intricacies of faculty research.

In increasing numbers, students are seeking the ability to enroll in courses of their choice from their own work sites and living rooms and to design individualized baccalaureate degrees with faculty from more than one institution.[28] This option, joined with the opportunities afforded by corporate providers of higher education, challenges new chief academic officers to become more aggressive global managers of the relationship among curricula, communications, and cost.

3. *An institutional entrepreneur.* The adjective "entrepreneur" was probably mentioned more frequently in our interviews with deans and vice presidents than any other descriptor. There is a pervasive view that chief academic officers have moved beyond simply serving as advisors to presidents to positions of collaborating with state legislatures in the development of systemwide policies and the procurement of multimillion dollar grants. In the process, the provost must motivate campus personnel to improve the quality of academic and student affairs within a context of declining public confidence and noncollegial competition.

4. *A student affairs advocate.* Effective chief academic officers of the future will build new forms of official partnership between offices of student and academic affairs to enable the institution to deliver a more coherent educational experience. As noted earlier, some chief academic and student affairs officers have already begun to join their budgets and programs into more comprehensive systems. Reasons that such collaborations may fail are varied: lack of time and orientation, faculty autonomy, internal distrust. However, reasons they should succeed are equally critical: dated curricula, inadequate advising, and the chance to enhance a student's own involvement in learning through new forms of mentoring and collaborative goal setting.[29]

Particularly in light of the changing needs of low-skilled and non–traditionally aged students, some faculty members are realizing that "professional development" no longer simply means a sabbatical for focused research purposes but also "in-service" time spent on instructional methodology and syllabus development. Chief academic officers can use this realization as an opportunity to encourage faculty colleagues to redefine their view of the relationship between curricular and cocurricular experiences.

5. *A savvy fund-raiser.* "Savvy" does not imply simply an academic administrator who has become familiar with the language of institutional advancement. For several generations, deans and provosts have been working in partnership with campus grant writers and alumni recruiters to increase annual levels of giving. In the year 2000, chief academic officers will coordinate and manipulate deeper linkages among faculty, curriculum, and the institution's financial structures. More specifically, academic vice presidents will focus less on the basic act of raising funds and more on shaping new alliances among state legislatures, private corporations, alumni chapters, philanthropic organizations, and faculty committees in order to build more extended, and longer-lived, resource networks. Many provosts and deans are designing professional "advisory boards" to include local and regional prospects and then structuring innovative campus "retreats" to join the strengths of their internal faculty governance systems with the resources of these outside professionals.

6. *A supporter of "selected excellence."* The new chief academic officer must provide the leadership and vision to designate the areas of quality an institution can continue to support as well as those program areas to be redefined or retrenched. "Selected excellence" has come to represent the difficult resource allocation choices almost every institu-

tion has had to make during the 1990s. The Pew Higher Education Roundtable describes this process as a pursuit of more "agile" institutions as higher education has too often defined progress in terms of "addition rather than substitution or subtraction."[30]

Historically, chief academic officers have not led initiatives to reduce the number of faculty or programs; increasingly, however, the academic vice president is being forced to choose between one department and another as funding sources and student majors shrink in number. The well-publicized "lattice and rachet" of senior faculty teaching fewer, smaller sections as younger instructors gradually become more specialized in focus as their own careers progress, has created unprecedented financial challenges for academic administrators who must finally reduce the scope of what once seemed an ever expanding educational enterprise.

7. *A legal interpreter.* When interviewed, many chief academic officers observed that a majority of the professional development resources they had purchased over the past ten years addressed the rise of legal problems in higher education. This is a comment not only on various hostilities within the academic "society" for which the academic vice president is responsible but also on the inadequate training he or she received in preparation for the position.

As both campus and society have become more litigious, and as federal regulations have grown more complex, it has become imperative for a chief academic officer to become conversant in laws affecting hiring and labor grievance issues, affirmative action, sexual harassment, financial aid, and accommodating those with disabilities, among other concerns. More critically, he or she must learn how to maintain academic excellence within a "regulatory jungle" without entering the trap of acting as an unofficial attorney. While future chief academic officers will most likely utilize the services of university counsel more than their predecessors, a telling difference will be the degree to which those services are enlisted *proactively.*

8. *A public intellectual.* Contemporary chief academic officers have experienced a sweeping redefinition of the professional expectations that apply to them as academicians. As representatives of higher education's "public intellectuals," some have been described as "searching for a new language and literary forms. . . . turning to autobiographical essays, trade books and articles for the op-ed pages of daily newspapers."[31] While search committees still cling to a doctorate in a traditional discipline as the preferred training for the position, provosts are increasingly

asked to engage in and decisively shape the national debate on the leadership and management of colleges and universities through their research, presentations, and publications.

9. *A shaper of the new consensus.* While the collegium survives in name at many institutions, fewer aspects of campus life appear to be governed by it. A chief academic officer must increasingly arbitrate among constituencies alien to, and at cross purposes with, a higher education institution. Confronted by conservative student news agencies, fundamentalist religious groups, and for-profit corporations seeking space to hold "educational seminars" on campuses, academic vice presidents often need formal training in mediation and conflict resolution to maintain a harmonious learning environment. In fact, is harmony even possible within many higher education communities? As the age difference between "traditional" students and their professors increases, and intractable problems such as domestic abuse and urban crime redefine the campus experience at many institutions, a new consensus coordinated by the provost is urgently needed among students, parents, faculty, and trustees that acknowledges and incorporates these evolutions in campus culture.

10. *A visionary pragmatist.* Within the consensus outlined above, a chief academic officer will need to act boldly and definitively to accomplish various educational objectives. Tenured faculty members may need to be shifted from dying departments to healthy ones; faculty advisors could be assigned to academic counseling offices, and librarians may be trained to manage institutional research. Skillful deans will look beyond former responsibilities and job descriptions to create fluid, shifting networks of campus professionals.[32]

As long ago as the 1940s, deans noted how they were ceasing to serve as the intellectual leaders on their campuses in light of the postwar expansion of their administrative responsibilities. Fifty years later, the stereotype of the American dean has been transformed into the distinctly more complex identity of chief academic officer. During the intervening period, although administration has gradually become a profession for many, the responsibilities of intellectual leadership have not diminished, as the following chapters illustrate. In fact, to view these chief academic officers as being separated from the values of either faculty or classroom would be inaccurate. Rather, through new choices that demonstrate educational leadership and managerial vision, these men and women are challenging their campuses to provide effective programs for complex and demanding constituencies.

Faculty Relations and Professional Development: Best Practices for the Chief Academic Officer

Roy A. Austensen

The complex interactions between the chief academic officer and the faculty contain more ambiguity and paradox than do any of the other administrative relationships in a college or university. If, as the title suggests, the provost is one who is "placed before" the members of the faculty, it is nonetheless also true that no chief academic officer can function effectively without the respect and support of teachers and scholars who view themselves as colleagues rather than subordinates. Indeed, the overall title of this work, "First among Equals," conveys some of these same ironies. As it has evolved over the past century, the relationship between the provost or academic dean and the faculty is one of the defining characteristics separating a college or university from organizations in almost every other sector of American life. Since the days of colonial institutions, the predominant culture on the nation's campuses has been collegial, and the addition of the research focus of the German university at the end of the nineteenth century only strengthened this quality by identifying it strongly with the academic disciplines. As William H. Bergquist observes in *The Four Cultures of the Academy*, "Faculty members who live primarily in a collegial culture generally assume that effective leadership is exerted through the complex give-and-take of campus politics."[1]

Within this setting, the chief academic officer must act as a partner with the faculty while serving as its principal leader. To the degree that the provost is a manager, he or she manages more through diplomacy and negotiation than through the exercise of administrative authority. Most colleges and universities have developed sophisticated, often complicated, systems through which members of the faculty share in the governance of their institutions, typically via committees and assemblies such as a faculty senate. Within these political structures, the chief academic officer participates in extensive deliberations that Bergquist characterizes as "intricate—almost baroque."[2] Nonetheless, the influence of an academic vice president will be felt in the allocation of financial resources to departments; the hiring of new faculty; the orientation and mentoring of new faculty members; and the awarding of sabbaticals, research leaves, release time, and other perquisites of academic life. Senior academic officers with responsibilities for admissions, student affairs, business affairs, electronic information services, and other major administrative areas will have additional resources with which to achieve academic objectives, although this can also result in less time to manage relations with the faculty. Whatever the scope of their administrative responsibilities, however, chief academic officers must never lose sight of the centrality of the faculty in each activity shaping the college or university's educational mission.

Leadership and Management within the Collegial Culture

Although there can be great variety between the responsibilities of the provost at a large research university and the academic dean at a small liberal arts college, there are many tasks that every chief academic officer, no matter what the institutional category, must fulfill. What differentiates a list of best practices in the 1990s from those of previous decades is a realization that the scope and rate of change on campuses are greater than at any time since the massive influx of students immediately after the Second World War. If Robert Zemsky, William Massy, Arthur Levine, and other observers are correct, the changes that our higher education system must accommodate to address these new demographic, economic, social, technological, and political realities must be of a transformative nature if institutions are to survive.[3] Six practices reflect these new necessities.

Link Faculty Recruitment to Institutional Mission

One of the most frequently cited causes of what Zemsky has described as the "academic ratchet"—a tendency of colleges and universities to expand academic programs and services in an uncontrolled and uncoordinated manner—has been the virtual autonomy of academic departments in the recruitment and hiring of new faculty.[4] While the dean or provost exercises control over the number of positions approved for hiring, the identification of suitable candidates and, as important, the determination of the disciplinary specialty or subspecialty to be sought, is governed by the individual department. The result has been a fragmentation of many institutions into aggregates of unrelated academic specialties in which there is neither coherence nor scholarly community. Moreover, this process of hiring new faculty members offers few opportunities for a chief academic officer to ensure that young professionals are oriented in how to contribute to the educational mission of the institution beyond their own scholarship.

Affirmative action programs to achieve racial, ethnic, and gender diversity goals have provided an important check on departmental autonomy via search committees that follow institution-wide norms and procedures in the recruitment of new faculty. While the achievements of some of these traditional programs have remained modest, their successes over the past two decades could only have been accomplished with strong support and collaboration between chief academic and affirmative action officers. Building on this foundation, innovative "affirmative action" plans are now also being applied to achieve other kinds of institutional objectives.

For example, the University of Notre Dame recently conducted a strategic planning exercise entitled *Colloquy for the Year 2000*, in which the university recommitted itself to its Roman Catholic character and identified goals for hiring faculty who are interested in Christian higher education and who are prepared to support Notre Dame's institutional mission as well as to practice their academic discipline.[5] The Lilly Fellows Program at Valparaiso University extends this concept by providing postdoctoral appointments for young academics who have an interest in exploring the possibility of teaching in a church-related college or university. Fellows receive two-year appointments to teach at the university, where they are assigned a formal faculty mentor, participate in a weekly colloquium organized by a visiting senior fellow from another church-related institution, and attend national and regional meetings organized by the Lilly Fellows Network. The network is a consortium of approximately fifty church-related colleges and universities representing a variety of Christian denominations and each region of the country. Through this program, member institutions of the Lilly Fellows Network are able to identify several hundred young academics with an interest in church-related higher education, thereby providing them with a pool of potential faculty candidates.[6]

As constituents of both public and private institutions have increasingly demanded greater accountability and focus on institutional mission, the need to recruit faculty members who can identify with this broader agenda and directly support it through their teaching, scholarship, and professional activities has become a priority for chief academic officers. Having said this, it should also be noted that on many campuses academic disciplines and the departmental structure itself continue to

---

Best Practices for the Chief Academic Officer and the Faculty

- Link faculty recruitment to institutional mission
- Provide for the comprehensive orientation of new faculty members
- Promote ongoing faculty development
- Ensure the integrity of faculty evaluation processes
- Ensure the appropriate assessment of teaching and learning
- Promote high morale among members of the faculty

---

play persuasive roles in the challenges and compromises that shape the professional development process. Thus, in the absence of an overall consensus on the future direction of an institution, an academic vice president must be able to negotiate successfully among trustees, the president, and the faculty, subgroups of which may themselves be deeply polarized. Whatever the campus culture, however, the recruitment of faculty members who are willing and able to support the mission of their institution as defined by the state, the trustees, and other major stakeholders, including colleagues in their own department, is one of the foremost responsibilities for contemporary chief academic officers.[7]

Provide for the Comprehensive Orientation of New Faculty Members

An urgent topic in discussions on the quality of life at American colleges and universities since the 1980s has been the need for greater community. The works of Robert Bellah and Parker Palmer have been essential texts in this conversation, as have the publications of the Carnegie Foundation for the Advancement of Teaching.[8] In *College: The Undergraduate Experience in America*, Ernest Boyer stresses the importance of orientation programs for introducing new students into a community "whose structure, privileges, and responsibilities have been evolving for almost a millennium."[9] Similarly, in *Campus Life*, Boyer's first principle to define the nature of a campus community is that it should be "an educationally *purposeful* community, a place where faculty and students share academic goals and work together to strengthen teaching and learning on the campus."[10]

The task of building "an educationally purposeful community" requires that both teachers and students are initiated into the culture and traditions of the campus. This is typically accomplished through a combination of methods, from informal mentoring by senior colleagues to formal, comprehensive orientation programs. At some universities, faculty orientation is conducted by the personnel office, with a few administrators participating, and tends to be less formal than that at liberal arts colleges, where orientation programs often extend throughout the new faculty member's first year.[11] The growing concern for better faculty orientation was demonstrated at a large state university in the Midwest a few years ago when several academic departments asked the dean of the graduate school if new tenure-track faculty members could attend the orientation workshops on teaching created for graduate assistants. Since that time, the program has been expanded to include sessions designed specifically for new faculty, and many senior members of the faculty now attend as well.

An exemplary orientation program for new faculty was created by Gerald Gibson, vice president and dean of the college at Roanoke College. Gibson later included many of the ideas he developed for Roanoke's "First-Year Faculty Sessions" in his book *Good Start*,[12] which outlines a faculty orientation program incorporating sessions on institutional mission, teaching effectiveness, scholarship, citizenship and service, campus politics, management of time and stress, and promotion and tenure. Although Gibson's framework was developed primarily for a liberal arts college, his suggestions can readily be adapted for other types of institutions. In a research university setting, his ideas could be implemented at the college or department levels. The fundamental message of *Good Start* is one that should inform any orientation program for new faculty: "'Teaching' is the name given to what is really a slightly different career, the *faculty* career. Teaching is part of a package. To teach, one must become a faculty member, and accepting that assignment means accepting responsibility not only for what goes on in the classroom and laboratory and studio and gymnasium, but also for the conditions in which teaching and learning take place."[13]

Promote Ongoing Faculty Development

In an era of drastically changing expectations, both on campuses and in the communities surrounding them, there has emerged no greater challenge for chief academic officers than the ongoing professional development of members of the faculty. While many organized professional development programs date back to the 1960s or earlier, the original intent of most of these initiatives was to work with individual faculty members to promote good teaching. Since then, however, the scope of professional "development" has expanded greatly, with a focus on the vitality of the faculty as a whole.[14] During the 1990s, the need for internal faculty development programs has become even greater as outside sources of funding for both research and teaching projects have declined or disappeared. Following a major shift in the strategic priorities of both the federal government and private foundations, faculty members at even the country's most prestigious research universities have found it increasingly difficult to fund their teaching and research activities. This situation has become even more difficult for teachers at comprehensive institutions and liberal arts colleges. Public and private sources simply can no longer provide the levels of support needed to promote creativity and change at the institutional level. Additional pressure is also now exerted by trustees and state coordinating boards in their demands for post-tenure review, which is inevitably linked to faculty development, as the experience of institutions with successful post-tenure review programs has demonstrated.[15]

Opportunities for personal development and professional renewal are important at every stage of an academic career. Younger professors often need assistance to establish a research program, and they invariably benefit from both formal and informal programs on teaching effectiveness. Senior faculty scholars may need support if they have reached a plateau in their research and are no longer able to attract outside funding. All segments of the faculty can benefit from opportunities to develop new curricula and learn about applications of new technologies for teaching and learning. Faculty development programs are essential to address those symptoms associated with the aging of the American professoriate, including general frustration and fatigue, intellectual stagnation, even cynicism. Bergquist suggests that a major challenge to maintaining the collegial culture is the disillusionment experienced by classroom teachers regarding the gap between the realities of professional advancement and the ideals that prompted them to choose a career in higher education.

> Administrators are never as wise or as responsible as they could be. Colleagues are never as bright, well read, or articulate as they ought to be. Students are never as appreciative of a liberal arts education as they should be; certainly they are not as competent and well- prepared as the despairing faculty member would like them to be. This conflict between what they would like and what they actually confront is particularly difficult for many faculty members to reconcile, for their whole orientation in life is toward the ideal rather than reality—the possible rather than the actual.[16]

While most colleges and universities now have some model of professional development, including sabbaticals, paid and unpaid leaves for research, summer research fellowships, teaching improvement grants, travel support, and publication funds, the challenge of the 1990s has been to expand these programs to integrate new technologies into the teaching and learning process, to update curricula, and to involve faculty members more integrally in the ways their institutions accomplish their missions.

Ensure the Integrity of Faculty Evaluation Processes

All recommendations for salary increases, promotions, and tenure come to the chief academic officer, who must evaluate each one prior to forwarding it to the president with a decision to approve or disapprove. In the process, the provost or dean must ensure that members of the faculty have been evaluated fairly and in accordance with the terms of the faculty handbook while simultaneously creating and preserving a learning environment in which students are served in a manner consistent with the mission of the institution. Chief academic officers must be thoroughly familiar with the faculty handbook as well as the national standards of the American Association of University Professors, particularly as they relate to the granting or denial of tenure. While specific standards for merit raises, promotions, and tenure will vary among different categories of colleges and universities, it is essential that institutional expectations are clearly articulated and disseminated in written form to every new faculty member. These expectations are communicated most effectively at the initial interview.

Faculty members need to know specifically what is to be evaluated, when, and by whom. In a collegial culture, the professoriate normally will have played a major role in establishing these standards and processes, and faculty committees will work with administrators to monitor the effectiveness of the system and to recommend changes as needed. Chief academic officers must take an active role in every institutional process related to faculty evaluation to ensure that procedures are adhered to at each level. Failure to do so can lead to lapses that compromise the legitimacy of promotion and tenure decisions, leaving the institution vulnerable to expensive and time-consuming litigation. To avoid problems arising out of department- and college-level decisions, chief academic officers should coordinate biannual workshops on faculty evaluation for deans, chairpersons, and faculty members who serve on promotion and tenure committees.

As importantly, chief academic officers must acknowledge and address the gradual shift away from research as the most important faculty activity. For nearly half a century, original research and publication have been viewed as the hallmarks of excellence in a faculty career, as the principal vehicle for faculty mobility, and as a major contributor to the prestige of many institutions. Also, because of the assumed nexus of research and good teaching, some selective liberal arts colleges even went so far as to describe themselves as "research liberal arts colleges."[17] Major forces have contributed to the weakening of this paradigm in favor of greater emphasis on teaching as the principal focus of higher education; yet, for the most part, the pressure to elevate teaching—and downgrade research—has come from outside the academy via legislatures, coordinating boards, and trustees.

The most influential contribution to the national conversation about the nature and importance of research in higher education has been that of Ernest L. Boyer, whose book *Scholarship Reconsidered* has been the most widely disseminated publication in the history of the Carnegie Foundation for the Advancement of Teaching.[18] Boyer advocates preserving research as a legitimate activity of college and university faculties by subsuming it into the larger concept of scholarship. In this way, original research becomes the scholarship of discovery, one of four principal forms, along with application, integration, and teaching, which hold legitimate places in the work of higher education institutions. Boyer maintains that this view of scholarship is more appropriate to changing conditions in both the nation and the world, and he expresses confidence that faculty members at American colleges and universities will embrace the belief that teaching, integration, and application should be regarded as equal in significance to discovery.

> There is growing evidence that professors want, and need, better ways for the full range of their aspirations and commitments to be acknowledged. Faculty are expressing serious reservations about the enterprise to which they have committed their professional lives. This deeply rooted professional concern reflects, we believe, recognition that teaching is crucial, that integrative studies are increasingly consequential, and that, in addition to research, the work of the academy must relate to the world beyond the campus.[19]

Chief academic officers must be both conversant with and involved in the national debate over the relative importance of teaching, research, and service in the evaluation of faculty and its impact on the mission of their institutions. Ultimately, it will be the mission of each college or university, rather than nationally defined norms, that will determine the proper balance among faculty activities. In addition, academic vice presidents should consider sponsoring a campuswide discussion at least once annually on faculty roles and rewards, drawing on Boyer's research as well as studies sponsored by the American Association for Higher Education and locally developed strategic plans.[20]

Ensure the Appropriate Assessment of Teaching and Learning

One can hardly think of a time in this century when colleges and universities did not, in some manner, assess the achievement of their faculty and students. Assessment of student performance was a major concern particularly during the 1930s and 1940s, involving topics such as rating scales, profiles, measures of critical thinking, and inventories of life goals. However, it was during the 1980s that assessment qua assessment became a national movement, emphasizing the need to determine an institution's effectiveness in promoting student learning rather than merely charting the progress of individual students. This shift in emphasis took its cue from many sources both inside and outside of higher education. On campuses, there were concerns that existing testing methods no longer fairly suited the diverse characteristics of the student population. The changes in the curriculum, with new perspectives on general education and Western civilization, and the addition of programs and courses in new fields, such as women's and ethnic studies, produced the need to identify different outcomes and the means to evaluate them. External influences on assessment arose in political concerns regarding the competitiveness of college-educated Americans in the global economy. There was also a growing public perception that colleges and universities were not as effective as they should be, primarily because professors did not teach well enough and students no longer learned with the skill and dedication of their parents. As a result, by 1990, assessment was one of the leading movements in American higher education. Less than a decade later, it has become a standard element of both the internal and external evaluation of courses, programs, and entire institutions. Regional as well as specialized accrediting bodies now require or at least strongly recommend a wide variety of assessment strategies as a part of their accreditation reviews.[21]

As a result of this movement, assessment plans are currently in place in most institutions. Indeed, a 1993 report by the American Council on Education indicates that 97 percent of American colleges and universities are engaged in some form of new assessment activities.[22] The chief academic officer's principal roles in the campus assessment process are those of leadership, facilitation, and coordination. Reports on assessment to regional accrediting associations will need to be assembled and finished in the office of the provost. The responsibility to ensure that all of the institution's assessment activities are being performed, that data are being collected, and that the individuals and committees responsible for assessment are fulfilling their functions appropriately will also fall to the chief academic officer. Properly understood, assessment is not simply an exercise to placate regional accrediting agencies; rather, it is a means to achieve a variety of complex institutional and departmental goals, from the improvement of teaching in individual courses to a transformation of the curriculum and creation of a student-centered learning environment across the campus. An academic vice president's role in the assessment process may vary according to type of institution, yet standard expectations will remain, such as working closely with the faculty at each stage of the development process and recognizing that the program, once created, must be managed, evaluated, and revised as student needs, faculty interests, and institutional priorities evolve.

Promote High Morale among Members of the Faculty

Even during the early 1960s, viewed by many as this century's golden age for higher education, faculty dissatisfaction with their administrations was discernible. G. Bruce Dearing observed in an article in the *Journal of General Education* in 1963, "Indeed, virtually anything that can honestly be said about the relationship of the dean to the faculty in contemporary American higher education can be subsumed under the rubric of 'growing tension between faculty and administration.'"[23] While low faculty morale is not always a sign of tension between a faculty and administration, it is nonetheless a warning signal for a provost.

Much of what a senior academic officer can do to promote positive attitudes among faculty members is merely symbolic, but no less important because of this. For example, deans and provosts should continually seek opportunities to recognize faculty achievements. Convocations and award ceremonies should be used to honor professors who have received tenure, promotions, appointments to endowed chairs, election to significant offices, announcements of fellowships and grants, and other marks of distinction. Prior to this, chief academic officers must also ensure that faculty members who could be successful candidates for awards in teaching or community service receive timely nominations for these recognitions. Consistently, in language and action, the chief academic officer should affirm both the primacy of institutional mission and the roles faculty members play in achieving it.

Beyond this level of symbols, provosts must act as leaders of the faculty in ways that clearly demonstrate their commitment to the ideals that shape the campus's academic culture. To accomplish this, it will be necessary to articulate the aspirations of classroom teachers with genuine conviction and to link their goals to institutional mission. In this setting, the chief academic officer is uniquely positioned to translate the excellence behind these accomplishments to the broader constituencies of the college or university.

Through symbols and language, a provost can promote a higher level of faculty morale, but strategic actions will also be necessary. On issues such as compensation, support services, facilities, equipment, and working conditions, the chief academic officer must ensure that the academic mission of the institution is supported appropriately, and this will often mean providing rising levels of resources for the faculty. Failure to do so, especially relative to competitor institutions, will lead to a decline in the quality of faculty productivity over time. Conversely, blind advocacy for one constituency may lead to a loss of credibility with the institution's chief executive and financial officers; thus, it will be imperative that the provost gather comprehensive data in developing proposals and preserve a balanced view in presenting them.

Maintaining high faculty morale in an era of retrenchment and "downsizing" is an extraordinary challenge. Nevertheless, the chief academic officer will need to demonstrate leadership by guaranteeing as much faculty participation as possible in key educational policy decisions and by ensuring that "re-engineering" plans do not violate the academic and personnel processes that have defined the collegial culture of the campus. To accomplish these objectives, it may be necessary to revise practices that members of the faculty view as sacrosanct, and if so, these changes must be negotiated and implemented through careful and meaningful consultation. Without this, senior academic officers risk turning their colleges and universities into "repressive, uninspired places to work or learn," as Bergquist characterizes educational institutions dominated by a managerial culture.[24]

New Roles and Rewards amid Fundamental Change

The prospects for college and university faculty during the next two decades present a paradox for chief academic officers. Faculty members will be under increasing pressure to adapt to the fundamental changes affecting American society and, more specifically, to those which are transforming higher education. Many observers are already positing that the entire structure of faculty roles and rewards will be redesigned, including the assumptive pattern of faculty careers that has dominated the academic community since the 1950s. Not surprisingly, the institution of tenure is being seriously questioned in this debate and is likely to be modified—possibly even eliminated—as a result of the close scrutiny it is receiving from state legislatures, boards of trustees, and the national media. In the midst of these developments, chief academic officers are being confronted by a series of highly controversial issues that are testing to an unprecedented degree their abilities to lead the faculty.

At the same time, several emerging trends in higher education offer chief academic officers new opportunities to expand the influence of faculty in the management of their institutions through greater participation in campus planning, budgeting, and student affairs. One consequence of the great expansion of higher education in the 1950s and 1960s was an increased separation between the roles of teaching and administration, with faculty concentrating more heavily on research, curriculum, and matters of recruitment, promotion, and tenure. All other aspects of managing a college or university were left to full-time administrators, including financial affairs, admissions, counseling, career services, financial aid, and cocurricular activities. Many student-focused activities were gradually gathered into a powerful unit called student affairs or student development and over which faculty members had little or no influence.

Ironically, some of the same pressures that have threatened faculty employment security have also produced noticeable increases in their influence on administrative policy making. Even though some of the most difficult re-engineering decisions necessarily must be made by the president and governing board, increasingly, chief executive officers are broadening the campus consultation process to include faculty in strategic planning exercises. Even more striking has been the expansion of the administrative role of the chief academic officer to the equivalent of a chief operating officer.[25] Administrative reorganization at some institutions has placed responsibility for student affairs and business affairs under the provost. As a result, many chief academic officers now have unprecedented opportunities to place faculty members in positions of influence in the management of their institutions. More than one observer has noted that the decline of a national faculty culture based on research, loyalty to the discipline, and the protection of tenure will be followed by the rise of a new culture based on student learning, loyalty to the institution, and forms of tenure that are local rather than national. In this process, the divide between faculty and administration will be narrowed significantly through increased faculty participation in managerial activities and collaborations with other campus constituencies. Emerging trends in significant areas illustrate this transition.

Post-tenure Review Processes

It is still too early to predict the long-term impact of post-tenure review policies on the status of faculty members at institutions that adhere to the standards of the American Association of University Professors.

Emerging Trends for the Chief Academic Officer and the Faculty

- Post-tenure review processes will become more prevalent
- Faculty "work" will be defined with greater variety and flexibility
- Faculty will participate in institutional planning and budgeting processes to a greater degree
- Student learning will become a greater focus of faculty pedagogy and research
- Faculty involvement in service learning programs will increase

---

Under such a policy, tenured faculty members are required to participate in a review of their performance, typically every three to five years. The process provides the opportunity for an individual to assess her or his accomplishments over an extended period of time and to establish major goals for the future. If the review determines that a faculty member's performance has not been at an acceptable level, remediation is usually recommended, including specific activities and a timetable for their accomplishment. A faculty member with an unacceptable teaching performance over several years would be asked to collaborate in the creation of a professional development plan including attendance at a workshop on teaching effectiveness, participation in a teaching and learning center, or working with a colleague mentor. A scholar whose research activities have diminished or ended might receive a start-up grant from an internal fund to initiate a new project. While some, if not many, tenured faculty members might have concerns about the concept of the periodic review, by far the most controversial aspect of such a policy will be whether a faculty member who fails to improve or adapt to new missional priorities over a stipulated period of time could lose tenured status and be dismissed. Put differently, the advocates of post-tenure review are suggesting that nonperformance over time should be added to moral turpitude, professional incompetence, and neglect of duty as sufficient cause for the loss of tenure.[26]

Legislatures, governing boards, and corporate officers now calling for change in higher education have come to regard the system of tenure as a major impediment to increasing productivity in higher education. In addition, widespread corporate "downsizing" in recent years has contributed to a belief that lifetime tenure is a status that is both unfair and inefficient, particularly in light of an institutional cost structure whose annual increases have rivaled those of the health care industry. Inside the academy, the elimination of a mandatory retirement age for faculty members has also given the "lifetime" aspect of tenure a deeper meaning, raising new concerns about the performance of an aging professoriate and a lack of opportunity for younger scholars.

Chief academic officers can easily find themselves caught in the middle of the debate over post-tenure review, unable to satisfy either critics or defenders. In order to avoid this, it will be necessary to remain well informed on the latest national developments related to this issue and to remain familiar with examples of what other institutions have accomplished in this area.[27] Provosts must also be prepared to build reasonable compromises with critics of tenure, encouraging them to express their expectations in terms of achievable goals and outcomes. As William Plater observes, "So, let's understand that the future of tenure depends first on our talking about it. We should agree from the outset that the term is itself highly charged as a symbol and that it is a symbol with polar meanings within and without the academy and that the competing mythic systems which the term represents have irreconcilable opposing values."[28] Finally, chief academic officers must link post-tenure review to larger concerns about faculty roles and rewards, especially in the context of activities that further institutional mission. The success of the post-tenure review system at the University of Hawaii at Manoa has been attributed precisely to these forms of collaboration within an institution. As Madeleine Goodman concludes, "the key to the success of the program thus far has been the shared recognition of the value of professionalism, the need for accountability, and the possibility of improvement through consultation, support, and the clear articulation of academic standards."[29]

Definitions of Faculty "Work"

If post-tenure review represents the most dramatic example of the changes now confronting the faculties of American colleges and universities, the broader context behind those changes is probably illustrated most clearly in "New Pathways: Faculty Careers and Employment in the 21st Century," a major project of the American Association for Higher Education (AAHE). In a draft paper he presented to the 1996 AAHE Conference on Faculty Roles and Rewards, R. Eugene Rice, the director of the New Pathways project, describes its purpose as "exploring ways of putting into place a multidimensional academic career that will potentially be more resilient and self-renewing for faculty, while also enhancing the capacity of our colleges and universities to meet the changing educational needs of our students and the knowledge requirements of a society committed to be democratic."[30] Rice and others have come to believe that the incremental approach to change in American higher education will remain inadequate as long as it represents simply adding new initiatives to existing structures. They foresee a major transformation of the professoriate based both on broadening the definition of scholarship according to Boyer's guidelines and restructuring of the concept of a faculty career. In Rice's view, the new definition of scholarship will not only incorporate new modes of teaching, integration, and application, but will also reflect ways of learning that proceed from reflection, observation, active practice, and forms of "concrete, connected knowing," as well as traditional analytic knowledge.

The impact of these changes on the academic workplace will be substantial, challenging some of the basic assumptions on which colleges and universities have been organized and managed.[31] Rice suggests there will be four major shifts in the dominant academic culture: from an emphasis on faculty to an emphasis on learning, from faculty autonomy to increased involvement in the institution, from individual work cultures to collaboration, and from a tradition of separateness to greater responsibility for public life.[32] In this new academic workplace, members of the faculty will have opportunities to become more complete and connected scholars, pursuing varieties of work that link them more closely to colleagues, students, and the larger community. They will practice a more interactive, collaborative style of teaching that utilizes experience-based learning and new information technologies. This new faculty "work" will also move more easily across disciplinary boundaries as well as outside of higher education, providing extended opportunities for careers in industry, business, and government.[33]

Additionally, as studies increasingly demonstrate the vital interdependence of in-class and out-of-class activities to the success of the learning process, some institutions are considering the merger of their academic and student affairs operations to serve as a catalyst for other initiatives to improve the learning environment as a whole.[34] Such models could include: adding the chief student affairs officer to the council of academic deans, adding a faculty senate representative to the student affairs council, or creating joint task forces to address policy issues affecting both areas. Respecting the fact that faculty culture is not changed easily, this process can be designed as a professional development initiative as well as another redefinition of institutional roles and rewards.

The concept of the "New American College," less than a decade old, has already contributed to several transformations of the professoriate. Frank Wong, vice president for academic affairs at the University of Redlands, developed the concept with Ernest Boyer and a group of chief academic officers of private, comprehensive colleges and universities. Boyer believes these institutions to be unique in their combination of elements from the English and German higher education models on which the standard liberal arts college and research university are based. They develop faculties and curricula infused with the spirit of liberal learning while also maintaining fully accredited professional and graduate programs. They remain small enough to provide a personalized learning environment and yet large enough to offer a wide selection of academic program choices to an increasingly diverse student body. Moreover, their size, character, and mission make it possible for them to respond to changing educational needs far more quickly than larger, public institutions.

In addition to being uniquely American institutions, these New American Colleges offer laboratories for the ideas Boyer develops in *Scholarship Reconsidered*, particularly regarding the concepts of integration and connection. What Boyer, Wong, and others observe in these institutions are models to re-establish important connections within the academy, first, by connecting general education with specialized education; second, by connecting teaching and learning to a greater degree in specific academic disciplines, thus ensuring more coherence and connection within the curriculum; third, by connecting academic and student cultures in order to recreate the kind of community that exists in a liberal arts college; fourth, by reaching out to the various external communities surrounding college campuses and responding to their needs; and fifth, by defining a college education as part of a web of learning, integrally connected to the secondary education that preceded it and to the continuing lifelong learning which follows.[35] On a broader scale, Wong and Boyer both believe that these principles can be applied in some format to any college or university and, in this manner, constitute one important reform of the current higher education system.

Faculty Participation in Institutional Planning and Budgeting Processes

Meaningful faculty participation in planning and budgeting processes varies considerably according to the type of institution and the culture of the individual campus.[36] Clearly, the general attitude has been, as Kent Chabotar describes, "administrators are paid to manage the campus—which includes preparing a budget—while faculty teach and students learn."[37] Chabotar identifies three principal models for faculty participation in budget planning: informational, consultative, and participative. In the informational model, faculty are provided with reports on budgets and other planning decisions but do not contribute to the decision-making process. The consultative approach provides for interactive communication, but administrators still make the final decisions.

In the participative process, various constituencies within the institution consider comprehensive data and make suggestions to a budget committee that includes members of both the faculty and administration. Typically, this group prepares a pro forma budget and recommends it to the president, who may accept it as is or modify it prior to submitting it to the trustees.

The participative model offers numerous advantages to institutions attempting to accomplish their missions more effectively while also becoming more efficient in the use of their human resources. In recommending that colleges and universities consider this model, Chabotar outlines nine stages of implementation:

1. create a budget committee

2. establish clear guidelines

3. allow sufficient time

4. provide adequate data and staff support

5. arrange for public forums during the process

6. involve the board of trustees

7. arrange for overlapping membership in the shared governance system

8. keep the mission, vision, and strategic plan in focus

9. implement the participative process slowly and gradually[38]

A Greater Focus on Student Learning

An analysis of the documents produced by faculty-administration roundtable discussions sponsored by the Pew Charitable Trust at thirty-two colleges and universities between 1993 and 1996 produced three concluding themes, one of which was "the need to focus on the enhancement of curriculum and pedagogy and on the fostering of successful student learning."[39] Five principal strategies were identified to achieve this goal:

- Address changes in students' educational needs resulting from changes in workforce and skill requirements, as well as from the range of backgrounds, educational preparation, and learning styles that current students reflect.

- Apply the capacities of technology to enhance teaching and learning, extending both the range and quality of learning experiences students may have in the course of attaining a degree.

- Assess student learning more effectively through the development of measures which gauge student achievement beyond the classroom context.

- Focus on the curriculum to develop coherent learning experiences combining in-depth study in the major with a general education program which integrates knowledge within and across disciplines.

- Foster pedagogical innovation to enable more effective delivery of education, in part through the creation of enhanced linkages among departments, as well as among members of a single department.[40]

A decade-long project sponsored by the Fund for the Improvement of Post-Secondary Education and the Ford Foundation reached similar conclusions about the centrality of student learning and learning styles to the future success of the higher education enterprise and the need for significant change in faculty teaching styles to address this new focus. In their report, *Turning Professors into Teachers*, Joseph Katz and Mildred Henry identify seven principles of student learning that faculty must apply to their teaching if it is to be effective: active learning, individualization, participation, the process of inquiry, the ability to inquire with other people, mutual support, and the recognition that learning is an intensely emotional experience. They conclude that improving student learning necessarily involves continuing faculty professional development and recommend a process through which faculty members can learn to create a successful pedagogy cooperatively with students and faculty colleagues.[41]

American colleges and universities need to pay even greater attention than they already do to the changing ways students learn. Failure to do so on the part of faculties and their chief academic officers will eventually result in the creation of new educational delivery systems—and for-profit organizations ready to implement them—that ignore our traditional, costly campuses and move to cheaper, more convenient "classrooms" in homes and work sites.

Faculty Involvement in Service Learning Programs

The value of internships, cooperative education, field experiences, and other forms of experiential learning has been well-recognized since the 1960s, especially in fields in which a practicum experience prior to graduation is a requirement to acquire professional certification and employment. In recent years, however, this concept has also been adapted to the needs of students in the arts and sciences, thus providing opportunities for undergraduates in these majors to gain practical experience in a wide variety of professional occupations. Within this context, service learning is a newer concept that connects student learning with community service.[42] Like the other forms of experiential learning, this model also joins theory with practice and involves the student in active learning experiences. What has differentiated service learning from prior programs is the commitment of its experiential component to address unmet community needs and to develop a sense of social responsibility among students. Through experiences in service learning, students also develop skills in solving community problems. Boyer stresses the importance of service in an undergraduate program and recommends that every degree recipient complete a service project.

> We conclude that today's undergraduates urgently need to see the relationship between what they learn and how they live. Specifically, we recommend that every student complete a service project—involving volunteer work in the community or at the college—as an integral part of his or her undergraduate experience. The goal is to help students see that they are not only autonomous individuals but also members of a larger community to which they are accountable.[43]

With support from national and state-based organizations such as Campus Compact, the Partnership for Service-Learning, and the Corporation for National and Community Service, an increasing number of colleges and universities have incorporated service learning into their undergraduate programs in one of three ways: by integrating service into existing courses, by organizing service learning as a formal discipline or area of study, or by affiliating service learning courses with an interdisciplinary campus institute or center dedicated to issues of leadership and citizenship. Colleges and universities that have experienced the most success in integrating service learning concepts into their curricula report that the most important criterion for success is to develop a plan that is consistent with the institution's mission and openly accepted by students, faculty, and administrators as an authentic expression of that mission. While administrative support is essential, faculty participation in both the planning and the implementation is even more important. As is the case in many areas of campus life, creating an impression that the program is being driven by the administration can produce a negative effect. Gradual implementation of a well-conceived plan by a group of committed faculty and students appears to be the most successful route to the establishment of a sustainable service learning program.[44]

Similar to the new partnerships between academic and student affairs noted previously, service learning programs present expanded opportunities to connect members of the faculty more closely to the student culture of the institution. While some provosts may discover that their campus cultures are not naturally inclined toward service learning activities, others may find passionate support from certain departments or the college as a whole. While even the most ardent advocates of this initiative concede it is not a panacea to address many of the shortcomings in a typical undergraduate experience, they still contend that it is one of the most effective strategies now available to connect good citizenship and community support with academic instruction.

Conclusion: New Challenges, New Opportunities

From the perspective of relationships with the faculty, many of the trends now shaping American higher education confront chief academic officers with more challenges than opportunities. Many provosts would be grateful simply for more time to enhance faculty development and student learning without damaging—much less destroying—the collegial culture that sustained their institutions for decades prior to their arrival. And like colleagues on the faculty, chief academic officers are also often skeptics, recognizing the cant and faddishness behind many of the recent agendas for educational reform.

Anyone in the 1950s who believed that colleges and universities would revert to what they had been in the 1930s once the majority of World War II veterans had graduated failed to perceive the transformative impact the war and its aftermath would have both on American society and its higher education institutions. Global competition, student diversity, mounting economic pressures, and the enticements of technology signal a similar, inescapable moment of transformation for contemporary colleges and universities. Like it or not, chief academic officers will be among those closest to the center of the process, and they should view it as a singular opportunity to preserve the best of the present system while achieving needed reforms. Provosts, deans, and academic vice presidents must not leave these tasks to others. Rather, they must simultaneously teach and lead, working collaboratively with faculty to design the new American college or university for the next century.

Leveraging Resources to Enhance Quality: Curriculum Development and Educational Technologies

James R. Coffman

The U.S. higher education system is regarded from many perspectives as the premier example in the world. This is based, in part, on the fact that upwards of half a million international students travel here annually for some part of their postsecondary educations, according to the *Chronicle of Higher Education*. However, the view that American undergraduate education is in decline is also widespread and growing.[1] One critic makes the interesting observation that the huge enrollment increases of the 1960s and 1970s necessitated doubling the size of many faculties and, as a direct result, the quality of education declined.[2] It was during this same period that increased demands for and opportunities in research burgeoned, largely due to federal funding policies. As we approach the close of an uncertain century, new advances in curriculum design and educational technologies, along with a focused reconsideration of the values and work ethic of higher education institutions will be critical to reversing the impact of these fiscal, political, and demographic trends.[3] As one provost recently observed, taxpayers and tuition payers are "here to remind us they own the place and want to inspect the property. They also want us to know they will not be putting any more money into it, expect a lot more from what they have already invested, and may even take some of it back."

Changes in the academic culture of higher education, particularly among career-oriented faculty and consumer-driven students, have created unprecedented challenges for chief academic officers. Provosts, academic vice presidents, and deans of instruction are collectively experiencing an educational paradigm shift that will redefine how a successful college or university achieves its mission.

Managing the Shift: The Need for Curricular Change

Demographics in Transition

After a period of decline, the number of high school graduates nationally is now increasing, a trend that will persist until well after the turn of the century. At the same time, dislocation of new students across state lines will likely increase. While the number of high school graduates nationwide will increase by approximately 20 percent, this number will vary from state to state. California, Texas, and Florida, for example, will experience much larger increases at a time when public funding for higher education remains in crisis. More than half of the graduating seniors in most southern states will be minorities.[4] In the face of this overall increase, most regions have experienced a reluctance by taxpayers to increase funding; in some states, in fact, the movement has become a revolt. Funds are less available and a tax-averse mind-set has become dominant at the federal and state levels. An increasing number of students must be served with fewer resources as deans and academic vice presidents are being pressured by aggressive calls for quality and accountability.

To compound these challenges, the number of nontraditional students is increasing, including those seeking completion of a degree started years before and place-bound workers in pursuit of a bachelor's or advanced degree. As America's middle class shrinks, the distribution between upper and lower class will be determined largely by access to, and ability to use, information.[5] Even elite institutions should prepare for advances from the private sector, including nonaccredited, for-profit organizations willing to tailor their curricula specifically to the needs of those who ask, and pay, for it.

Media-Saturated Students

It is important for chief academic officers to remember that the present generation of college-age high school graduates grew up on a diet of six to eight hours of television daily. Some read well, some do not, but virtually all retain an affinity for, and trust in, television. They are also far more computer literate than any generation before them. These skills have been honed on video games, which results in a high level of comfort with computing, as well as voice and video combinations. While current seventeen- and eighteen-year-olds are America's first truly computer-literate generation, the fact remains that the country's K-12 systems have fostered these learning skills at a faster and more efficient rate than most of the colleges and universities in their communities.

Taxpayer and Parent Concerns

The parents of these technologically literate students have growing reasons for concern. The cost of a baccalaureate degree is escalating beyond their ability to afford it, precisely as insufficient state resources have caused substantial budget reductions. In many instances, these shortfalls have been partly addressed by aggressive, larger than usual, tuition increases. A growing number of campus critics have taken note of these sharp increases in cost, and they have voiced genuine concerns as to whether higher education has lost its focus on the primary reason for its existence: quality teaching. Some sources cite small teaching loads, time spent consulting, research of questionable value, excessive dependence on teaching assistants, and lack of career commitment and classroom ability on the part of some in the professoriate as reasons for poor return on the educational dollar and questionable value of the "end product."[6]

Teaching and Research as Competitors

External demographic, political, and fiscal issues have been compounded by the fact that the academy has succumbed to the self-defeating circular argument about the relative values of teaching and research. Since the 1960s, a consensus has developed that universities value research, scholarship, and creative work more than teaching. The perception is that scholarship has become almost completely aligned with research. Regardless of individual views, it is fair to say that research has become far more important than teaching for career mobility among faculty at the country's 3,550 colleges, community colleges, and universities. This has produced a declining level of incentive to direct extra time and effort toward innovative, high-quality instruction. Ernest L. Boyer makes a valuable contribution to the reconsideration of scholarship by providing chief academic officers, in particular, with the opportunity to emphasize the complementarities among teaching, research, and scholarship.[7] Many provosts and academic vice presidents acknowledge that a new level of faculty leadership will be required to "redefine" scholarship on a national level. In addition, greater amounts of institutional resources will need to be directed toward instructional needs with less going to marginally valuable research and scholarship. Many chief academic officers instinctively avoid such unpleasant decisions yet also must admit that the stakes have been permanently ratcheted upward for individual faculty members, as well as institutions as a whole, regarding both curriculum enhancement and new technologies.

Governing boards, federal agencies, chief executives, and student consumers are all discovering that curriculum design and the methods by which information is delivered and received play a pivotal role in meeting the needs of learners in the new environment. Success will be achieved by implementing change that is accompanied by high incentives for faculty. These incentives must be clearly incorporated into their evaluation, annual salary adjustment, promotion, and tenure processes. At the same time, it is obvious to any chief academic officer that change cannot occur in ways that compromise institutional competitiveness for extramural research funds, as this will undermine the college or university's ability to provide equipment, computing support, graduate stipends, and new degree programs, to say nothing of failing to produce in another prominent area of public expectation.

Overcoming Inflexible Curricula

There is a growing belief among many higher education practitioners that their curricula have become too long and inflexible.[8] In response, some institutions are implementing shorter, more flexible degree-completion programs. On other campuses, some are calling for a national discourse on the undergraduate student as a lifelong learner. At many institutions, curricula have evolved over time within long-established parameters that are heavily influenced by individual faculty interests and accreditation pressures. Conversely, vice presidents and deans on many campuses would acknowledge that the learning needs of students have not been a consistent aspect of curriculum development dialogues in recent years. Faculty members know the most about how a given discipline is evolving and how its curriculum must be adapted; however, the incentive to maintain the status quo has clearly increased on campuses of every type and mission in light of current economic conditions and the employment security needs of a gradually aging professoriate.

The Impact of Information Increases on
Curriculum Development

An explosion of new information is reshaping the learning needs of students along with modes of delivery in most courses. Undertaking change within this context is a formidable challenge for an institution's academic managers; however, it is not inconsistent with other learning objectives now emerging, such as the development of communication skills, problem-solving abilities, and information management skills. Accomplishing these objectives within a curriculum some believe already too crowded may require a significant restructuring in the ways student learning takes place. Faculty will need to change how they spend their talent and time, for example, emphasizing skills that students cannot learn by themselves or from each other.[9]

Developing Strategies for Change

Assessment: One of the Chief Academic Officer's Management Information Tools

The academic vice president must have an effective means to shape campus debates on curriculum enhancement and the incorporation of new instructional technologies. Of particular importance is ensuring a direct link between the assessment of basic skills, general education parameters, and the requirements of each major. When provided with direct evidence of a need to change teaching styles, adequate time to retool and prepare revised syllabi, and the invitation to lead the institution's curriculum development process, faculty members will contribute with imagination and innovation. However, to remain effective, assessment programs must also include mechanisms for feedback to the most basic institutional level—individual academic departments.

Curricular decisions remain the domain of the faculty, with the sometimes subtle, sometimes overt influence of a chief academic officer in the membership appointments to curriculum and academic standards committees. However, while an assessment program may be largely the responsibility of a provost or vice president for instruction, when implemented in collaboration with deans, department heads, and teaching faculty, it can provide the critical evidence for needed changes while demonstrating accountability to students, parents, regents, and legislators. It also should be integrated with personnel, fiscal, and technological decision-making processes.

Leveraging Resources through Time, Place, and Method

Undergraduates live in increasingly varied settings, on campus and off, nearby and distant. A growing variety of educational delivery media are now available to interact with them, including print, videotape, satellite transmission, compressed video, local cable systems, nationwide satellite programs, low power television, and the Internet. Many of these media are used with increasing frequency, whether the students are in a college residence hall or studying abroad. The need for a national infrastructure of informational technology has been noted by Carol A. Twigg.[10] As this diversity of place and methodology has emerged, the definition of "campus" as a learning place has also experienced a permanent redefinition. For example, since distance learning technologies can serve students on and off a campus simultaneously, an added benefit to the "virtual classroom" model will be to reduce housing pressures on many crowded university campuses without incurring enrollment declines.

Emerging Trends in Curriculum Development and Educational Technologies

- The number of high school graduates is going up, to a projected 20 percent increase soon after 2000
- Future students will be much more computer literate and oriented toward television and interactive technology
- Taxpayers and tuition payers have become cynical about a perceived lack of attention to teaching, in contrast to such other pursuits as research
- The typical curriculum has become too long and inflexible
- The information explosion has proven to be a reality, and it will continue to impact the needs of students

---

In order to increase the quality of the student learning experience in the face of rising enrollments, shrinking resources, and other demands on the learners' time, new approaches to leveraging the time of both full- and part-time faculty members need to be implemented. Professional development opportunities must accompany these new models. One way to achieve this might involve increasing the number of applications of a single work product, such as a class preparation, multimedia product, or lecture, by simulcasting over compressed video with two-way video and audio. This method leverages both quality and lack thereof, so it is imperative, at least initially, that only faculty who volunteer to teach in this manner, and are effective at it, are introduced into these technologies. This will allow other instructors to observe the potential of this format and to consider the benefits of a course or seminar in "television teaching methods," for instance.

The most cost-effective way to replicate a high-quality classroom preparation is to use videotape. The advantages are obvious, as class interaction and enrichment materials can be included in the finished product. Videotape presentations have acquired an unfavorable reputation on some campuses because of poor technique or inexperience. Students and faculty both note the low learning value in simply taping "talking heads." However, if other visual materials, including class interaction and graphics are edited into the final product, video presentations can be deployed in multiple applications and can be worth significantly more than the modest financial investment required for production.

Such a product will allow faculty members to teach additional courses without additional preparation time, and, as materials become dated, they can be edited with relative ease and at lower costs. Sections of these courses may be assigned to teaching assistants yet maintain levels of quality reflective of senior professors. High-quality videotape can be used in courses taught via satellite, fiber, and compressed video, and students at distant sights can use videotape and communicate with the instructor by way of e-mail or a telephone bridge, individually or as part of a group. Learners who may participate just as easily in their homes as at a classroom site may also communicate with the instructor and other students over the Internet.

Leveraging Faculty Time and Talent Via Technology: A Case Study

An instructor teaches a course in computer security to a live class on campus. The class simultaneously is broadcast on satellite as part of a national program, broadcast as compressed video to a regional city, and taped for future use in the classroom, over satellite and compressed video, and through the mail. In this way, the remote students in the compressed video classroom have two-way interaction with the instructor, along with the students in the origination site, via both voice and video. Other remote students interact via the Internet at any time of the day or night with questions and comments. Those involved note with interest that the after-class interaction with the instructor is greater with the remote students who use e-mail than with local students.

On many campuses, instructors are still not experienced in or oriented to distance education methods, especially those who are not comfortable with rapid change or with the idea of working with media in the classroom. For them, the words "distance learning" usually evoke one interpretation: television. The automatic jump to television as the only means of distance learning is a serious miscalculation that becomes an obstacle not only to making progress but even to getting started. There are good reasons for this, as television is expensive in terms of the equipment and technical support, and many people are not comfortable working in front of a camera. Transmission costs may also be formidable.

However, television is only one asset in a comprehensive program of distance learning, whether it is low power or cable transmission, via satellite, fiber networks, or compressed video. Other valuable methods, with far less cost, include telephone conferencing (a telebridge system can accommodate class members from any site anywhere in the country), the Internet, print, mailed videotape, and CD-ROM. Without doubt, the World Wide Web is currently the most powerful single means of leveraging course material through multiple applications. Chief academic officers must avoid the "television-only" trap in favor of mixing media to develop the most cost-effective overall strategy for delivering a course at the highest level of quality to the greatest number of students. A small number of live transmissions via television can greatly enrich a course principally based on print, videotape, or CD-ROM, telephone bridging, and the Internet.

Some of the material in a mediated course such as the one described above can also be used in extension or other noncredit applications. The demand is great for focused, noncredit information, and many outreach organizations are now moving in the direction of new media applications. Even more important, on-campus students can enroll in distance learning courses along with off-campus students. For example, if an institution offered a course that utilized mailed tape, a web site, e-mail, and a telebridge, it could also benefit an on-campus student to enroll in that course if it is more convenient, not otherwise available, or if it fits his or her curricular sequence more efficiently, as long as the student has a telephone, a computer, and a VCR. While this type of course may not be appropriate for first- or even second-year students, it could have very productive applications to upper division and master's-degree candidates.

Leveraging Curricular Resources through Class Size and Time

Almost every college or university experiences a preference among students for classes that are offered from Monday through Thursday, from 9:00 A.M. to 4:00 P.M. Reasons for this range from a better distribution of leisure time to the need to work evenings and weekends by a growing percentage of all part-time students. Whatever the reasons on a specific campus, a great deal of classroom space; heating, cooling, and light bills; and some degree of faculty time are thus wasted. As the pressure for accountability rises, use of these resources will become more attractive to trustees, legislators, parents, and to students themselves, especially those for whom a concentrated degree sequence is important.

At the same time, the needs of nontraditional students are rising on a par with the average age of bachelor's degree enrollees generally. This is a larger issue in population centers, but any environment including large numbers of daytime workers or parents occupied with children has a growing need for class offerings on evenings and weekends. Thus, the opportunity exists on an increasing number of campuses to mix regularly enrolled, full-time students with nontraditional students in evening and weekend classes when evening degree sequences and traditional student courses coincide. Depending on how a given college structures and collects fees, considerable advantages can be accomplished in managing fixed costs, meeting shortfalls in course availability, and refinancing some of the instructional costs for full-time students.

Inappropriately small class sections will inexorably creep into the line schedule. While they sometimes can be justified, they often are simply a result of poor scheduling or maneuvering on the part of a faculty member with a specific area of interest outside the mainstream of institutional objectives. Thus, it is essential for the academic vice president to establish a simple, nonintrusive system to audit teaching productivity on an individual faculty basis. This is one of numerous reasons that the chief academic officer must also implement an aggressive institutional research function, as consistent and accurate data is critical in this regard. Elimination of some inappropriately small classes and decreasing the frequency of others can recoup substantial resources. When provided with adequate, reliable data from the institutional research offices, deans and department heads can act effectively to correct the problem while simultaneously responding to the calls for accountability from alumni, trustees, and the federal government. The combination of an effective assessment program and inventory of teaching productivity, coupled with an effective approach to the evaluation of teaching, places the chief academic officer in a strategic position to work effectively with the deans both in delegating the operational authority to manage academic programs and monitoring results through ongoing evaluation and feedback.

Leveraging Curricular Resources through Large Classes

Many chief academic officers concede that a greater percentage of the full-time faculty must teach greater numbers of student credit hours. Several of the above-mentioned strategies can help accomplish this objective. Another strategy is the effective and innovative use of large classes. The most common response to large classes is negative; objections are couched in terms of poor student interaction, lack of writing experience, fewer written assignments, and excessive use of grading by machine. However, the contention that active learning cannot be effectively accomplished in large classes simply is no longer true. Teaching large classes is a skill that can be learned, and in some courses, although not all, it is arguably better for an excellent teacher adept at engaging large classes in active learning processes to do so than to subdivide the group among a greater number of teachers who may teach at a much lower level of effectiveness, even with smaller numbers of students.

Definition of terms is important in considering the objectives related to the use of large classes. Active learning is not limited to writing. If a curricular objective includes the need for each student to write one or more extensive papers which the instructor will then evaluate and return, then classes over thirty or forty are daunting, and those over one hundred clearly will not work. However, in a significant number of instances when active learning is the objective, large classes may achieve institutional, as well as departmental, objectives extremely well. Critical ingredients include the imagination and ability of the faculty member in charge and professional development support from a dean or provost.

Considerable attention has been given to pedagogy in large-class environments.[11] Specific innovations, such as use of a roving microphone, in-class debates, small group responses to in-class questions, and participatory lecturing are but a few of many means through which experienced faculty can create an active learning environment in large classes.[12] Hardware and software configurations have also been developed to augment active learning in large classrooms.

As a final strategy, large class numbers can be divided into smaller "courses" within the larger course, with groups subject to rearrangement during the semester.[13] This can achieve learning objectives that go well beyond content, such as teamwork, information acquisition and management, critical thinking, and problem solving. The opportunity to teach students the value of synergistically pooling strengths can be as readily accomplished in teams derived from large classes as those from small ones.[14]

Managing the Connections between Curriculum Development and Resource Development: A Case Study

While curriculum remains the purview of the faculty, the need to debate, critique, and scrutinize curricular issues annually is held by multiple campus constituencies and serves as the best insurance against one faction's attempt to marginalize a degree program that could shape the potential for career success by thousands of students. At the same time, innovation and the willingness to adapt rapidly, or even to take a measured risk, is often overruled on tradition-bound campuses. The need to strike a pragmatic balance between these two concerns is a central responsibility of the chief academic officer. The challenge requires an effective working relationship with the faculty leadership, specifically the academic affairs and curriculum committees.

Since the largest line in a college or university budget is typically faculty salaries and the bulk of their time is devoted to teaching the curriculum, a vice president for academic affairs will naturally spend a significant amount of professional time managing the course and curriculum approval process. Large fiscal commitments can be made without money ever being mentioned as increments that seem small on a day-to-day basis become magnified over time. These expenditures are often unappreciated until the chief academic officer articulates the broader picture. Even then, however, the most common reaction is to look for yet more money to increase the number of replications of an outdated prerequisite without thinking to question the need for the program overall.

Suppose, for example, that the College of Engineering makes a convincing case that graduates cannot effectively write technical reports. In response, faculty members in Engineering revise the curriculum to include three semester credits of technical writing. This change is approved on its academic merits and is to be taught in the English Department, since to teach it in Engineering would set a precedent for establishing multiple, duplicative English units. The change is made during an enrollment decline, so it is feasible for the English Department to absorb the initial sections. However, an enrollment increase then ensues, with the greatest increase in Engineering, requiring the English Department to add sections of expository writing one and two and also two more sections of technical writing. At that time, faculty members in the Architecture Department recognize the need for a technical writing course for their fifth-year students. The proposal passes on its merits, but it calls for four more sections, requiring an additional instructor. The English Department cannot absorb this cost; in addition, if it is allocated another faculty position, its priority may be to add a position in another specialty because the number of English majors has also increased.

Enter the Assembly for the Accreditation of Collegiate Schools of Business. During an accreditation review, they have informed the dean of the College of Business that she has two problems: first, her college's curriculum is too heavy in business courses and second, the number of credit hours taught by each faculty member is above the guidelines. To avoid probation, the business faculty take two practical corrective measures. First, they redesign the curriculum to include more liberal arts courses, especially those that emphasize critical thinking and writing, such as philosophy, once again impacting the Arts and Sciences budget. Second, they raise the grade point average threshold for admittance into the business college, thereby decreasing the number of majors in the third year. Most of the now unsuccessful students become Arts and Sciences majors, heavily oriented toward the social sciences, which is already overrun by the general enrollment increase. Simultaneously, faculty responsible for other majors are rearranging the curriculum by adding prerequisite requirements for enrollment in specific courses, thus raising the demand for them.

Clearly, the chief academic officer must manage a process that will spin out of control if left to an approval system based principally on the academic merits of each isolated case, and he or she must do this in a way that does not result in tampering with the institution's core academic processes.

This can be accomplished by several methods. Given sufficient resources, the chief academic officer can maintain a pool of funds to follow credit-hour generation and let the process ebb and flow, while strategically moving funds toward newly developed pressure points. The main problem with this approach is that it leads to gamesmanship based on credit-hour production or avoidance, depending on the funding formula and availability of funds. This method can drive departments and programs apart and produce a corporate mentality to institutional operations with the curriculum subject to manipulation, based not on the needs of the student but on the most advantageous way to secure credit hour–driven funds.

A more effective strategy links budgeting to course approval, along with, but separate from, academic appraisal. If the course approval process includes parallel tracks of academic assessment and approval by the faculty at various stages, and documentation of indirect effects of curricular decisions and fund sourcing, then the chief academic officer and the faculty have an opportunity to carry out their responsibilities in concert. Of at least equal importance, the incentive for gamesmanship is reduced or eliminated. This outcome may be enhanced further by developing a system through which a core of widely used prerequisite "service" courses are withdrawn, for funding purposes, from each departmental budget and treated as an institution-wide responsibility. This will also make departments think twice about curricular changes, since they will encounter a direct feedback loop in terms of funding the prerequisites.

Elimination of credit hour–driven budgeting strategies within a college or university has a number of important advantages, principally, that curriculum changes are more likely to be made for academic reasons. This is especially true of institution-wide curriculum changes, prominent examples of which are the general education and core curricula. Others would include interdisciplinary programs, especially those that cross departmental lines.

Sources outside of higher education have begun to call for reconsiderations of the baccalaureate curriculum, proceeding from the point of view that it is too long, that its content is not necessarily derived from student needs,[15] and that faculty frequently are hired based upon their research expertise.[16] In many instances, even though a new faculty member will teach a course that the department must offer, he or she also will teach a course that is of particular professional interest. While this enriches the array of opportunities afforded students, it also consumes resources while expending faculty salaries. By definition, this begins to influence the nature of the curriculum. Add to this the impact of accreditation requirements on majors and their prerequisites and the pervasive belief that as new areas develop within a discipline courses must be added, and one can quickly discern how the curriculum of numerous colleges and universities has become elongated and inflexible. Simply put, too many bachelor degree programs reflect a combination of incremental additions and occasional fine-tuning without ever having been comprehensively scrutinized from the perspective of students as lifelong learners and citizens.

Connecting the Curriculum More Closely to Teaching and Learning

Program curricula are inextricably bound to the manner in which they are taught. The quality and efficiency of the student's learning experience can be enhanced most effectively through leveraging the use of faculty time, yet this will require most provosts and academic vice presidents to move beyond dated academic management models in which expectations are the same for all faculty in terms of specialization, service, and teaching load. George Winston observes in *Change* magazine that eliminating programs and reducing administrative costs, two measures that have received extensive attention in recent years, have very limited potential to save money.[17] However, restructuring the role of the faculty has significant potential even if the average workload of faculty members does not increase. By redirecting faculty time and talent to those areas where current students need it, while allowing them to take a much more active role in the teaching and learning process, makes much more effective use of educational resources, many of which can be leveraged even further through the use of distance learning technology.

Nationally, higher education leaders have become accustomed to holding similar expectations for all faculty in a department. Often, faculty are viewed as spending half their time in teaching and half in research, with whatever is left for "service." The theory has been that in an academic environment of this sort, every faculty member will invest and partake equally in the departmental mission. While most faculty prove themselves proficient to a greater or lesser degree in both teaching and research and scholarship, their intrinsic strengths, weaknesses, and areas of real interest and enthusiasm differ, and this becomes magnified over time. Some are eminently productive in the use of the time allotted to expectations of research and scholarship, others less so. And yet, as expectations remain the same for all, differences are manifested

Best Practices in Curriculum Development and Educational Technologies

- Ensure that all objectives and strategies are consistent with the overarching mission of the university
- Develop and maintain a management information system that includes strong assessment and institutional research components
- Leverage faculty time and talent through multiple applications, class size strategies, and technology
- Optimize the relationship between learning objectives and resources through an integrated organizational structure

in salary differentials and promotions, or lack thereof, along the path to full professorships.

Lack of productivity in time allocated for research and scholarship among tenured faculty represents a large block of wasted resources,[18] which is no longer affordable among highly competitive, midrange colleges and universities. Many academic vice presidents are quick to explain why this problem persists: The academic job market remains geared to research, not teaching. Some academic managers assume a pessimistic view of an individual institution's ability to change, yet, until each college or university begins to address this troubling dichotomy within its own academic culture, little real progress can occur in this area even though recent attention has been focused on a national market for those excelling in classroom teaching.[19]

In fact, a national market for innovative college and university teachers will emerge for one simple reason: Those who pay taxes and tuition will demand more quality than they are currently receiving, which will create the market by forcing competition among higher education institutions. This is not to say that quality scholarship will diminish. To the contrary, scholarship is being redefined in terms of both teaching and service. In fact, there will emerge an expanded role for productive research scholars, especially those who are rewarded with extramural funding, as institutions will continue to depend on them to fund laboratory equipment, computer centers, and graduate student stipends.

Major change in an institution's curriculum requires multiyear commitments of time and purpose on the part of numerous faculty members. Without this commitment, it will not happen, yet in terms of career advancement, these individuals will be accepting a risk to accomplish it. Their time, talent, and expertise are all they have to further their own interests, and if they dedicate one or all for a period of years on a project as encompassing as redefining a curriculum and implementing new technologies, they may pay a significant price. In particular, they will need assurances from their chief academic officer, dean, and department chair that this project is necessary and worthwhile to their career advancement. On many campuses, these assurances are difficult to provide at a time when the academy itself is experiencing so many uncertainties, many of which are shaping these same career opportunities. For these reasons, the chief academic officer must build credibility through support of this process and secure an equal level of support from the president and members of the governing board, a challenging task for even an experienced academic officer and one which can place her or him directly between anxious professors and aggressive trustees.

Developing Technology and Talent Collaboratively

In the context of the curriculum, technology achieves two principal purposes: higher quality and greater efficiency. Yet, faculty still populate both ends of the technological scale with some on the cutting edge and others still to turn on their first computer. Thus, reshaping the technological infrastructure of a college or university must also include changing the culture among personnel regarding its utilization. The provost or academic vice president will need to manage both of these initiatives, consistently and simultaneously, through institution-wide considerations of infrastructure needs and individualized faculty development plans.

Key factors in reshaping the infrastructure will be (1) central computing, the institutional network and its interface with national networks; (2) departmental and college-level computing needs; (3) telecommunications, including the college or university's telephone company or equivalent; (4) the voice network, including a telephone bridge or other telephone conferencing operation; and (5) a video production facility. All of these units should be consolidated into one structure with its key administrator reporting directly to the chief academic officer in order to coordinate development and maximize applications of the infrastructure across the curriculum most efficiently. With this accomplished, even smaller, less-affluent institutions can establish a research base while furthering their faculty development programs and technological support for new modes of teaching and learning.

This organizational structure adds a new and important responsibility to the scope of authority for many vice presidents for academic affairs, as the institution's other vice presidents and their administrative hierarchies will depend on the same computing infrastructure to operate major organizational systems, not to mention the ongoing needs of deans and department chairs. They must be able to depend on this infra-structure to serve, and adapt to, their evolving needs, and this can be accomplished most effectively by a collaborative electronic framework coordinated by the chief academic officer.

Conclusion: New Roles for the Chief Academic Officer

Increasingly, it is the campus's chief academic officer, most of whom have not been trained in technical disciplines, who must oversee an information system providing voice, video, and data management and production, both on campus and off, while simultaneously ensuring efficient hardware, software, and networking support for all administrative end-users. Hiring key administrators with the necessary combination of technical and people skills, as well as vision, is central to the chief academic officer's future success. Even on medium-sized campuses, this entails developing large multimedia, human resource, and student information systems, along with high-end computing, Internet connections, and day-to-day word processing and spreadsheet work for dozens of administrative units. Additionally, these systems are being developed at a time when many institutions are phasing out mainframe systems, or turning them into giant servers, in favor of smaller networked models.

While this structural approach to information and instruction technology promises to be a more efficient and feasible format, it brings with it a new set of policy determinations. For example, will the smaller computing units be lined up side-by-side in one central location, or will they be distributed across the campus and more closely associated with large end-user applications? Who will "own" the hardware, software, and operating systems? Who will be responsible for security? Which senior officer will control the data that is produced? Who will hire and supervise technical support people for desktop units and servers?

The overarching issue of how to finance such a comprehensive project over an extended period of annual budget cycles will challenge the vice presidents for academic affairs and finance beyond all others. In this regard, a Technology Advisory Board, which brings actual expertise to the institution in a manner consistent with the mission of shared governance, will be useful. Such an advisory group should report to the chief academic officer, or his or her chief information systems officer, who must constantly weigh its recommendations against program goals and budget limitations. Few academicians have been trained for this new responsibility, nor to build the common ground between on-campus and off-campus constituencies while managing the institution's overall academic enterprise with its competing administrative agendas.

As infrastructure and administrative configurations are being addressed, increasing faculty development support must also remain a priority. Two elements are essential to achieving this objective: individual success stories and money.[20] With titles such as *101 Success Stories of Information Technology in Higher Education*, various collections detailing impressive faculty innovations have begun to appear and may prove useful on campuses with constricted budgets and small instructional talent pools.[21]

In a faculty of any size, however, there will emerge individuals who apply new technology-based innovations to classic pedagogical issues, and it is critical for the chief academic officer to locate, cultivate, and encourage these professionals. As this group begins to grow, the provost or vice president must create an environment that advances their development, and self-confidence, for example, through institutional minigrants. These resources will prove to be well spent, as "early adopters" assume faculty leadership roles in mentoring others to develop their own technological solutions.

From the perspective of the chief academic officer, curriculum development and new educational technologies present an expanding set of challenges to effective leadership, and while these two components of the institution's academic mission provide the provost or academic vice president with an unprecedented set of resource combinations to achieve new models of teaching and learning, it is with the understanding that the long-term success of each combination, and collaboration, will be based in the talent and commitment of the institution's faculty.

CHAPTER FOUR

Academic Governance: The Art of Herding Cats

Mark G. Edelstein

Administration is frustrating. Closure is elusive, systems come undone, solutions create new problems, no group is ever satisfied without another being dissatisfied, and criticism about process can overwhelm substance.

—*Robert Birnbaum,* How Colleges Work

Nothing is more central to the success of a chief academic officer than an understanding of collegial governance. However dedicated, brilliant, and indefatigable, however experienced in curriculum planning, instructional innovation, and budgeting, an academic vice president will only be effective to the extent that he or she understands the institution's governance systems and is skillful at operating within them. The reason for this is simple: Governance constitutes the medium through which ideas are turned into actions on a campus. It is the way things happen and the way they get done. Broadly defined, the concept of "governance" encompasses all of the "structures and processes through which institutional participants interact with and influence each other and communicate with the larger environment."[1]

Fortunately, most chief academic officers come to their positions with an understanding of what governance is like in an academic setting. Many were formerly deans or department chairs and served as faculty members for a significant period of time, often exercising leadership in an academic senate or other governance body. In fact, an understanding of governance processes, whether consciously developed or simply intuited, may be one of the characteristics that distinguishes potential academic vice presidents from their colleagues.

For most chief academic officers, however, their new role will require a deeper and more subtle understanding of governance than was necessary in any previous position. The variety of challenges will be far greater, and the chief academic officer must be able not only to read a situation immediately and accurately but also to choose the single most appropriate action from a range of potential responses. When things "come undone," when a new issue arises at the eleventh hour, when a carefully developed consensus seems to fade and disappear before one's eyes, it is essential that a chief academic officer have the flexibility and multiple resources to construct another solution or approach from the debris with which he or she has been left.

New Roles for Faculty and Chief Academic Officers

Perhaps the most basic fact about governance in institutions of higher education is that it is dualistic. Trustees hold ultimate legal authority, much of which is delegated to the chief executive officer and through her or him to the rest of the administration. Based on this authority, the administration establishes the structures and processes through which the institutional mission is implemented. However, the faculty body also possesses authority in many areas, either because it has been specifically delegated by the trustees or because the faculty have traditionally assumed it. These two lines of authority are sometimes woven together effectively, with both the faculty and administration understanding the extent and limitation of their powers and avoiding unnecessary conflict and duplication of effort. At other times, the dualism engenders opposition and confusion, as both sides believe their authority is being undermined or their legitimate role usurped. When disputes over governance erupt, chief academic officers often find themselves caught in the middle, trying to explain the faculty perspective to the trustees or to the rest of the administration, trying to explain the trustee or administrative perspective to the faculty, and, of course, trying very hard not to look like a "stooge" to either side.

In the vast majority of American colleges and universities, faculty members now have a greater voice in governance than ever before. Much of this progress occurred early in the twentieth century when faculty became more professionalized and were delegated increasing authority, particularly in the areas of curriculum and academic personnel.[2] Even within two-year colleges, which often developed out of K-12 systems and tended to treat teachers more as employees than professionals, there has been a significant increase in faculty responsibility over the last several decades.

Faculty, however, are generally unimpressed by these changes. They trace their role back to the collegium of the medieval university, which they view as a true "community of scholars" functioning perfectly well with no administration whatsoever. From this Edenic perspective, administrators of today seem, at best, a necessary evil. The tendency among faculty members to believe that whatever authority they may have is only a shadow of the authority they should have is one of the things that makes governance such an inexhaustible topic of debate on many campuses. Most faculty don't actually believe that administrators are merely an excrescence on the system, and most administrators don't feel a corresponding contempt for the faculty's intrusions into administration, but it doesn't take much exposure to the kind of banter exchanged between faculty and administrators to realize that there is often something of those attitudes just below the surface of academic life. When discussions become heated, those attitudes are likely to break through.

Therefore, it becomes critical for a provost or academic vice president never to lose sight of two realities. The first is that there is a compelling rationale for the faculty's role in governance. It is only the faculty as a whole that has the necessary expertise to ensure the quality of curriculum, instruction, and research. While it may seem at times that administrators could act much more efficiently if they were allowed to simply "manage" their institutions, the reality is that the most important aspects of colleges and universities cannot be "managed." They involve far too much specialized knowledge. If the members of the faculty do not exert themselves to protect and enhance academic quality through their governance role, there is no way the administration can do so effectively.

The second thing that one should not lose sight of is that the faculty have a god-given right to criticize the administration, fairly or unfairly. They have the right to complain and disparage, to be sarcastic, cynical, carping, or snide. They do not need to be informed about the issues as they would within their own disciplines. Administration is not a discipline. Besides, as Henry Rosovsky observes, "Governance is a form of class treason, a leap from 'we' to 'they,' and a betrayal of our primary mission—teaching and research."[3] In the face of such a betrayal, it is natural to expect a certain amount of calumny and contempt. One must recognize that this is simply a symbolic response to a symbolic "treason," compounded by a perception of administrative dominance. References to "the bean-counting idiots in the administration building" may seem quite personal, but such statements are really just bullets fired into the air, and faculty often seem genuinely surprised when someone is injured by one of them. Reacting to such criticism is worse than futile, for it can create real conflicts where none existed before.

This does not mean that the criticism should simply be ignored, however. In fact, it is important to monitor its level quite closely as an indicator of faculty morale. Every campus will display its own level of ambient discontent, to which the chief academic officer must be closely attuned. The better one understands this ambient level, the more capable he or she will be of distinguishing the ordinary dissatisfactions of academic life from more serious, substantive complaints requiring immediate attention.

Reading the Institution

Effective chief academic officers become so by studying their institutions and learning their cultures. Clearly, the vice president for academic affairs or provost must know the history and traditions of a college, as well as its structures, policies, and procedures. Beyond this, however, he or she must also understand the culture—the "collective, mutually shaping patterns of norms, values, practices, beliefs, and assumptions that guide the behavior of individuals and groups in an institution of higher education and provide a frame of reference within which to interpret the meaning of events and actions on and off campus."[4] The longer one stays at an institution, the more one appreciates the force of its culture. Whether leaders can actually alter that culture may be open to question, but the importance of understanding the culture and aligning one's strategies with it is widely acknowledged. As W. G. Tierney points out, "To implement decisions, leaders must have a full, nuanced understanding of the organization's culture. Only then can they articulate decisions in a way that will speak to the needs of various constituencies and marshal their support."[5]

On many small campuses, to choose a simple example, the predominant description of the culture is "familial." Faculty members, particularly those who have been at the institution for a number of years, will often describe the college as "more like a family than an institution." Many things are implied in this description, an attitude of caring and concern toward one's colleagues, a tolerance for idiosyncratic and even nonproductive behavior, a sense of protectiveness, a resistance to outside influences. This aspect of institutional culture may be either positive or negative, which is to say that the "family" may be either functional or dysfunctional. If it is dysfunctional, an effective administration can help it to become functional, but no administration is going to change the basic orientation of the culture. Only time and growth can accomplish that. In this context, an academic vice president will be effective to the extent that his or her initiatives seem a natural outgrowth of that culture and are consistent with it.

The culture of an institution cannot be learned behind a desk. Particularly during one's first year, when a new chief academic officer may feel most overwhelmed by the pressures of paperwork and committee meetings, it is essential to be out walking around the campus, talking with people, hearing their stories, listening carefully for the myths and shared perceptions that bind the culture together. One needs to understand how the campus feels about itself and how it perceives the governance process, which groups feel empowered by the process and which feel alienated. Even when a provost comes to understand these things thoroughly, it will be crucial to stay tuned in to as many voices as possible. "Listen to gossip," Henry Rosovsky was advised early in his administrative career, "that is what all good deans do." Many experienced administrators have come to appreciate the "deep wisdom" that Rosovsky found in this advice.[6]

To be sure, as the chief academic officer is learning about the college community, that same community is learning about its chief academic officer. This is an important opportunity, therefore, to demonstrate to the campus that its academic leader is a careful and sympathetic listener, not someone seeking to impose ideas but rather one whose goal is to understand and reflect back to the institution its own highest potential. Creating this impression will often require a great deal of self-restraint because when one is new to a college or university and bears no responsibility for current practices, there seems to be so much that needs improving. The temptation to start "fixing" things may be very strong. Indeed, it may appear that the entire campus is waiting for the new academic vice president to act, to display that "dynamic leadership" for which he or she was appointed. "Acting is easy," as Birnbaum points out, "listening is hard, particularly for leaders who believe that the leadership role calls for them to tell other people what to do. But listening and influencing are reciprocal—the more administrators listen to others, the more others listen to them. We influence others by allowing ourselves to be influenced."[7] In a period such as this, when higher education faces major and fundamental challenges, the role of "change agent" may, in fact, be absolutely vital to an academic leader's position and to an institution, but one must first understand what needs to be changed and what can be changed. Often, one is most effective as a change agent when the role is developed gradually and approached obliquely. There is no merit whatsoever in creating unnecessary opposition, and even the most illogical practices and absurd policies will be defended when people feel threatened.

Certainly while one is in the initial stages of learning about an institution, it is advisable to withhold one's judgment on major issues. However, it can be very useful to pay attention to the small, concrete complaints that people voice and, whenever possible, take action to address those complaints. Often, it is these small issues—a poorly lit classroom, a cramped office, an inflexible policy in the bookstore—that wear on faculty, and taking steps to eliminate these annoyances will have several positive effects. First, these efforts buy goodwill, and although this commodity does not keep well, academic vice presidents and deans are well advised to maintain as large a store as possible. Second, such acts provide an opportunity for a new chief academic officer to demonstrate the ability to make things happen, to work effectively within the system, bringing about small but tangible improvements to the quality of campus life. This will make faculty much more inclined to provide support later when larger issues are addressed. Third, and perhaps most important, these efforts keep new academic administrators from addressing the larger issues before they really understand the institution and its culture, and thus may prevent their stumbling into a major disaster early in their tenure.

Some disagree with this approach and believe that they should use the "honeymoon" period to do difficult things, such as reorganizing their administrative structure, removing ineffective personnel, or launching a major revision of the curriculum. However, changes that seem clearly desirable when viewed from the outside of the institutional culture may seem very different when viewed from the inside, and it is dangerous to take major steps when one is not in a position to clearly anticipate the reaction. Also, when leaders initiate a change process, they don't necessarily know where it will stop or what all of the subsidiary effects will be. A person may think that all he or she is going to do is tear down a single wall, but until one really understands how the house is built, it is much safer to stick to interior decoration.

One does not really need a plan in order to begin a study of the college and its governance system. A chief academic officer might begin by consulting with the leaders of the academic senate and its committees, with department chairs and student government leaders, with representatives of the union if collective bargaining is in place, and with support staff or any other group that may have a role in campus governance. However, one must also go beyond these leaders in order to achieve a full sense of the college or university. The chief academic officer should talk with new and adjunct faculty, seek out those who are angry or disengaged and listen to their stories, and ask the opinion of those not normally asked. Even more important, academic vice presidents should visit classrooms, studios, and laboratories. Not only will they learn a great deal about the educational programs but they will also see faculty at their best. If later they find themselves at odds with particular faculty members and inclined to dismiss them as obstructive, petty, or irrational, it can be a valuable counterpoint to have observed them personally as brilliant and dedicated teachers.

Organizational Models

As the chief academic officer gathers more information about the institution, a conceptual framework will be helpful in organizing his or her knowledge and promoting a greater understanding of its governance system. One of the most useful frameworks for this purpose describes four types of organizational functioning in higher education: collegial, bureaucratic, political, and anarchic.[8] Although every institution includes aspects of all four models, one model tends to predominate on a campus, and the models correlate with four different types of postsecondary institutions:

1. *Collegial.* Most typical of smaller, liberal arts colleges, this model is organized in an egalitarian and democratic manner with little hierarchy. Interactions among the entire community are extensive and informal, and decisions are generally reached by consensus after thorough and lengthy deliberation. The function of the administration is to fulfill the will of the collegium. Institutional culture is cohesive.

2. *Bureaucratic.* Most typical of public community colleges, this model is more highly structured with a strong emphasis on the rationality of the organization, a clear chain of command, and formal processes for decision making. There is an extensive reliance on rules and policies, generally developed by the administration, which is dominant in the decision-making process. Institutional culture is coherent but comparatively shallow.

3. *Political.* Most typical of regional state universities, this model is characterized by a diffusion of power among groups and individuals, who may sometimes act autonomously but are largely interdependent. The power of any group or individual depends on the issue and the coalitions of common interest built around that issue. The senior administration and board may form a dominant coalition, but no group or individual dominates in all decisions, and decisions tend to be made through political means. While conflicts are constant, the fact that individuals belong to multiple groups and coalitions creates a balance and stability in the system. Institutional culture is less coherent because of ongoing competition among various interest groups.

4. *Anarchic.* Most typical of flagship universities, this model is best described as an "organized anarchy," with vaguely defined goals and processes and fluid participation within its many formal and informal

groups. People participate in decision making based on their interests, and authority may derive from numerous sources both internal and external to the university. The loose coupling of elements within the organization makes it difficult to trace clear patterns of decision-making. Institutional culture is more national and international than local and is based on the professional reputations and authority of the faculty.

It is useful to think about a college or university in terms of these models, particularly for those who have moved from one type of institution to another. No academic vice president would fall into the obvious trap of publicly comparing a new institution to a former one or touting the way things were done at the former institution. It is easier, however, to make the more subtle mistake of basing expectations on an entirely different model from the one being examined. A bureaucratic institution may seem hopelessly rule-bound to someone used to a more political environment, and either a political or anarchical institution may seem like a free-for-all to someone more used to the rationality of a bureaucratic environment. Therefore, it is important to understand the distinctions among the four models and to appreciate the strengths of each.

It is equally important to use the conceptual framework of these models judiciously and avoid unwarranted assumptions. While community colleges tend toward the structure of rational bureaucracies, they also reflect to widely varying degrees the collegial, political, and anarchic models. What appears to be an extremely disorganized community college may simply be a community college not principally bureaucratic in structure. It is necessary to think carefully about which model is dominant in a particular institution and then look for all the ways in which other models are evident as well. It is also very useful to try to understand why a college or university has developed into its particular blend, what forces have shaped its governance structure, and whether those forces will remain constant in the immediate future.

Despite important distinctions among the four models and the effects of history and circumstance in making each institution's governance system unique, there is a significant amount of cross-fertilization among institutions and several external factors that have moved all institutions in a common direction. Colleges and universities tend to emulate the most prestigious among them, and this tendency increases when there is close communication among institutions. In California, for example, where there is a great deal of interaction among the academic senates of the California Community Colleges, the California State University, and the University of California, the senates of the community colleges have come to resemble those of the university and state university in both structure and authority. As one might expect, since the community colleges tend more toward the bureaucratic model, the role of the senates is established in law and policy in ways that were never thought necessary within the more anarchic or political senior institutions. The senates of the three systems remain very distinctive, each reflecting the characteristics of the institution in which it exists, but at the same time they have grown increasingly similar in style and organization over the past two decades.

The national movement toward shared decision making in business and industry is also having an effect on colleges, as clerical staff and other constituencies request an increasingly greater voice in the decisions affecting their work. There is a growing belief that "participatory management" can improve organizational effectiveness, and this, along with a greater sensitivity to student rights and the expansion of traditional faculty governance, has moved most colleges and universities toward more open, participatory governance structures. More and more colleges are embracing the concept of governance expressed in the American Association of University Professors' "Joint Statement on Government of Colleges and Universities," in which constituencies share responsibility for governance based on their expertise and direct interest in a specific issue.[9] This direction creates a model for the governance of higher education, but there is an enormous distance between the model and the way groups actually operate on contemporary campuses.

One college president recently related a dream she had in which she was attempting to drive a city bus, one of the extra-long models, "loosely coupled" in the middle with an accordion-like connection. She was having great difficulty because the steering wheel was right in the middle of the bus rather than at the front, and all of the windows were so darkly tinted that she could only make out vague shapes outside the bus. Inside, there was a great deal of noise and confusion. All of the passengers were standing, many of them shouting directions to her and pointing toward different windows. Someone was crying, and a number of scuffles were going on among the passengers. In the distance, she heard gunfire. She referred to this as a "dream of governance."

Academic Senates: Six Guidelines for Success

For each chief academic officer, the most important aspect of governance will be the faculty senate, council, or equivalent body, as this is the structure through which authority is delegated to the faculty in the areas of curriculum, instruction, faculty status, and the educational aspects of student life.[10] Since these areas also constitute the core of the senior academic officer's responsibilities, his or her effectiveness will depend heavily on the functioning of the faculty through its senate. An academic vice president must learn to work effectively with governing boards and unions and will find it helpful to have good relationships with student organizations and any groups representing members of the staff. However, an academic vice president is not in a primary position with any of these bodies and does have the same overlap of responsibilities. An academic vice president must work through the senate or take the longer path around it, and must expect that the senate will react, sometimes explosively, to virtually everything that he or she does or tries to do. Whether the relationship between the academic vice president and the faculty senate is good or bad, they are joined at the hip, and thus the functioning of the senate is something which the academic vice president must give a great deal of thought to.

Faculty senates are often criticized not only by administrators but by faculty as well for being ineffectual, obstructionist, or overly political. All of these criticisms are justified to some extent. Senates sometimes attract faculty members more interested in political intrigue than academic policy, and when these representatives dominate, they can drive away others whose contributions could be more positive. Senate participation, which may require a great deal of time, does little to enhance one's academic career, so it is not surprising when some of the most respected scholars and teachers on a campus decide that they would rather commit their energies elsewhere.

Some senates lack a clear sense of purpose. When a governance body is not consciously and actively committed to its role in protecting and enhancing academic quality, it can fall into the easier role of "gatekeeper" or administrative critic. In those instances, rather than developing their own initiatives, faculty representatives simply react to those of the administration, adopting a skeptical, if not cynical, posture to obscure the fact they often do not have the time or expertise to master the complex regulatory or budgetary issues behind the policies they are considering. When senates operate in this manner, there is a great temptation for administrators to simply ignore them or to thank them for their "constructive criticism and many helpful suggestions," and then to move on without the slightest change in direction. After all, an administrator may reason, the "silent majority" of reasonable faculty members seem to approve or at least accede to this direction. Why try to convince a consistently negative minority?

The answer, of course, is obvious if one thinks of leadership not just in terms of achieving a particular end but in terms of developing an institutional commitment to that end. When one is dealing with issues related to academic policy, there is no way that such a commitment can be built without the active cooperation of the body elected to represent the faculty on those issues. If an academic senate is ineffective and not helping to move its institution in the right direction, it must be strengthened. Even if there are other groups on campus capably representing faculty interests, such as unions or department chairs, for example, the role of the senate remains crucial because the specific interests of the senate are closest to the central purposes of the institution.

There are several "best practices" that an academic vice president can implement in collaboration with members of the faculty to improve the functioning of a faculty senate.

Demonstrate Respect for the Senate and Its Governance Role

The chief academic officer should frequently recognize publicly the importance of the senate's functions with regard to curriculum, instruction, academic standards and policies, and faculty qualifications. This kind of recognition not only increases the stature of the senate but also helps to define a senate's appropriate role by emphasizing certain functions more than others. Seeking the senate's advice and approval on all appropriate matters, ensuring that the senate's accomplishments are well publicized, and seeing that its leaders are prominently featured at campus activities are all ways to enhance the prestige of this body and to attract participation by the institution's most effective faculty leaders.

Share Information to Improve Trust and to Help the Senate Focus on Issues

Beyond keeping the faculty as a whole informed, the chief academic officer should continually provide information and access to senate leaders. This is yet another way to confer status upon faculty leaders, and, more importantly, to decrease the effects of misinformation and rumor. Including faculty senate leaders in various deans' meetings and other administrative forums improves trust and helps to promote the shared perception of reality necessary for institutional change. Information may also be used to help the senate focus on issues of academic significance. The type of information and date that a chief academic officer provides to the senate should have a significant impact on its agenda.

Help to Develop New Academic Leaders

The academic vice president should seek out and help to prepare new academic leaders by providing staff development opportunities and resources to improve their understanding of the governance system and of major educational issues. This should be viewed as both a long-term

---

Best Practices in Academic Governance

- Use multiple frames through which to view the institution and all situations that arise because virtually every situation has a structural, political, human resource, and symbolic dimension
- Never lose sight of the fact that it is the institutional culture and not simply specific structures of governance that must adapt to meet new challenges
- Evaluate all governance processes in terms of whether they promote or obstruct the transition to a learning-central and student-centered institution
- Embrace the principles of shared governance and open communication with all constituencies; abandon the notion that sharing authority diminishes authority
- Work to delineate clearly the responsibilities and primary interests of all constituencies in the governance process and to establish the mechanisms to ensure that accountability is always tied to authority
- Establish "rolling coalitions" made of of as many groups and individuals as possible in order to keep the change process moving forward
- Maintain balance through perspective, humor, and a tolerance for ambiguity because satisfactory resolutions will be few and even an efficient collegiality will seem to function slowly compared to the pace at which new challenges arise

---

and inclusive activity, since not only junior faculty members but also those from disciplines and backgrounds under-represented in the current leadership should be identified and nurtured in leadership roles. Tenure and promotion policies should also reflect and support an institutional commitment to fostering effective faculty leadership.

Assist Senate in Improving Processes and Continuity

Faculty senates can sometimes become bogged down in repetitive discussions simply because of a lack of effective process. Vaguely worded resolutions are sent forth and then forgotten, as faculty participants become increasingly frustrated by their apparent inability to accomplish meaningful objectives. The structural problems of ineffective senates can be obvious from an external perspective and yet not well understood by their faculty leaders, who are typically untrained for their positions, have limited time to devote to senate activities, serve relatively brief terms, and are beset by apparently compelling issues that demand all of their attention. A provost or academic vice president can help in this situation by ensuring adequate clerical and financial support for senate activities and by working with the leadership, if it is amenable, to develop an organizational structure and procedures that create a bias for action and decision making. Changing the way an agenda is structured, creating a system to track decisions and resolutions, establishing continuity in leadership, and training inexperienced senators in the complexities of parliamentary procedure all can make concrete differences within a single semester of senate operations.

Provide Staff Development Opportunities

There is a wide range of staff development activities useful in strengthening academic senates, and chief academic officers are often more likely to be aware of these activities than senate leaders and to control the resources necessary to implement them. A number of national conferences, publications, and organizations focus on governance and educational leadership development. Chief academic officers should assume responsibility for informing faculty senate leaders about these opportunities and encouraging their participation.

Delegate Meaningful Authority to the Senate

The most effective senates focus their energies and clearly understand the distinction between their role and the role of the administration. Where those distinctions are not clear, chief academic officers should consider the development of policies delegating specific authority to the senate and defining its role. When the authority of the faculty is recognized not just in custom but also in policy, the requisite delineation may be much easier to maintain. Such policies define the senate's functions by what they omit as well as by what they include and can be used as a touchstone for senate interests and activities. Provosts should also consider carefully the kinds of tasks delegated to a senate, ensuring that they are sufficiently defined and structured to create a reasonable expectation of success.

Time, however, is an important factor in all changes in governance systems. While changes in the structures and policies of campus governance can sometimes be accomplished relatively quickly, it may take considerably longer for patterns of behavior to adjust to new realities, particularly where there has been an ongoing level of distrust between faculty and administration. At one college, when a new vice president moved immediately to enhance the authority of the senate, the efforts led to an unexpected amount of conflict and frustration. The problem was not with the nature of the changes but with the fact that they were made too rapidly and without sufficient attention to the campus's current climate and longer-term culture. The faculty, feeling that they had long been criticized unfairly by the administration for a lack of professionalism, sought a demonstration of respect more than a change in policy. Because they had little trust in members of the administration or their motives, the faculty did not appreciate the significance of their new authority. Since the college was not predominantly bureaucratic in orientation, a change in rules that was not preceded by a perceptible change in attitude simply confused the faculty. The vice president, expecting cooperation from the newly empowered faculty, became increasingly critical of senate leaders for patterns of behavior that had, in reality, been many years in the making. His criticism merely reinforced the faculty view that nothing had changed and mitigated against the developments he sought. Meanwhile, frustration about a lack of "dramatic" progress made it difficult to see the more subtle, positive signs that were emerging.

These efforts to strengthen the faculty's role in governance could have been considerably more effective had they been made more gradually, with greater awareness of the institutional culture's emphasis on personal connection, and with more tolerance for the time it can take to accomplish such changes. Tolerance for the pace of change in higher education is something that every chief academic officer needs. That truism, however, leads directly to the critical paradox confronting administrators today, for such tolerance is also extremely dangerous in an era when the external pressures for change threaten to overwhelm all but the most adaptive institutions.

Effective Governance and the Challenge of Change

For a majority of educational leaders, the most obvious fact about managing campuses at the end of the century is that colleges and universities face a growing crisis that their structures and traditions have left them ill-prepared to meet. The Pew Higher Education Roundtable, in its publication, *Policy Perspectives*, has focused on the nature of this crisis and, in a widely discussed essay entitled, "To Dance with Change," concludes that "no institution will emerge unscathed from its confrontation with an external environment that is substantially altered and in many ways more hostile to colleges and universities."[11] According to this analysis, three forces contribute to the new environment: "a rising anxiety about jobs and careers among Americans of all ages, the emergence of a technology that promises to create both new forms and new suppliers of postsecondary education, and a seemingly irresistible impulse on the part of policy makers and public agencies to rely on markets and market-like mechanisms to define the public good."[12] These forces, combined with other changes in demographics, social values, public expectations, and the financing of higher education, would constitute a daunt-

Emerging Trends in Academic Governance

- Changes in the external environment will create pressures for restructuring that will have a fundamental impact on existing governance structures
- Governance systems will become less obstructive and more oriented toward action as all constituencies define more clearly the areas of governance in which their roles should be primary and those in which their roles should be secondary
- As organizations become less hierarchical, governance systems will continue to become more inclusive, moving toward models of shared governance involving all constituents in substantive decision making
- All those involved in the governance system will be required to demonstrate responsibility and accountability commensurate with their authority
- Governance systems will become more open as both technology and restructuring make a much greater amount of information available to all constituencies
- Governance systems will become increasingly decentralized as access to information increases and the time allowed for decision making decreases

ing challenge even if the pace of change were only a fraction of what it actually is.

The speed with which change is occurring, in fact, seems almost to stun some institutions. Colleges and universities in California, long sheltered under the umbrella of the state's Master Plan for Higher Education, are finding it very difficult to come to terms with the idea that their future is now being driven by "market-like mechanisms" rather than educational policy decisions based on the public good. There is an expectation that sooner or later the governor, the legislature, or other policy leaders must step forward to repair and renew the 1960 Master Plan, since the minor modifications made during the late 1980s were clearly inadequate to address the complexities confronting colleges today. To many observers, it is still inconceivable that the state could abandon its longstanding public policy commitments to open access, educational equity, and a coherent statewide plan for higher education. Yet, that is exactly what is occurring.

Without significant restructuring, California's—and America's—colleges will not be able to meet the challenge they confront—a challenge requiring not only that they provide a higher quality of education but that they do so at a lower cost, while simultaneously protecting, to the greatest extent possible, both access and equity. Our colleges and universities, of course, are resistant to such restructuring. Their modes of governance do not exactly make them "agile" institutions. Indeed, they seem designed to turn as slowly and ponderously as huge ships. This "steadiness," which has been their great strength, may have become one of their greatest liabilities. "The internal politics of most institutions," as another Pew article points out, "tend toward inaction—toward a status quo that evolves from the sum of individual behaviors rather than from a set of principles deliberately imposed. The instinct of faculty is to defer decisions, to preserve their own collegiality by waiting until a viable consensus has been formed."[13] In the next five to ten years, chief academic officers must do much more than facilitate the development of a new consensus; they also must affect the decision-making process itself. They have to find ways both to work within and to modify traditional academic governance systems in order to create the more flexible, responsive, and dynamic institutions required by a highly competitive, information- and technology-based society.

While there are many different terms for this restructuring and multiple views on what it entails, there is general agreement among educational leaders that restructuring must involve radical changes in the roles of both faculty members and administrators. Administrations will need to become more efficient, decentralized, and "flat," reducing overhead and encouraging initiative by replacing the "command and control culture" with one that fosters decision-making at the lowest possible level.[14] Faculty members will need to shift their basic orientation from one that is teaching-centered to one that is learning-centered, a change which initially sounds simple but which has the most profound implications for the way education is delivered and assessed. Faculty, serving as designers of educational programs and services as well as student guides and facilitators, will spend much less time behind a lectern but actually work with greater numbers of students in more focused ways. Students will do more independent learning through a wide range of interactive technologies both on campus and in their homes and will be assessed solely in terms of their learning rather than partially on "seat-time." While traditional modes of delivery, such as lectures and seminars, will continue, they will constitute only one option in a system that allows learners at every skill level much greater flexibility. Colleges will assume increased responsibility for student learning and define their accountability not in terms of how much instruction they have provided but how much learning actually occurred.

While fundamental changes in the role of administration, particularly in large universities, will be extremely difficult to effect, changes in the role of the faculty will be both more challenging and more important. Alan Guskin, chancellor of Antioch University, states, "Restructuring the role of faculty members will, at first, prove to be a monumental undertaking. All of the incentives seem against doing so—except, in the end, survival." Part of the challenge is that faculty have so much control, not just collectively but individually, over what and how they teach. "Survival depends on radical change," Guskin says, "yet the people needing to change the most are in control of the decision-making processes that must deal with the change."[15] However much it may sound like an oxymoron, our goal must be for a more efficient collegiality in campus governance, one that allows for full debate on important academic issues and delegates appropriate decision-making to faculty bodies but limits the ability of individuals to reject or undermine all decisions they do not personally support.

If our institutions are not as agile and flexible as we would like them to be in this era of change, chief academic officers had better be. Their difficult jobs have become much more difficult. Working with board members, presidents, administrative colleagues, and faculty leaders, chief academic officers must develop a new vision of their institutions and of faculty roles within them. They must then employ every means possible to communicate that vision and infuse it into the campus culture, while addressing the natural tendency of an academic audience to reduce the call for fundamental reform to something that can be more easily dismissed, such as a demand for "greater efficiency" or more "business-like" practices.

However compellingly it is explained and however clearly it is understood, many faculty members will feel deeply threatened by any new conception of their role. Thus, provosts and academic vice presidents will need to depend, increasingly, on a series of "rolling coalitions," which are constantly dissolving and reforming, rather than on a steady base of constituent support. In the midst of this change, a certain number of individuals or groups will be angry or opposed on any given day. The chief academic officer must ensure that the number never reaches a critical mass, that yesterday's antagonist has some reason to be supportive today. To accomplish this, he or she must move quickly and adroitly, working simultaneously with all groups involved in campus governance and with a wide range of individual faculty, students, and staff members. Initiatives taken down a single path can be blocked much more easily than those proceeding down multiple routes. Also, since most faculty members belong to multiple constituencies, they will generally not become locked into permanent opposition as long as some of those constituencies are being satisfied.

Guided by a clear sense of how the college or university must adapt, academic managers should be prepared to press forward aggressively, and then to retreat or stand aside so that reactions do not become hardened. As most academic vice presidents discover in working with members of the faculty, it is pointless to try to push them into a specific action however high the price of inaction may be. One must, at the same time, pull, nudge, cajole, explain, sympathize, reward, demonstrate, motivate, and lead. The focus must be on *directions* rather than *positions*. In fact, at times one must be satisfied with movement regardless of direction if the alternative is stasis. A vice president for academic affairs calling for change and flexibility can hardly afford to be rigid. It is not merely a bad example; it is a self-defeating strategy. "The best managers and leaders," as Lee G. Bolman and Terrence Deal note, "create and sustain a tension-filled balance between two extremes. They combine core values with elastic strategies."[16]

In fact, an effective way to avoid rigidity is to make a point of examining issues or situations through each of the "frames" that Bolman and Deal discuss in their book *Reframing Organizations*. The four frames—structural, human resource, political, and symbolic—correspond to the perspectives of the four major schools of organizational theory, and it is important to ensure that one is viewing issues from all of these perspectives. Just as a particular organizational model tends to predominate within a college or university, a particular frame will predominate in the way an individual views organizations. If that frame is structural, "reframing" a situation in terms of its human resource, political, or symbolic implications will reveal significantly different issues and concerns as well as helping one to understand the range of reactions likely to be generated. Using multiple frames is a way for leaders to "complicate themselves,"[17] which not only enhances their perception but also enlarges the way their actions are perceived.

Conclusion: The Chief Academic Officer and Governance Systems

Chief academic officers should pay special attention to the symbolic frame since governance systems involve such a high degree of symbolic interaction. At one institution, where the president had been, by tradition, a member of the academic senate, a new chief executive decided that he would not attend senate meetings because his presence at the lengthy sessions seemed merely symbolic. However, to faculty leaders, the participation of the president in senate deliberations and his availability to respond to direct questions represented the essence of governance at that institution. When the president's decision became clear to the senate, its members passed and forwarded to the trustees a resolution that, ostensibly, bore no relation to that decision but which the faculty knew would be embarrassing to the president. The chief executive understood the message and quickly revised his opinion of participation in senate meetings. In this instance, either a political or a symbolic perspective could have led him to reconsider, but if he were only capable of viewing issues through the structural frame, the senate's action might have seemed inexplicable or merely vindictive. Had he missed the intended message, his presidency could have failed in its first months.

At another institution, the new president made a powerful statement by choosing to move his office to the library rather than occupying the office of his predecessor located in the administration building. The former president had been unpopular, leaving a fragmented and ineffective administration. By moving his office away from the administration building, the new president sent a signal to the faculty that his leadership would be substantively different from that of his predecessor, and by choosing the library he positioned himself at the academic core of the college, displaying a sense of educational values not lost upon the faculty. The move inconvenienced the rest of the administration and made the president less accessible to them, but this warning to them was also part of his symbolic intent. The office of Harvard's president is in the "Yard," right in the middle of both history and the freshman dorms. The office of the University of California's president is miles from the Berkeley campus, in a modern, antiseptic office tower in Oakland. Both settings have a symbolic impact that partly reflects and partly creates the reality of those institutions.

While academic vice presidents may not have much control over where presidents choose to locate their offices, they can control the symbolic implications of many aspects of the campus's educational environment. They need to consider issues with an awareness of their symbolic implications and to manage the symbols of their environments, sometimes to inspire change and sometimes to cushion its effects. Academic vice presidents must use every tool available to them in their efforts to create the kind of restructuring required of institutions, and they must continuously look for new opportunities to "plant" change or nurture its growth. Staff development and sabbatical opportunities, support funds, new positions, and every bit of discretionary authority or influence the vice president may possess must be used to foster this restructuring. No activity or expenditure is really neutral, for the things that do not promote change simply strengthen the conviction that nothing is really very different and nothing very different must be done.

Because trustees can serve as critical allies in the restructuring effort, chief academic officers should think frequently about how they can use their access to board agendas and their ability to influence those agendas both to increase the board's level of awareness and to ensure that its authority and influence have the greatest effect. When campus systems tend toward inaction, governing boards can provide a critical stimulus by means of the issues they focus upon, the questions they ask, and the evidence they require. However, agenda items must be structured in ways that make the stimulus effective. Even when boards are fully committed to the goals of restructuring and improving educational accountability, trustees may not know how to express those goals in language convincing to members of the faculty. Simply calling for "greater efficiency" or "higher productivity" is counterproductive; it reinforces the faculty's suspicion that restructuring simply means downsizing through laying off a percentage of current faculty and increasing the workload of those who remain. Ensuring that trustees support the change process and that they know how to express their support in constructive and meaningful ways is primarily the task of the president, but since so much of the discussion must focus on the fundamental question of how best to deliver education, the academic vice president also has a critical role to play. The conversation between faculty members and trustees must be carefully shaped, and the chief academic officer can assist in that through the issues and reports presented to the board as well as through those presented to the faculty.

The goal of efficient collegiality in governance requires a campuswide understanding of the challenges now facing higher education and a commitment to rethink all existing campus governance structures and practices on an ongoing basis. It requires that faculty forego what has been described as the "hollowed collegiality" of their academic departments, the superficial aspects of collegiality which protect individual privileges but seldom lead to "the more substantial discussions necessary to improve undergraduate education," or to a "sense of collective responsibility" among the faculty.[18] Faculty must be willing to transcend everything that protects them from engaging the fundamental questions of what and how students learn and what relationships exist between student learning and faculty work. Faculty and administrators must work together to delineate clearly the appropriate authority of faculty within a shared governance model as well as the specific responsibilities attached to each area of authority.

Boards and administrators, in turn, must move beyond the forms of shared governance to its essence, which requires much more openness in decision making than is practiced on most campuses. Providing access to information and to processes is not enough; board members and administrators must be truly open to the influence of others and willing to consider with the utmost seriousness opinions that threaten their most cherished projects, beliefs, and ideas. They must not only be honest and fair themselves; they must trust others to be so. In an essay on governance, Kenneth Mortimer and Annette Caruso make the crucial point that "the legitimacy of academic governance is based on mutual trust and cooperation among participants," and that "to maintain essential patterns of legitimacy and trust," institutions must approach governance "with a high degree of openness," which is the "natural enemy of arbitrariness and the natural ally of the struggle for trust and legitimacy."[19]

There is no escaping the fact, however, that the road to this new vision of higher education is a dangerous and arduous one. Not all colleges will survive; nor will all of the academic leaders who work to restructure and renew their institutions. Change is stressful and difficult, and a good deal of discomfort is necessary before most people will even consider it. We may honor "change agents" in these difficult times, but we also make them pay the price for the discomfort they have created. Academic vice presidents must recognize that doing their jobs well means fundamental changes to their institutions, and this will put them in significant jeopardy. They must be able not merely to tolerate but to enjoy that jeopardy, just as they must enjoy and find order in the chaos that is an inescapable part of their professional lives. The only real balance for administrators in times such as these comes from imbalance, from their ability to appreciate rather than resist the multitude of forces around them and yet never lose sight of their basic goals.

II

The Leadership Team

Shaping the Leadership Team: The President, Governing Board, and Chief Academic Officer

Alice Bourke Hayes

In delivering the mission of a college or university, the president and the chief academic officer head the leadership team. Even though they are often removed from the learning events that occur in classrooms, libraries, laboratories, and residence halls, their decisions and interactions with faculty, students, and staff members shape the core learning environment on campus. Therefore, this team of two is central to the institution's academic enterprise.

The relationship between the president and the chief academic officer takes many forms.[1] Traditionally, it has been a leader/follower relationship, with the president assuming an active role in designing the academic plan, and the chief academic officer following those directions. This has been particularly the case in smaller institutions in which the president is a former chief academic officer. Contemporary experience and scholarship have demonstrated, however, that the most satisfactory relationship for many chief academic officers is a genuinely collaborative one. In institutions in which the president spends much of her or his time off campus on executive responsibilities such as external relations, fund-raising, and financial affairs, the chief academic officer will typically set the internal agenda for academic affairs, and the relationship to the president is basically a reporting one. Although one might predict that a collaborative team would be more effective than a directive one in implementing goals and providing campus leadership, over the long term, this expectation is not necessarily supported by data. Studies have shown that any of these relationships *can* be productive.[2]

While the president and the chief academic officer are bonded by a formal reporting structure, it must also be acknowledged that business and family situations, civic and political affairs, and race and gender

---

Best Practices between the President and the Chief Academic Officer

- Respect the president's time
- Maintain a policy of no surprises, no secrets
- Be a problem preventer
- If that does not work, be a problem solver
- If that does not work, be a crisis manager
- Provide alternatives when making recommendations
- Support the president's views with deans and faculty

---

issues will affect the dynamic of their personal and professional relationships. While these individuals may never become close friends, each needs to be seen by the other as capable and powerful,[3] as the collegiality that develops between them will be needed at numerous junctures as a source of support and even inspiration. When the president and the chief academic officer can rely on each other for shared understanding, the bond between them becomes a critical resource in times of difficulty, unforeseen and otherwise. To accomplish this, these two officers *must* reserve time for each other amid extremely busy schedules and demanding interactions with literally hundreds of members of the immediate and extended campus community. To perform most effectively, they will need to express to each other their deepest fears and highest goals. Similarly, they must be able to vent frustration and celebrate success. While at times one or both may experience the loneliness that accompanies leadership, such as the myth of being lonely at the top, one vice president has wryly observed, "The myth is that there is a top. As for lonely, there is seldom enough loneliness!"[4]

Whatever the history and parameters of their relationship, there must be close and frequent communication between these two individuals in order to accomplish the institution's academic agenda. Both have crowded calendars, demanding schedules, and few opportunities for casual interaction, thus regularly scheduled meetings are essential. In a small or even medium-sized institution, they may be able to meet daily or two to three times per week by visiting each other's offices frequently and without formality. In a larger university, it may be necessary to schedule a formal appointment at least biweekly. Even though the chief academic officer and the president may meet frequently as members of other groups, it remains important for the provost or academic vice president to have access to the undivided attention of the chief executive officer at regular intervals. While it will not always be practical to develop a formal agenda for these meetings, the chief academic officer should be careful to respect the president's time. While it would not be unusual to spend one to two hours reviewing individual faculty performance or the minutes of a faculty meeting or dean's council, contemporary chief executives are often unable to allocate sufficient time for these discussions. For this reason alone, the chief academic officer should have a clear sense of the issues he or she wants to share in each discussion and consistently make sure that the single most important one is raised, reviewed, and resolved.

Communication

The president needs to be informed clearly and concisely of any "hot" situations on campus or in the local environment that are likely to come to her or his attention in the near future. In essence, the rule should be: No surprises; no secrets. In the ideal situation, there would never be anything "hot," as crises would have been prevented by the smooth guidance and careful planning of the leadership team; however, on most campuses, efforts to prevent or solve problems are not always successful.

Instinctively, a chief academic officer may attempt to manage the situation away from the president's attention. However, before the provost or dean can bring the situation under control, the president may be cornered by a news reporter with a portable television camera or approached by a member of the community in an open forum.[5] Every word from the president will be assumed to reflect a fully informed, well-considered answer. More timely communication from the chief academic officer would ensure that this is in fact the case.

When proactivity has not worked to either prevent or solve a problem, the provost will need to demonstrate skills as a crisis manager. The chief academic officer and president will need to work together to convene a standing crisis management team, including the public relations officer, legal counsel, the student development officer, and other appropriate senior officers, to develop best case/worst case scenarios and implement appropriate action and communication plans.

Action Items

At any point in the academic year, there will be several initiatives on which the chief academic officer and the president are collaborating. These may include the strategic plan, the annual budget, student outcomes assessment, academic program reviews, and accreditation visits. The president needs to receive regular updates on these initiatives, and to know, well in advance of both the board and the public, any concerns regarding campus governance. All policy proposals that will affect faculty, students, and staff members need to be reviewed with the chief executive officer before implementation.

Other topics, calling simply for communication, may be handled via routine memorandums. The president may rely on an assistant to handle these issues. This situation must be handled carefully so that the staff member works well with the chief academic officer and does not unintentionally interfere with that individual's communication with the president. The president's assistant cannot always be helpful, since he or she is usually not fully informed about many of the sensitive issues that the chief academic officer needs to discuss with the president. At the same time, the assistant can adjust schedules and otherwise facilitate response from the president if he or she understands that the chief academic officer must have priority of access. A good working relationship with the president's assistant will save time at critical junctures for both the president and the chief academic officer.

The natural tendency for campus managers is to focus on events of the day, particularly what is urgent or problematic. This often results in the neglect of the broader task of shaping the institution's future. If meetings with the president become overwhelmed with daily issues, the chief academic officer should devise a separate time or series of meetings to focus on strategic and long-term planning issues. Particularly helpful would be to plan an off-campus retreat for the president and the chief academic officer to clarify future initiatives and directions.

Resolving Different Points of View

Even if he or she once served as a faculty member, the president will not always view an issue from the same perspective as the provost. In fact, there will almost certainly be times when the senior academic officer is convinced that the president is not pursuing the best course of action. Yet, as chief academic officer, he or she must speak for the larger institution rather than for his or her own personal views. In that leadership capacity, he or she should support the president's views publicly, leaving to private conversation the exploration of alternative views. A pattern of failing to do so is a danger sign that should not be ignored.

Who's in Charge? A Case Study

A large independent institution faced a period of financial stress, and decisions had to be made to identify programs that would be discontinued. The view of the president was that the undergraduate programs, as the heart of the university, should not be touched. Graduate programs were desirable but expensive and not an essential component of university mission; therefore they bear the brunt of the cutbacks.

The academic vice president fundamentally agreed with the president that cutbacks were essential, but believed that deciding how the cutbacks were implemented should be her responsibility rather than the president's. She thought it would be better to retain all of the programs at a reduced level by budget cuts across the board. She presented the situation to the faculty and sought their recommendations for cutbacks. She openly admitted to the faculty that she did not agree with the president that programs should be eliminated. The deans and faculty were reluctant to identify any programs, their own or others, as inessential. The president, faced with financial pressures, initiated a hiring freeze across the institution. Strong departments that were growing and experiencing heavy teaching loads were unable to meet the demands placed on them without reducing research and passing over scholarly opportunities. Discussions bogged down in frustration and inertia.

Correspondence between the president and the academic vice president became vitriolic. Eventually, since no priority programs were identified by the academic vice president, the president made unilateral decisions about which programs to eliminate. As a result of the freeze and these cutbacks, several other programs suffered deterioration, the president lost the esteem of the faculty, the academic vice president was relieved of her position, and a process that would inevitably have been painful became even more so.

Comment. Clearly, this scenario has played at many institutions and presents a classic conflict between the chief academic and chief executive officers. In most instances, the view of the president will prevail, and the chief academic officer who cannot or will not support the president will not continue in that position for long. The alternative scenario in which the faculty and deans rise up in support of the chief academic officer and reject the president's authority is an unlikely one on most campuses.

Admittedly, this situation presented a difficult challenge for both the chief academic officer and the president. None of the parties involved wanted to make the necessary decisions. In a similar situation, the provost of Columbia University noted "a high level of motivated unwillingness of any academic unit to criticize any other—at least when the stakes are as high as reductions in size or possible program elimination."[6] Similarly, the president of Stanford found, "In a recent round of harsh budget cuts at Stanford, we involved a group of distinguished faculty from all fields. They worked hard and faithfully with us on all aspects of the process. . . . They frequently worried that we were cutting too much 'across the boards,' and not singling out whole programs for elimination; yet, they could not develop a consensus on which programs should go."[7] For a chief academic officer to expect the faculty to determine priorities that she herself is unwilling to determine, or to accept across-the-board cuts without damage to programs, is unrealistic.

In a difficult case like this, in which neither the president nor the provost could propose a course of action that would escape criticism and campus conflict, it would have helped if these individuals had displayed a shared understanding of the roles of graduate and undergraduate education at the institution. This basic question of mission should have been reviewed and addressed early in their working relationship. With some clarity about the institution's educational mission, a more extended discussion between the provost and president about specific alternatives, before opening up discussion with the faculty, could have identified the least disruptive courses of action and placed the president and the chief academic officer in collaborative roles to address the problem.

Different Management Styles

In the case discussed above, the president and the provost clearly had different perceptions of the mission of the institution. Consequently, they were in direct conflict about an appropriate course of action. In some cases, however, discord is not present, but the two senior administrators may have different working styles. One may be impulsive and crisis-oriented, while the other is a methodical planner. A gregarious administrator who enjoys group discussions and consultative approaches to issues may have difficulty working with an administrator who prefers to think things through quietly and reach a decision in isolation. Some administrators have a highly developed sensitivity to others and may make intuitive decisions, which can pose a significant challenge to a data-oriented, process-driven manager. When management styles are very different and there is no disposition to accommodate, it may not be possible to develop an effective team. If, however, the administrators can find a way to use their different styles to add new dimensions to their effectiveness, these differences can become an asset. In fact, they may produce a more effective senior administrative team than one in which everyone thinks and acts along similar lines.

Within the complexities of professional working relationships, the ability to work effectively with the president and other members of the leadership team is a highly valued management skill. In this context, there are several challenges that a chief academic officer may need to address at one or more points in a career:

1. *Acknowledge differences openly and build on them.* The two administrators will quickly perceive that they do not approach issues the same way. If they can be candid about this, it may be turned into an asset. Sometimes an administrative team can be helped by the kind of understanding achieved by a Myers-Briggs inventory, or the Boltons' analysis of work styles. With some appreciation of the styles and strengths of colleagues, the administrators will realize that no single approach is "right" or "wrong," but that rather these are alternative ways to handle responsibilities.

Once differences are admitted and an effort to understand and appreciate one another is in process, the administrators can modify behaviors and delegate appropriate tasks in ways which utilize the skills of each one. When the visionary leader communicates an exciting dream for the future, the data cruncher can share the enthusiasm while developing an effective business plan.

2. *Be realistic about professional strengths and weaknesses.* The process of leading the academic sector of an institution can be made more difficult for a provost if the president demands skills that he or she does not possess. Often, the chief academic officer will need to understand the president to the point that he or she can predict how the chief executive will both act and react. In some cases, it may be possible to work more effectively by adapting working styles. However, if the president's needs do not match the chief academic officer's talents, style, or ability to adapt on a given project, the dean or provost must address this situation by coordinating the efforts of colleagues toward this objective. He or she may need to identify a public speaker, a budget analyst, or simply a patient listener in a given area to meet the president's expectations. At the same time, an academic vice president must also recognize in sending a colleague to meet with the president on a given issue that he or she still retains professional responsibility for the outcomes of the decision. Responsibility for academic affairs cannot and should not be delegated.

3. *Acknowledge that some conflicts cannot be resolved.* If the president continually assigns work that is not part of an agreed-upon position description or is hostile to the chief academic officer because of an issue such as race or gender, the situation should not be allowed to continue. While institutions typically maintain grievance procedures to address this, the chief academic officer, if possible, should bring the matter directly to the president's attention for immediate resolution. If the problem continues, a grievance should be initiated.

To protect his or her career, a chief academic officer should address situations such as this with extreme care. In all interactions, efforts should be made to resolve differences. If necessary, a mutually trusted colleague can be invited to witness, and even defuse, critical discussions; however, provosts must be honest with themselves concerning conflicts that cannot be resolved. If the basic relationship has become personally and professionally unproductive despite serious and focused efforts to improve it, it may be necessary to restructure the current model significantly or even to dissolve the relationship and seek a more favorable alternative.

The Chief Academic Officer and the Cabinet: Shaping Effective Relationships

The senior officers of a college or university are an interdependent group and must coordinate their cross-functional activities to accomplish the common goals of the institution. To achieve this coordination, the team members should meet and collaborate in both formal and informal settings, they should disagree civilly when necessary, and they should accept joint responsibility for the results of efforts across each area of institutional operations.

Everyone employed at a college or university now "participates" in higher education and affects student retention. The bursar, the public safety officer, the swim coach, and the admissions officer, for example, all have interactions with students that shape their personal development. Increasingly, research has documented how much students learn outside of the classroom. Teamwork, service to the community, leadership, the bonds of friendship, and ties to the alma mater are developed in the many interactions that occur across the campus. Each student whose needs are not handled sensitively by a financial aid officer, who cannot prepare for examinations in the evening because of lax residence hall supervision, or who is denied access to a faculty advisor by a departmental secretary is negatively affected by an unsupportive learning environment. Whatever model of administration is followed by an institution, the chief academic officer must be able to work effectively with his or her colleagues at the cabinet level to overcome these challenges to student success.

The Chief Financial Officer

It is impossible for a chief academic officer to be effective without a clear understanding of the uses, management, and allocation of resources. Many deans and academic vice presidents enter their positions with little budget management experience, having been chosen instead for their academic leadership skills. Yet, the financial responsibilities of the position can be daunting. While the busywork can be handled by a staff member, the vision and planning involved in budget development cannot be delegated to an assistant. The chief financial officer can be a valuable aid to the chief academic officer in helping her or him understand the institution's financial systems. If the chief financial officer is brought into a close working relationship with the chief academic officer, he or she will be able to help this individual to develop resources in a time of need, to develop methods to finance major projects, and to provide expert advice on methods to handle the operating budget. An open budget process and frequent meetings should promote good working relationships.

The Student Affairs Officer

The relationship between the student affairs officer and the chief academic officer must be an effective one in its shaping of the student learning environment. Yet, sometimes the chief academic officer and members of the faculty do not appreciate the importance of either the office of student development or student life activities. At some level, academic officers realize that students must receive an orientation to campus, have a full residence life, maintain good health and fitness, develop their social and leadership skills, work, study, and grow through their college experience. However, all of that goes on outside the classroom, library, and laboratories in which much of the academic community is involved, and sometimes the two dimensions of campus life are viewed as competing for the attention and energies of the students.

In an effective working relationship, academic administrators and the faculty are invited to participate in student life programming and serve as advisors to organizations, as speakers in residence hall programs, and as volunteers in community service activities. Being involved generates appreciation of these aspects of college life. The chief academic and chief student affairs officers and their senior staffs should meet at regular intervals to plan and develop the events of the academic year collaboratively. As a result, a shared sense of responsibility for student development will increase.

The College Relations Officer

Too often, the chief academic officer confines her or his attention to the internal affairs of the institution. Yet, who could be a better spokesperson for the development of academic programs, the needs of the faculty, and the achievements of the students? The provost or academic vice president should be encouraged to become actively involved in institutional development activities. Meeting with alumni, major donors, foundations, and media representatives can be a time-consuming burden, but it is also an important method to fulfill the goals of the academic sector. The chief academic officer should meet frequently with the university relations officer to discuss program goals, grant opportunities, public relations, and ways in which academic administrators and faculty can promote the mission and objectives of the institution. Simply attending and perhaps speaking at a few alumni meetings and receptions each year constitutes a valuable contribution to this sector of organizational operations. It also provides excellent opportunities to articulate the needs of the faculty concerning grants for instructional resources to the college or university relations officer.

The Human Resources Officer

In most institutions, the management of faculty is handled by academic administrators, and the management of all other staff is handled by a human resources officer. Typically, there are several unique features of faculty administration related to contracts, tenure, and promotion that do not apply to other staff members. In light of this separation, occasionally there may develop a barrier, either real or perceived, between the human resources administrators and the college's academic leadership. Yet, benefits administration is typically institution-wide, and such functions as payroll and tuition benefits are also handled by the human resources office. Similarly, recruitment, hiring, and management of secretarial, clerical, and technical staff is usually administered by the human resources office. Staff evaluation and salary increases are handled by the supervising administrator, but administration of salary increases, discipline actions, and terminations are usually handled by the human resources office. Affirmative action and legal services are also usually located in this office. In light of the occasional, sometimes persistent ambiguity in these relationships, it is important for the chief academic officer and the human resources officer to meet regularly to discuss shared concerns, to delineate individual responsibilities, and to achieve a productive institutional working environment.

The Athletics Director

Athletics is a division that may report to the chief academic officer, the student affairs officer, the public relations officer, or the business and finance officer. While there can be much variation regarding where athletics connects with the organizational structure, it is readily recognized that athletics interacts closely with academic affairs on every campus, regardless of size and mission. In light of this, the chief academic officer needs to remain attentive to maintenance of admissions standards; the class schedules of student athletes; the management of financial aid; and tutoring, retention, and graduation rates. National athletic organizations have explicitly recognized the priority of academic considerations in planning athletic activities. Yet, the continuing enthusiasm for athletics by students, alumni, and members of the extended institutional community can present significant challenges to the academic operation of a college or university. Many institutions maintain an extensive athletics advisory board system and hire a faculty athletics representative to provide oversight to the activities of the athletics programs and to serve as a resource to the academic vice president regarding connections among athletic endeavors, the faculty, and the classroom.

The Chief Academic Officer and the Board of Trustees: New Accountabilities, New Agendas

For a vice president of instruction or provost, trained to work with other academics, interaction with trustees is typically an experience demanding new skills. Cyril Houle describes this discovery candidly. "As staff members move up in a hierarchy, they gradually begin truly to perceive what they have always superficially known; a group of part-time nonspecialist people who behave in idiosyncratic ways and are chosen according to no known system of merit ranking (other than, perhaps, wealth or social position) is in full charge of the institution, making basic decisions about its future and controlling the work life of the highly skilled and educated people who make up the staff."[8] Although this view presents the situation with humor, in fact, trustees bring perspectives to the operation of the institution that are very different from those of the chief academic officer and members of the faculty, and each is essential for a college or university to achieve its educational objectives.

It All Depends on the Rain: A Case Study

After three years of careful development by a faculty committee and review and approval by the dean, the university academic council, and the provost, an academic program proposal was brought to the board of trustees of a large state university. The provost was enthusiastic about the proposal and believed that it would be an effective and important component of the university's academic programs in the future.

Before the meeting began, she asked a member of the academic committee of the board what his view of the proposal was, and whether the program was likely to be approved. "Well," the trustee said, "it all depends on the rain." The provost was startled and somewhat bewildered by the reply. The trustee, who had served in the state legislature, then carefully laid out the sequence of events that he thought would be necessary for the success of the proposal. His first requirement was at least twenty inches of rain during the growing season. The rain would determine the crop yields in the state. The crop yields would determine state tax revenues. The availability of general revenues would determine the possibility of increases in the funding allocations for higher education, and thereby for the new program. He further noted that, if crop yields failed, another alternative would be the success of a proposed state lottery that could support the general revenue fund. The provost realized with some despair that the implementation of her program depended not on the growth of academic knowledge or the potential for interdisciplinary development but rather on a throw of the dice or the price of beans.

Comment. Situations in which one or more trustees inserts a note of financial reality into an academic prospect are occurring more frequently on campuses in every sector of higher education. In some instances, a program must be terminated, even though it continues to maintain high academic quality, because of a decline in student interest and consequent lack of tuition revenue to support the necessary faculty and resources. For a new dean of the college, it can be a formative moment to observe trustees considering the legal, financial, and social dimensions of an academic program proposal.

In earlier centuries, as a means to balance the interests of the university with those of the community in which it was located, institutions of higher education were ruled by powerful guilds of students who exercised considerable control over the faculty.[9] The gradual transition to public control by a governing board over the past two hundred years has, in general, produced superior management, enhanced public support, and provided clearer focus on the social purposes of a college or university.

Most presidents expect that interactions with trustees will be through their office. Ordinarily, senior administrators will not directly approach trustees without the president's knowledge and approval, and all contacts with trustees should be reported back to the president.[10] Peter F. Drucker recommends that no restrictions be placed on contacts between the board and the staff, but he also stresses that when those contacts occur, the president must be informed.[11] Trustees serve as advisors to the president, while the president remains directly responsible to them. Presidents will differ in their attitudes on officer contact with the board. This should be openly discussed among members of the leadership team and

---

Best Practices between the Board and the Chief Academic Officer

- Ensure that all contact with the board goes through the president
- Use board expertise and community influence to support academic programs
- Present materials in a brief, concise format rather than in formal academic style
- Bring only complete proposals to the board
- Ensure that trustees meet deans and faculty leaders on an annual basis at least

---

guidelines must be provided. When good understanding and confidence develop between the president, the chairperson of the academic committee, and the chief academic officer, the academic agenda is effectively furthered.

Quarterly Report

The chief academic officer will typically be invited to provide both the president and board members with quarterly reports which summarize the major initiatives underway in each school and department. Reports should be positive in tone, informative, and preferably brief. Documents of this type are not the place to make excuses for unsuccessful efforts, to lobby for future initiatives, or to pontificate on issues in higher education. Trustees expect to receive a breadth of knowledge about the institution's current status, including those topics which cannot be covered in depth at respective committee meetings. In order to represent the college in the external community, trustees must be continually updated on new programs and academic initiatives.

The Board Meeting

Although the chief academic officer has an important role to play in board committee meetings, presidents differ regarding the attendance of senior officers at the board meeting itself. Many presidents will expect cabinet members, including the chief academic officer, to be in attendance. These administrative officers are not members of the board, and they do not officially participate in the meeting. They are present to respond to questions and provide information as requested. They may sit in a separate part of the room or wait in an adjacent room where they can be available to respond to any questions from board members.

Information to Be Provided to the Board

Trustees often come to a college or university from the disparate worlds of business, medicine, law, engineering, and other endeavors. They are often unaware of many of the details of higher education management, although in recent years many boards have become more activist in their roles, with the membership taking its stewardship responsibilities more seriously. At a minimum, members need to know the basic operating structures of a college or university so that they can clearly and accurately distinguish them from those that govern their own areas of professional responsibility.

One approach now used at many universities includes the presentation of abbreviated sets of data in the form of "dashboard indicators." These indicators clarify trends in enrollment, tuition revenues, degrees awarded, and percentage of faculty with tenure, for example, so that trustees can determine the critical trajectories in each operational area. A second approach provides trustees with a copy of the "fact book" institutional administrators use for their own decision making. These books may contain more information than the trustees will need, but they can serve as an ongoing reference over successive semesters.

A general rule is to provide trustees with the opportunity to review any major document that the institution plans to distribute publicly. This provides them with necessary "talking points" when they meet with people in the external community while also indicating to them the pact of academic progress among students and faculty. Trustees should be placed on mailing lists for those institutional publications that are substantive, but they should not be burdened with every flyer, newsletter, and announcement produced over the course of the academic year. Guidelines for what should be mailed out can be worked out with the university relations officer and the chairperson of the academic committee of the board.

Committee Meetings

Usually the provost or academic vice president will have responsibility to staff the academic committee of the board. These committee meetings are valuable opportunities to involve the trustees in what is going on on campus, to seek their advice and approval on academic initiatives, and help them get to know the real life of the university. As staff to the committee, the chief academic officer should assure that the trustees have all the support they need to make their time commitment effective. When a trustee first joins the committee, he or she should be fully informed as to the committee's areas of responsibility and the kinds of decisions its members will be expected to make. Whatever information he or she seeks should be supplied, and the individual should be introduced to all members of the committee and, equally important, to the academic officers of the institution. Usually, orientation to the work of the committee is provided by the chief academic officer and the committee chairperson. The committee meeting provides an opportunity to seek advice and approval from the trustees on such issues as new programs, degrees, policies, and strategic plans. The committee should also review executive summaries of reports to accrediting organizations, and, in the process, can become more informed and effective spokespersons for the institution when representing it in external settings.

The chief academic officer should also be prepared to attend meetings of other committees of the board as appropriate. Topics of discussion at the student affairs committee, the development committee, or the finance committee may call for her or his participation. While the vice president for academic affairs is not usually appointed to the finance committee, as an example, he or she may be asked to be present when that committee considers the academic affairs budget in order to provide information in more detail than the vice president for finance is likely to be able to give.

Orientation of the Board

The senior academic officer has an important contribution to make in the development and orientation of the board. Often, he or she is the individual best positioned to provide an overview of the history, mission, and values of the institution.[12] This review should also include presentations on the organizational structure of the academic sector and the specific roles and responsibilities of deans, chairpersons, and faculty councils and committees. The strategic plans of the departments or schools and how they fit into the institution's strategic plans can also be included. Experienced board members should be involved in conducting the key aspects of the orientation program, formats for which should include video conferencing, videotapes, briefing papers, retreats, one-on-one discussions, tours of the facilities, and attendance at outside educational programs offered by such professional organizations as the Association of Governing Boards of Universities and Colleges and the Governance Institute.

Frequently, trustees will not be familiar with academic traditions and operations, yet they may be aware of and sensitive to criticisms and negative opinions of higher education institutions in the media. In a 1994 speech before the Business/Higher Education Forum, the chief executive officer of a major corporation commented:

I had a dream the other night . . . a nightmare. The nightmare was I dreamed I was the CEO . . . and had to run the corporation like a university. In my dream . . . many employees in the line organization—the academy—had guaranteed lifetime employment . . . sometimes called tenure. . . . A quick study of a few departments suggested that some employees were paid simply for showing up a couple times a week. . . . In my nightmare . . . business results were not defined in terms of sales or profit or meeting the customers' needs, but rather in terms of how big individual departments were, what kind of recognition they received, how many books or articles in journals were published, and how many contracts or what we called grants were received from the government.

The speaker, Richard J. Mahoney, challenges universities to redesign to reduce costs, eliminate the unnecessary, and focus on core functions.[13] Mahoney serves on the finance committee of the board of a major research university, nevertheless, these words are testimony to how strange and even nightmarish many university traditions and values appear to a corporate observer.

As part of the orientation of new board members, the chief academic officer should not only provide basic information about the schools, programs, and activities of the institution, he or she should also try to communicate the values and expectations of the faculty. Faculty workload, especially, is an area unfamiliar to trustees, and they will require background to understand how "workload" includes not only class hours but also research and professional activities as well as service responsibilities. Some trustees will assume that a professor teaching nine credit hours per semester actually "works" nine hours a week, not realizing that faculty "work" also includes the time to select materials for those classroom contact hours; the time to read and grade student examinations, essays, and reports; the time to review the latest literature in her or his field; the hours of office time made available to individual students for tutoring, discussion, and counseling; and the time to plan and discuss curriculum development projects with colleagues in the department. Many trustees come from the corporate sector and demonstrate a familiarity with teaching based only on the classroom contact they recall from their own undergraduate years. Trustees in this category can provide a formidable challenge to the chief academic officer's "orientation" skills.

Participation by faculty in student activities, professional organizations, and community activities is also an integral part of academic life often not communicated to trustees. Presentations to the board by active scholars will not only provide trustees with a better understanding of research, creative writing, consulting and laboratory work but also will provide a sense of pride in the achievements their trusteeship supports. As they have opportunities to learn more about what the faculty are doing, they will naturally develop more ways to contribute to the success of these activities. The chief academic officer can then use board expertise and community influence to support programs. Well-informed trustees also contribute to college life by correcting misrepresentations and bringing attention to the positive activities of the faculty.

The Power of Shared Governance

Despite familiarity with concepts such as "quality circles" and considerable enthusiasm for "continuous quality improvement," shared governance is still a new and unfamiliar method to many trustees. Universities have decades of experience in using the insights and counsel of the faculty and professional staff in shaping the policies that govern academic life, and trustees may be surprised at the extent to which the president and provost seek and respond to the views of the faculty. Generally, trustees instinctively respect the authority of the faculty in academic issues, but they are not as familiar with the influence of a faculty senate, council, or assembly to determine policies and make personnel decisions.

During the orientation of new trustees, the chief academic officer should thoroughly explain the academic tradition of shared governance, taking particular care to frame it for listeners from a corporate, hierarchical environment. The joint statement by the American Association of University Professors, the American Council on Education, and the Association of Governing Boards of Universities and Colleges acknowledges "the variety and complexity of the tasks performed by institutions of higher education," and observes the "inescapable interdependence between governing boards, administrators, faculty, students, and others. The relationship calls for adequate communication among these components and full opportunity for appropriate joint planning and effort."[14]

Particularly mysterious to some trustees are the concepts of peer review and tenure. The requirement of academic freedom is also worth delineating, as trustees may be familiar with the idea, but they may not understand its limits and its significance.

The Parameters of Academic Program Review

Most colleges and universities implement some form of cyclical academic program review through which each degree and department is assessed by internal or external professionals. These reviews provide the unit with critical feedback and provide the chief academic officer with information helpful in planning the future of each area under her or his authority. This process can sometimes produce a decision to discontinue, modify, or significantly expand a degree program. In such cases, this needs to be brought to the board with full background data, including its immediate public relations impact and long-term financial implications.

In addition to oversight for existing degree authorities, many boards will expect to consider proactively new program proposals. In presenting such proposals to the board, the chief academic officer forwards materials developed within the college or university in the course of academic program review, including her or his own rationale for implementation. Depending on the procedures of the institution, these materials should include a narrative that justifies the need for the program and documents the resources to sustain it; a list of required courses, course descriptions, and recommended sequences; the curriculum vitae of the faculty who will initially teach in the program; and recommendations from the curriculum committee, the department head, pertinent deans, and the chief academic officer.

Interesting and useful as all of this information is, it will not provide answers to many of the core questions trustees will pose. Some will obligingly read all the material that the chief academic officer sends and narrow it to three basic concerns:

1. *Cost.* How much will the program cost? The major costs will be for personnel: new faculty, professional staff, graduate assistants, work/study students, technical and secretarial staff. Next, essential resources should be considered: library demands, computing support, laboratory equipment, classroom and office space. In addition, there will be operating costs: insurance demands, maintenance costs, utilities, administrative offices costs, residence halls and dining service demands.

2. *Revenue.* How much revenue will the program generate? The trustees will expect to see projected enrollments, a market study to substantiate the projections, a review of the competition, estimates of tuition revenue at start-up and when in full operation, estimates of projected grants or sales of services, and estimates of return on investment.

3. *Strategy.* What benefits will accrue from offering the program? Will this program position the college or university favorably in its immediate community? The broader academic community? The national higher education environment? What strategic issues must be considered?

In response, the academic vice president must be able to present materials in a format appropriate for a business decision rather than an academic committee meeting. Trustees usually will, and should, have great confidence in the ability of the faculty and academic administration to make a proposal that is academically sound. They will then view their responsibility as one to determine whether it is in the best interests of the institution legally, politically, financially, and in terms of broader community concerns. They will consider whether the institution can support the new program, whether the proposal includes all of the factors need for its success, how the program will help the broader community, how it will contribute to the financial strength of the institution, and whether it will position the college or university more or less favorably in its current political environment.

In particular, trustees will assume responsibility for financial oversight.[15] Thus, it will be imperative for the chief academic officer to work with the faculty finance committee to develop a detailed pro forma budget statement that can be used effectively in a trustee context. Once such a statement has been developed and approved, the provost or academic vice president can provide this format to deans and faculty program developers for use in their planning as the degree undergoes various internal stages of development.

The decision as to the appropriate time for involvement of the board in the development of new proposals should be made in consultation with the president and the chairperson of the committee. In some institutions, boards will seek early involvement in deciding whether to encourage the school to proceed.[16] At other institutions, the board will not become involved until the proposal has been internally reviewed, approved, and brought to them for final action. As a rule, the more significant its financial implications, the earlier a proposal should be shared with the board. A recent study proposed that "boards should clarify the level of policy, performance review, and major decisions they wish to reserve for themselves and delegate the rest of the decision-making to the president and faculty."[17] In either case, whether it is a request to plan or a request to approve, the chief academic officer is responsible for ensuring that all the information necessary to make an appropriate decision has been provided.

Board Participation in the Accreditation Process

Most professional accreditation and regional institutional accreditation site visitors will request meetings with members of the board. Clearly, this interaction is most effective when the trustees have been thoroughly prepared. Usually, only the members of the academic committee of the board will review the self-study document, or its executive summary, before it is submitted to the accrediting body. However, any trustee who is going to be involved in a site visitation should be given a written summary and a comprehensive briefing before the event. The chief academic officer's briefing should provide background information on the accrediting body and the importance of the accreditation to the college or university's ability to continue to attract students, to offer degrees, and to receive federal and philanthropic support. He or she should also review the criteria for accreditation and give a concise summary of the institution's ability to fulfill these criteria. Less informed trustees may sometimes become alarmed because the self-study reveals one or more problem areas. The job of a vice president for academic affairs will be to reassure them that it is the mandate of those on the self-study team to identify areas of concern as well as those of strength.

Communicating Board Decisions

The chief academic officer should keep deans and faculty informed of board decisions while preserving confidentiality regarding the substance of board discussions. A provost or academic dean accepts the challenge to represent the president and the board to the college community and simultaneously to represent the will of the faculty to the board. Since most deans and faculty leaders have contact with board members only when they are presenting a proposal for approval, tensions may sometimes arise due to lack of community and familiarity. Faculty may complain they have no knowledge of board activities until after the board has made its decision. This is another classic conflict reflective of a campus environment, and it remains the responsibility of a chief academic officer to mediate successfully the authority of the board and the prerogatives of the faculty.

Emerging Trends for Boards and Chief Executives

Many of the problems facing America's health care industry today will confront our country's higher education institutions by the turn of the century. The health care community faces complaints about uncontrollable high costs, yet hospitals no longer receive the kind of financial support from federal and state governments that they once enjoyed. Hospital administrators find that operating costs are increasing because of the expense of the latest and best equipment and technologies, high salaries and fringe benefits, and the costs of liabilities. Similarly, colleges and universities face increasing complaints about higher costs and the affordability of a degree. Yet, higher education also no longer receives the amount of financial support from federal and state governments that it once enjoyed. Campus administrators assume ever higher operating costs due to new technologies and competitive salary structures to name just two major forces.

The response of the health care community to these pressures has been to initiate the following four strategies: (1) reduce length of stay and thereby the cost of treatment; (2) provide health services in lower cost ambulatory settings rather than a hospital whenever possible; (3) network or merge with other institutions to reduce costs; (4) reduce hospital beds, staff, and budgets. These stringent measures have become necessary to survive in the current aggressive payment market that has replaced the traditional fee-for-service system.

Chief academic officers will be wise to adapt proactively similar strategies. As a starting point, they should aggressively seek opportunities to reduce costs; to share costs through consortia, affiliations, and strategic alliances; and to deliver degree programs in more individualized, sometimes even unorthodox, formats. Distance learning and alternate sites, schedules, and curricula, for example, can produce unprecedented savings through collaboration and shared staff and equipment.

Put differently, there will be a greater use of business practices in college and university administration by the year 2000. Early indicators of this include the new emphasis by accrediting organizations on the assessment of student learning outcomes, the increasing accountability required by the new federal Higher Education guidelines and the State Postsecondary Review Entities (SPREs), and the new Financial Accounting Standards Board guidelines for presenting financial statements in a format familiar to the business community. In fact, many higher education boards which have reviewed these new financial statements have been supportive of them as they are simpler to use than the fund accounting methods currently in use. In return, with a firmer sense of the business operations of the institution and a clearer view of its cash flow, trustees will be able to provide more pertinent and useful advice to their colleges and universities.

At the same time, it is apparent that higher education institutions have begun to experience new criticisms of traditional academic practices. The tradition of tenure has now become vulnerable to criticism and dissolution on some campuses. In every region of the country, several institutions are now in the process of eliminating the structure of tenure and replacing it with rolling, multiyear contracts or even annual reviews of departmental needs. The chief academic officer who supports tenure needs to be prepared to explain the circumstances in which tenure should be now awarded. Trustees should be fully briefed on the reasons to continue tenure as well as the alternative personnel and staffing options now replacing it on some campuses. While many faculty members continue to view tenure primarily in terms of academic freedom and job security, trustees may view it from the perspective of needing a qualified labor force to deliver academic excellence in degree programs. Another vulnerable personnel issue will be the annual teaching load, something which is frequently misunderstood by those outside of higher education working fifty or sixty-hour weeks in a company or small business. As faculty recognize that their working conditions are coming under increasing scrutiny, calls for more faculty participation at the board level inevitably will emerge, especially on budget and strategic planning committees.

The American Association of Governing Boards, the national organization for college and university trustees, recommends as a matter of principle opposition to representation by internal constituencies as voting trustees in light of potential conflicts of interest.[18] At the same time, the AGB proposes that boards consider and create other ways in which faculty members can become responsible and reliable partners in the institution's decision-making and policy-formulation processes. Suggestions include the formation of a faculty executive committee or faculty membership on appropriate committees of the board. Provosts and academic vice presidents can shape the academic cultures on their campuses through support for these alternatives.

The removal of the cap on retirement age for faculty, effective in 1994, has produced new awareness of the burden of the fixed cost of faculty salaries. In previous years, tenure ended when the faculty member reached the age of retirement, yet, now that there is no age for retirement, a faculty member may retain tenure as long as he or she considers himself or herself able to work. As senior faculty members are compensated at significantly higher levels than their junior colleagues, their continued activity on many faculties has resulted in a ratcheting upward of the salary component of annual budgets. As trustees have been consulted more regularly regarding retirement plans, salary increments, fringe benefits, and incentives, they have, quietly but firmly, also become more involved in compensation issues on their campuses.

The complexity of both the strategic planning and daily management issues facing university administrators today often demands forms of specialized knowledge that neither a president nor chief academic officer can provide. An institution may find itself preparing for an intricate, politically charged revenue bond issue, an unforeseen, time-consuming lawsuit, or the design of a new campus center which requires in-depth and expert advice well beyond the scope of its academic environment. In these instances, a sensitive investigation or controversial campus building plan can be addressed more effectively by outside professionals. As trustees may be more familiar with consultants whose expertise is in the corporate sector, the chief academic officer should be prepared to work collaboratively with both governing board members and these experts to assure that the needs of the academic sector are understood and reflected in their recommendations.

Conclusion

The increasing professionalization of academic leadership challenges the chief academic officer to work with the president and trustees as a collaborator who understands that higher education institutions are now multimillion dollar corporations requiring tough and visionary decision making. For an academic vice president or provost, the challenge will be to manage effectively while enhancing the teaching and learning experiences of both faculty and students.

Creating Common Ground: Student Development, Academic Affairs, and Institutional Diversity

Paula Hooper Mayhew

Diversity and multiculturalism have been issues of transforming concern on college and university campuses since the early 1980s. Few in higher education have escaped choosing sides in the debate between what Allan Bloom terms "a loss of commitment to transcendent values"[1] based on the Western canon and Maxine Greene's articulation of a multicultural and inclusive "curriculum for human beings."[2] As each side has formulated increasingly impassioned arguments, the nation's colleges and universities diversify at a steady rate, continuing a trend that began when returning soldiers from World War II enrolled under the GI Bill. Although this trend toward diversification is now more than half a century old, it is the increasing presence of African Americans and other historically disadvantaged students on campuses that has sparked the most recent, and vitriolic, debate.

The increase in diversity among students in the American higher education system poses both challenges and stumbling blocks for academic leaders striving to create a newly fashioned, yet shared, sense of academic community. In the majority of colleges and universities, the chief academic officer now bears the final responsibility to develop multicultural initiatives and support the educational needs of diverse student populations. Increasingly, provosts and academic vice presidents must initiate and sustain institution-wide teaching and learning environments for members of a complex and evolving campus "community." While developing programs to assess demonstrable student academic achievement, chief academic officers must also coordinate the budget, curriculum, and faculty personnel so that the potential for broad-based student success will be realized. Ensuring individual academic achievement in this environment requires the ability to create an almost magical integration of social, intellectual, and community life—an academic objective with multiple levels that is far easier to describe than to achieve.

The presence of "others" in academia has made the task of sustaining community far more daunting than in the decades prior to the Second World War. As leaders of the traditionally white, often male, American higher education community, contemporary chief academic officers have had to reevaluate virtually every aspect of our social and intellectual lives in order to meet the needs of new populations of students. Furthermore, as this task has grown more difficult since the late 1980s, many academic managers remain far from satisfied with the outcomes: Retention and graduation rates remain far too low among nonwhite students and those with low socioeconomic status in every sector of the country and in every category of institution.

Although the necessity to do so is clear, the commitment to keep the larger social and educational issues of the decade central to one's work as a provost or dean is easily overwhelmed by the day-to-day, reactive chores of administrative life. Consequently, it is not surprising that many chief academic officers find it practically impossible to provide consistent, integrative leadership in student development and issues of diversity, particularly since institutions possess so little shared historical consciousness surrounding these issues. Although many academic vice presidents still think as teachers and learners, it is simply too easy to allow one's concern for—and commitment to—the educational development of students to be vitiated in the struggles with the very bureaucratic systems one has helped to create. Thus, effective senior officers must create ongoing systems to promote student diversity in the contexts of academic leadership and faculty development.

Analyzing the chief academic officer's ability to accomplish institutional priorities within this context requires an articulation of educational "best practices" and emerging trends. This chapter explores the multiple dimensions of these responsibilities for provosts and deans as well as providing guidelines on which to model successful programs.

Creating New Partnerships between Academic and Student Affairs

Since 1970, American higher education cannot claim success in meeting the goal of creating an informed citizenry, especially with regard to educationally and economically disadvantaged students as well as those who are the first in their families to attend college. Despite more than two decades of concerted effort, few senior academic officers are satisfied with the extent to which their institutions serve and educate individuals from educationally disenfranchised backgrounds, especially urban and rural poor and people of color. Having attempted to address the learning issues of these students through traditional coursework, both remedial and targeted, many deans realized that revisiting the curriculum was a necessary yet insufficient response to these students' needs. Gradually, several innovative colleges and universities incorporated the resources of the student development professionals on their campuses into academic programming initiatives.

Prior to initiating this practice, most higher education institutions had relied on senior professors to serve as temporary, rotating deans in the area of "services" to students, usually asking them to enforce academic standards and adjudicate cases of disciplinary infractions. Aided by growth in the number of professionals in the field first called "student services" and now known as "student development," many postsecondary institutions began to divide the academic and social aspects of college life into separate spheres. The administrative priorities of the "academic dean's office" and "student services office" diverged by mutual agreement, with one focusing on curricular and progression issues and the other on cocurricular programs and residence life. Unfortunately, both groups furthered the fiction that financial issues affecting students were an ancillary third province, better kept confidential from faculty advisors and other service providers in order to "protect" the student. As a result, increasingly complex student needs became divided along the lines of a dated campus hierarchy with academic services retaining an isolated primacy, student "services" viewed as secondary, and financial planning relegated to a mechanical, noneducational procedure.

Further reinforcing both separation and hierarchy, new professionals entering these three areas—academic, student development, and financial—underwent significantly different and unrelated training for the work they would eventually do. Research confirms that these groups now hold widely divergent career expectations, which tends to minimize collaboration and isolate functions over the course of careers. Thus, at many institutions, one office continues to make referrals to maximize the use of its own administrators' and service deliverers' time, often with little knowledge of, or regard for, the work of the other two areas of operation.

Underlying this businesslike but unintegrated use of campus personnel, a fundamental problem exists which becomes more starkly apparent as institutions mature: The more diverse a student population becomes in terms of age, economic, marital, and cultural background, the more diverse its expectations also become. By the year 2000, increasing numbers of students will possess only thirdhand knowledge of what college or university life is actually like, and it will be knowledge culled from the undifferentiated array of popular beliefs and images that "explain" college to those who have never attended. As deans of admission and others increasingly utilize the full force of the media to shape a rhetoric that bonds education with democracy as "values" integral to the American system, it follows that growing number of undergraduates will assume their futures will be compromised without a baccalaureate degree. Those in coming generations will not only need to complete their degree requirements but also to learn what is reasonable to expect from the college "experience" as well as what will be expected of them in terms of individual responsibility, community building, and civility.

To compound these challenges, a steadily rising percentage of students are completing their postsecondary degrees on a part-time basis with their "real" social identities no longer proceeding from their identities as students. For these workers and family members, studies are valued, but attending college is, of necessity, a secondary commitment.

In distinguishing between large categories of traditional students and returning, "nontraditional" students, chief academic officers must acknowledge a diversity not only of age and experience but also of expectations. The most obvious difference is well known: rite-of-passage students care enormously about on-campus opportunities to meet and socialize with people of their own age. Most nontraditional students either prefer to lead, or are forced by circumstances to lead, social lives off-campus. Clearly, numerous policy decisions, annual programs, and budget-planning exercises will be shaped by this reality.

Other differences between these two populations are less obvious, but nonetheless defining. Traditional students *expect* to have intense one-on-one interactions with professors and campus officials, and they retain a vision of higher education that centers on their individual growth. They demand personalized academic and social services and ongoing relationships, no matter how slight, with the people in the institution through which they are achieving identity.

Conversely, nontraditional students demonstrate needs connected to saving, rather than spending, time. With greater numbers of businesses beyond the campus providing automated systems to enhance customer service, nontraditional learners are finding it increasingly difficult to adapt to systems requiring face-to-face interactions like in-person advisement and proofs of immunization. Time is an omnipresent factor in every requirement posed by their institutions, and impatience frequently characterizes interchanges with a campus bureaucracy that is less than user-friendly.

Individuals for whom the designation "student" is not a primary distinguishing characteristic are also particularly unsuited to following the often antiquated paths set for them in deciphering college degree–completion systems. Unless one is familiar with their histories, it can be difficult to grasp how a college or university "thinks." In part because only a portion of their lives can be devoted to this degree-completion process, many nontraditional students have neither the time nor the patience to make fine distinctions among social, academic, and financial problems. They do not comprehend that most higher education institutions mark firm boundaries in these areas, and they become frustrated by the assumption that they are supposed to realize how these systems work. Often, these boundaries have become blurred, or even dysfunctional, for nontraditional students, and persistent attrition rates may be viewed as their response to a system that has, for them, outlived its usefulness yet remains central to traditional students.

A new, more effective model to address the educational priorities of both of these student groups is clearly indicated. In response, some colleges and universities now view academic affairs, student development, and financial aid as a unified matrix of related services rather than as separate entities. More frequently, enrollment management task forces, once comprised of admissions professionals only, now include a team of academic administrators, student recruiters, faculty advisors, student development officers, and financial aid counselors. This new, collaborative approach to creating positive teaching and learning environments has expanded the responsibilities of chief academic officers to encompass almost every aspect of student life—psychological, academic, financial, and even social needs and expectations. For an academic dean primarily experienced in faculty personnel and curriculum development discussions, assuming an institutional leadership position within this new, more complex educational environment can be extraordinarily daunting, no matter what his or her professional preparation.

The need for a chief academic officer to integrate the traditionally distinct worlds of academic, financial, and student affairs has grown into an imperative if colleges and universities intend to remain competitive among current consumers. Under the focused leadership of a provost or academic vice president, institutions can achieve a more effective "one college" model centering on the whole student experience and addressing the need to create a campus culture that purposefully coordinates student development and academic mission. In this manner, student accomplishments within a diverse, multicultural institution are encouraged and supported by the clear statement and implementation of these shared goals.

Developing Academic Systems to Support Diverse
Student Constituencies

Alexander Astin has shown that once students' characteristics are adjusted for differences at entry, the *kind* of college in which they enroll has little direct causal effect on their achievement.[3] Nonetheless, American colleges and universities cover a wide spectrum in terms of diversity, ranging from open access to highly selective, and their programs for diverse students differ significantly, as well. Some universities accept large numbers of students from historically disadvantaged minorities who enter with educational deficits; many regional comprehensive institutions maintain enrollment mixtures of diverse students in need of remediation; and the category of highly selective colleges welcomes small numbers of students from educationally disadvantaged minorities, most of whom have demonstrated high academic achievement. Whatever the institutional type and tradition, however, the chief academic officer now holds the central responsibility to devise policies that achieve diversity as well as academic quality within the organizational culture.

In 1990, Richard Richardson and Elizabeth Fisk Skinner of the National Center for Postsecondary Research and Improvement considered ten public institutions whose graduation rates in the 1980s for African American, Hispanic, or Native American students were above average for their states. In reporting the results of the study,[4] they developed a model that represents the process of institutional adaptation to diversity, taking into account concerns related to issues of selectivity and quality.

Using the Richardson and Skinner model as a basic method to measure institutional effectiveness on this issue, a provost or academic vice president can assess the interventions that have proved most useful for his or her category of institution. Richardson and Skinner note that "within any institution the particular choice of achievement and diversity strategies depends upon mission,"[5] and their findings clearly demonstrate that even subtle differences in institutional practices was the primary reason some institutions achieved superior outcomes.

In 1991, Richardson developed a "Model of Institutional Adaptation to Student Diversity." It describes the ways in which educational mission and policy environment shape the implementation of partnerships between academic and student affairs.[6] Richardson's revised model clarifies paths for institutions not only to ameliorate potential conflicts between achievement and diversity but, more importantly, to encourage achievements that *accommodate* diversity. Simply put, his research suggests that selective institutions need not emphasize achievement at the expense of diversity, nor that nonselective institutions build diversity by sacrificing academic accomplishments. With collaborative leadership by the chief academic and chief student affairs officers, both types of institutions can design programs that provide a balance of attention on both achievement and diversity, thus creating the possibility for a new level of positive outcomes.

Setting Priorities for Student Development in the Context of Academic Affairs

What else "really matters" when setting priorities and providing academic leadership in the area of student development? Astin provides an extended analysis of this question centering on issues such as personality and self-concept, patterns of behavior, academic and cognitive development, career aspirations, and attitudes, values, and beliefs. Important for chief academic officers are Astin's findings on what he terms "peer group effect" and the "diversity issue." Utilizing a very large sample of full-time undergraduates of traditional college age, his research reveals that "the student's peer group is the single most potent source of influence on growth and development during the undergraduate years."[7] In his view, the influence of the peer group is far more important to positive student development than institutional type and structure (for example, size, private versus public, university versus college), which are *not* direct causal factors in most student outcomes.[8]

On first reading, this finding causes concern among both faculty and admissions officers. If students in similar circumstances with common needs and interests show the greatest degree of academic success in college, then homogeneity of the student body would seem to be a more important goal than diversity. In fact, however, Astin's data demonstrate that "students' values, beliefs, and aspirations tend to change in the direction of the dominant values, beliefs, and aspirations of the peer group."[9] Therefore, it is of the greatest significance to promote and support an orientation toward diversity in each aspect of institutional life in order to help establish a peer climate that both exemplifies this value and encourages academic achievement. Astin's study confirms the hypothesis that both institutional and individual commitments to diversity are associated with greater self-reported gains in cognitive and affective development, with increased satisfaction in most areas of the college experience, and with increased commitment to promoting racial understanding.

In short, the weight of the empirical evidence shows that the actual effect on student development of emphasizing diversity and of student participation in diversity are overwhelming. . . . The findings of this study suggest that there are many developmental benefits that accrue to students when institutions encourage and support an emphasis on multiculturalism and diversity.[10]

Best Practice: Strengthen the Peer Group

We can extrapolate from Astin's findings, when setting academic priorities to achieve student success. It is clear that creating multiple opportunities to consolidate peer group relations within a value system that honors diversity should be emphasized. However, what if a given institution is like so many others in each sector of the country and is characterized by a broad mixture of some traditional and many nontraditional, commuting students whose socioeconomic status requires either full- or part-time work while attending classes nights and weekends? How does one assure positive student development, as well as academic accomplishment, among people whose identities as students are not as important as their roles as parents and workers, or whose personal histories may include prior attendance at one or more institutions, each one a failed attempt at degree-completion? Answering these questions has become the inescapable assignment of a chief academic officer. No matter how many task forces and special study groups may be created, it is the provost or vice president for academic affairs who most often must assume the critical responsibility for student achievement in its broadest sense. Outlined below are several models that articulate plans to achieve institutional diversity and enhanced learning outcomes.

One notable model of a peer group focused in support of student achievement has been that for "returning women." These programs, first developed in the 1970s, have been largely successful for middle-class females collectively designated as "returning women," although many are, in fact, entering college for the first time. This "returning woman" model, now providing postsecondary education for several hundred thousand American females, is reduced to its core elements to help chief academic officers extend its success to more diverse academic constituencies.

A Program Model for Student Development and Academic Achievement

Build Programs That Target Work and Success

In the case of returning women, although most programs were open from the start to men and women of all colors and socioeconomic backgrounds, they "spoke" most effectively to the needs of middle-class females in their thirties and forties who found themselves victims of the

---

Best Practices in Student Development and Academic Affairs

- Target programs for diverse students and acknowledge the special needs of the population they are designed to serve
- Value multiculturalism and diversity because they can create ideological bonds that enhance community among diverse students
- Ensure that first-generation-to-college and socially and economically deprived students are comfortable as they enter an institution and learn how college works
- Allocate ongoing resources to fund mutually reinforcing systems to provide academic and social supports for diverse students

---

"feminine mystique."[11] A review of the materials currently used for recruitment of students to many of these programs continues to show direct appeals to middle-class values centered on work and success. The target population for these programs is a middle-class woman between twenty-five and forty-five who desires an education in order to secure a middle-class position, yet who still clearly identifies herself in relation to male power and success.

Create Programs with Ideological Coherence and Marketing Will Follow

While new ways to discuss self-esteem, life-planning, divorce, and single parenthood continue to provide the rhetorical underpinnings for the back-to-college experience for many of America's "new" undergraduates, this rhetoric has proved far less appealing to poor and lower middle-class working women and has been virtually useless with most males considering a career change.

Make Re-entry to College a Simple Process and Transitions Back to the Classroom Comfortable

Successful programs are developed and continue to be staffed at every level by academic women and men who stress their similarity to, and identity with, the returning population enrolling at their institutions. Significant amounts of time and energy are devoted to demonstrating that attending college is a manageable process and to creating links between new students and successful students from similar backgrounds already enrolled. Since testing is often one of the greatest psychological barriers for these new constituencies, interviews that explore motivation and self-knowledge can be utilized in place of traditional entrance exams and diagnostic testing, for example.

Create Academic and Student Development Systems That Reinforce One Another

As Astin has shown, there is now ample evidence demonstrating that involvement is the key to educational attainment for *all* students. Using evidence from clinical settings and from their beginnings, effective returning women's programs purposely incorporated the types of academic "involvement" appropriate to their participants. In many instances, returning women responded particularly well to highly interactive learning experiences in groups of twenty or fewer. Over time, groups that highly value peer learning have become the hallmark of the educational experience for these undergraduates.[12] Conversely, one criticism of this method has been that classes are sometimes hard to distinguish from support groups.

On a broader scale, returning students overall typically respond well to support groups, as long as environments are not hierarchically structured and judgments can be suspended. Leaders who identify directly with the issues of that constituency, and who are identified with them in return, quickly earn necessary levels of trust. In order to establish this connection, facilitators of support groups, no matter what the issue— time management, study skills, school-to-work transitions—learn to share their own stories before asking new students to take academic or personal risks. In sum, provosts and deans may find these guidelines useful both in reconsidering basic assumptions about the learning environment on their campuses and in upgrading programs that, on closer analysis, no longer achieve retention goals, student support, or appropriate levels of academic quality.

Conclusion: Emerging Trends in Student Development and Academic Affairs

Although there have been ongoing challenges to its actions, in 1995, the University of California at Berkeley abolished its decades-old program to give preference in admissions to students from historically disadvantaged minorities. This event has grown to symbolize a growing national disaffection with higher education programs aimed at social change while also signaling a retreat from collegiate affirmative action programs, especially in highly competitive institutions supported by public monies. Still, population statistics for the years 2000 to 2020 continue to show significant growth among groups previously under-

Emerging Trends in Student Development and Academic Affairs

- Affirmative action programs for disadvantaged students will continue to be under attack, especially in public universities
- Multicultural approaches to teaching and learning will be better linked to institutional goals for student development and academic mission
- Governmental agencies as well as regional accrediting bodies will increasingly demand evidence of success in student learning outcomes and the application of institutional assessment instruments
- The demand for federal and state funds for higher education will force public institutions to be more selective in admissions, challenging private institutions to diversify their student bodies and increase tuition discounting
- Students entering colleges and universities will come from more diverse backgrounds than at any time in the history of our higher education system
- High school–college articulation programs will be judged successful only if they demonstrate an integration of both academic and student service objectives to enhance self-esteem, personal development, and academic preparation

represented in American higher education. Almost certainly, public institutions less prestigious than Berkeley and virtually all but the top 1 or 2 percent of competitive private institutions will continue affirmative attempts to enroll, educate, and graduate increasingly diverse students.

In order to serve this population of diverse students, multicultural approaches to teaching and learning will become more closely linked to institutional goals for student development and academic mission. The disappearance of compartmentalization of social and academic programs begun in the 1980s will, of necessity, continue to accelerate as colleges and universities struggle to recast themselves to serve students with more complex educational needs and expectations. Private foundations will continue their work to support programs to diversify the curriculum and to link this curricular change with institutional reform.

Governmental entities as well as regional accrediting bodies will increasingly demand evidence of plans that join academic affairs and student affairs in partnership. Even if the federal Department of Education is abolished and the regulation of higher education is assigned to individual states, colleges and universities will increasingly need to demonstrate student achievement and institutional effectiveness to some regulating governmental body. In the present climate of low public confidence in higher education, colleges and universities will need to prove they are able to educate the diversity of students they enroll, and that they can do so with scarcer state funding and fewer federal supports than at any time since World War II.

The demand for shrinking federal and state funds to support higher education will force some public institutions into increased selectivity in admissions, a trend that does not bode well for students from groups even now underrepresented in American public colleges and universities. Historically, the mission of our public institutions has been to broaden the educational franchise for new Americans and minorities of both genders. With raised admissions hurdles in state- and city-supported institutions, however, more and more students who would otherwise have sought admission to public colleges and universities may seek access to private higher education institutions whose missions have not necessarily focused on academically and economically marginal students or, for that matter, on the idea that their particular brand of higher education is one means to remediate social ills. Therefore, private colleges and universities embracing diversity in both mission and campus culture could have first choice among students who may be excluded from public institutions and who are ready to "spend" their educational entitlements in the private sector where they find programs and services tailored to their needs.

While students entering colleges and universities across the country will come from more diverse backgrounds than at any point in our history, the rate of this diversification will far outpace the growth of diversity among full-time faculty members. For a longstanding set of reasons, American higher education institutions have failed to attract, educate, and grant degrees to students from historically disadvantaged backgrounds who are then drawn into collegiate teaching. Although some innovative programs in teacher training and professional development are emerging in various graduate programs, it is unlikely this trend will shift to any great degree in the near future. As a result, in the year 2000, chief academic officers will still be conceptualizing strategies to help faculty members deal successfully with students whose backgrounds and preparations are significantly different from their own.

College and university orientation programs will increasingly be asked to integrate academic and student service objectives to enhance self-esteem, personal development, career focus, and academic preparation among new learners.

Few members of the academic community have the opportunity of oversight enjoyed by chief academic officers. They are so placed to have the luxury of envisioning institutions as entireties, not simply as fragmented faculties, departments, and student bodies. They must learn to capitalize on this privileged perspective and to emphasize their roles as creators and implementors of constructive, democratizing institutional change. In so doing, they must work to reconcile the conflicting claims of scholarship and socialization, and to shape the exciting possibilities inherent in teaching and learning for professors and students alike. As the new century begins, the role of the chief academic officer in integrating academic programs and campus services for our increasingly multicultural and diverse student populations will continue to pose insistent challenges filled with exhilarating prospects for innovation and change.

CHAPTER SEVEN

Enrollment Management

Michael A. Baer and Peter A. Stace

Chief academic officers have always worried about admissions projections even though for much of this century enrollment yields have been reasonably predictable with recent historical data as an indicator of the size and configuration of entering first-year classes. Of course, this has not stopped provosts and academic vice presidents from worrying about this issue, and about the retention of upper-class students, and about the contributions both groups make to the institution's financial resources.

In the 1990s, for a variety of reasons, both chief academic and chief enrollment officers have lost the stability of prior enrollment patterns. Foremost among factors that have changed the higher education enrollment environment is a demographic decline in the number of students turning eighteen each year. In fact, since the mid-1980s, there has been a steady and significant decrease in the number of eighteen-year-olds in the United States. In some regions, the effect has been dramatic for academic, admissions, and budget planners. As figure 7.1 indicates, in the Northeast, the decrease from 1987 to 1994 was 23 percent, and in some states it will be 2007 before the levels of 1987 are again achieved among traditional student-age populations.

Sheer numbers is not the only demographic change that will effect future enrollments, however. Even among traditional-age students, an unprecedented shift is predicted within less than a decade in the configuration of those seeking a baccalaureate degree. A far greater proportion of applicants will come from the minority populations, first-generation college families, and those with modest incomes. As well, continued increases are also expected among non–traditionally-aged students both in undergraduate and graduate programs. As a bachelor degree becomes the mandatory credential for career entry in most fields,

117

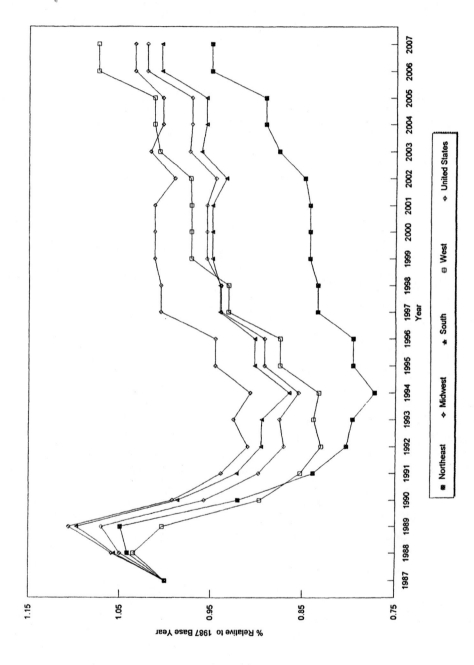

Figure 7.1. Population reaching age 18 by region through the year 2007.

there will be increasing pressure to maintain lower tuition increases and higher financial aid packages to allow students of less-than-average means to enroll in a choice of quality higher education institutions. Decisions regarding program offerings, strategic audiences, financial aid competitiveness, and the willingness to invest in developmental support programs for underprepared groups and other special populations will impact both the enrollment level and enrollment mix of every college and university.

These new, more complex managerial decisions demand the expertise of someone who understands demographics, who can evaluate different markets and their populations, who understands how to communicate skillfully with prospective students and those who advise them, and who stays current on the details of federal financial aid policies. This individual must also understand the economic models used to package the institution's own financial aid resources with federal monies to attract the types of students the institution has targeted.

Enrollment Management: New Systems, New Agendas

Enrollment management is a relatively new entry in the lexicon of higher education administration.[1] It first appeared on the scene in the late 1970s as concerns about the dire demographic projections and declining numbers of high school graduates challenged the perspective from which campuses had become accustomed to viewing the admission function. Depending on the institution's academic reputation, admissions was viewed as either a selection office or a recruitment/sales unit. For enrollment-driven institutions most sensitive to this new environment, neither of these admissions models was adequate to the new challenges facing many campuses. Enrollment objectives could no longer be achieved by managing only the "front door" to the institution. In order to manage total enrollment and net revenue effectively, it became necessary for senior staff members to address the retention of currently enrolled students in addition to the recruitment of new entrants. To the extent an institution's retention rate improved, the institution became less reliant on new entrants and new markets to maintain desired enrollment levels and satisfy revenue projections. In the near future, however, retention and recruitment strategies will extend well beyond the traditional functions of an admission staff; it will require a collaborative approach by a newly configured enrollment management group capable of addressing the powerful dynamics now driving recruitment, retention, and revenue flows.

Clearly, for chief academic officers as well as the members of this new group, enrollment management is no longer simply selecting students for admissions, examining each family's finances, and deciding by rote formula what need that student has for financial support. Rather, the process has become far more shaped by strategy, starting with an assessment of an institution and then marketing what that campus realistically can offer to an appropriate segment of the potential student population through creative financial aid packaging.[2] Beyond this, those on the enrollment management team also must manage the integration of each student into the campus community to develop the bonds to increase academic success and ensure retention,[3] ultimately helping each graduate connect with employers through proactive career advising. This new strategy also fosters more involved alumni who consistently participate in the institution's development activities.

Increasingly, the institution's chief academic officer is responsible for all of these activities, and he or she should be directly involved in the development of policies related to them. In larger universities, however, the responsibilities for marketing, administrative services, and retention may be so broad that someone expert in this area must be engaged to maintain the enrollment management functions. A vice president for academic affairs who enlists a senior enrollment management officer to integrate admissions and financial aid, maintain records to track students, and manage the cocurricular student development process will be able to reserve significant time for curricular and faculty personnel issues that would otherwise receive less focused attention.

To manage its enrollment successfully, a college or university must understand its operating environment, and the decisions an institution makes regarding its academic programs and the investment of its resources should be viewed as significantly impacting its future attractiveness to students. In the current higher education market, each institution must make the choices to allow it to structure its own demographics to the extent possible. An institution that historically has catered to traditional student populations will need to make a set of sometimes unfamiliar decisions in an environment with fewer eighteen-year-olds. In an effort to continue to attract a similar student base, it may market more aggressively in a broader geographical area while simultaneously seeking new populations through the introduction of timely, consumer-driven degree programs. One college may elect to adjust its acceptance criteria so that it can accept a greater proportion of smaller high school graduating classes, while a larger university may decide to reaffirm earlier admissions criteria and, if necessary, restructure and reduce the size of its staff and faculty. An alternative approach might position the institution in relationships with community colleges to encourage transfer students and bolster enrollment levels in the upper division. Whatever strategy is chosen, the policies, programs, and services of the institution must be shaped carefully, consistently, and proactively to support that direction.

In examining new enrollment management options, a college or university must answer these types of questions:

1. Does the institution offer programs for nontraditional students?

2. Does the institution offer specialized programming for returning women?

3. Does the institution provide special study and lounge areas for commuting students and offer programs to help them provide support for one another?

4. Are classes scheduled throughout the entire day, including early morning, lunch hour, and early evening, to provide an attractive academic environment for students who work full time and still want to pursue a degree?

5. Have cultural support centers for minority, ethnic, and international student groups been established?

6. Is tutoring available for students who have not had adequate preparation in one or more basic skill areas?

7. Are faculty members both trained and willing to nurture students who might be attracted to the institution despite insufficient academic preparation?

8. Does the institution have programs to assist new students whose native language is not English?

In shaping responses to these policy issues, the chief academic officer and the institutional leadership team will need to consider multiple, sometimes overlapping factors. First, the overall environment in which the institution has been shaped educationally must be thoroughly considered. For instance, what are the regional demographics that provide the realistic potential student base, and what about regional competition? Will institutional changes make the college more competitive or less competitive vis à vis neighboring institutions? Are institutional resources adequate to accomplish all projected goals, or must difficult choices be made to achieve elements of the plan? One must also incorporate into the strategic plan the faculty's reaction to decisions. If the faculty as a whole are not likely to be supportive, are there cohorts of senior professors who can still nurture the process?

Each of these policy decisions should be viewed as one move in an ongoing game of chess, leading the institution down a path that will be difficult to reverse. Thus, it is paramount for the institution's enrollment policies and academic programs to be consistent. Any path recommended by a provost or academic vice president must incorporate the advice of faculty leaders who hold curricular expertise, as well as the enrollment management officer responsible for institutional recruitment practices.

The process of identifying and documenting those factors that draw students to a campus, agreeing on what constitutes quality, developing measures and standards accepted by the community, engaging necessary constituencies in the process, and building appropriate communication constitute the essence of successful enrollment management. As noted previously, the politics and economics of resource allocation at the highest levels of the institution will be key determinants of its eventual enrollment outcomes and must be carefully considered in structuring its enrollment management system. An effective enrollment management team will carry broad credibility with the institution's academic and financial leaders; will exercise the authority to implement costly, campus-wide strategies; and will regularly be invited to participate in decisions that may be outside its control but are central to achieving overall enrollment goals.

Organizationally, those elements that define the enrollment management group include the offices of admissions, financial aid, registrar, institutional research, and, increasingly, the bursar. Given the impact that financial aid discounts have on net revenue at most institutions, particularly those in the independent sector, it is also beneficial to enlist active participation by the chief budget officer so that he or she is well informed regarding the logic underlying primary marketing strategies as well as their revenue and expense potential. Depending on the size and mission of the institution, other offices and individuals shaping the student experience may also be included in the enrollment management group, and appropriate roles will need to be defined for each one.

New enrollment management systems employ a structure, sophistication, and degree of outreach quite different from the traditional admissions organization. In the external environment of the 1990s in which turbulence has replaced stability, and competition for students and funding has replaced cooperative concern for access and choice, prior assumptions and relationships no longer prevail. Internally, the press of dwindling resources demands attention to efficiencies that enhance service, such as computerization, while at the same time simplifying basic administrative processes for students. Entry-level and mid-management staff members must now demonstrate skills not previously required on a campus. Issues of professional development and employee turnover have become central considerations in the development of internal enrollment management organizations.

Recent technological enhancements have produced dramatic changes in the way enrollment management is accomplished administratively; this has lead to significant gains in both quality of service and economies of operation.[4] Once-separate offices are now merged into comprehensive units utilizing automated procedures to handle most routine student transactions via touch-tone phone, computer modem, and information kiosk. Beyond this, staff attention can focus on responding to individual situations not addressed by the system and on the production of strategic reports.

New Developments in Admissions

More than a decade ago, admissions officers began to undergo a metamorphosis from serving as gatekeepers shaping the "freshman" class in accordance with faculty wishes to acting as recruiters who aggressively pursue multiple categories of students to meet a budgeted "first-year" class size. Today, effective deans of admission must also exercise the skills of senior marketing managers. In a buyers' market, even the highest quality programs will not succeed unless they are sufficiently distinct from their competition and priced competitively. Traditionally, factors such as differentiation, responsiveness, and price competitiveness have not been pivotal considerations in the development of new academic programs, yet they have increasingly become the influences shaping both the attractiveness and eventual resource base for degree programs brought to an institution's curriculum committee. In response, senior admissions officers now must pursue a far more assertive role in strategic planning and policy formulations while designing marketing campaigning more complex than those of their predecessors. As tight budgets and scarce resources direct attention to the cost and revenue potential of new programs, it has also become wise to incorporate these market considerations in the early stages of the academic planning process.

Put simply, comprehensive admissions marketing must now begin earlier for all categories of students. Current research indicates that work must begin with disadvantaged youth as early as sixth grade if they are to regard higher education as part of their development and make course choices that keep that option viable. Bright students, particularly from affluent suburbs and independent schools, tend to narrow their choice set for college to fewer than ten schools by their sophomore years in high

---

Emerging Trends in Enrollment Management

- Improved retention and recruitment performance is becoming an institution-wide commitment expressed by the chief executive, academic, and financial leadership of the institution, but the rhetoric is not always supported by a system to monitor performance, eliminate unnecessary endeavors, and fund effective activities
- Financial aid awards, payment plans, and billing cycles are being aligned to smooth payment patterns for families and to support retention and recruitment objectives that enhance revenue flows
- Institutions are using telephone and computer technology to improve service to students by automating and simplifying routine financial aid, academic record, residence hall, bookstore, and bursar transactions, providing 24-hour access to their records, and facilitating electronic communication with faculty and staff
- Increasingly, families expect higher education institutions to provide the same level of attention to customer service, and the prompt, courteous handling of their needs, that they demand of other institutions at which they make similar levels of expenditure
- Funding reductions, new technology, government regulation, and public skepticism will continue to make change—however unwelcome—the new constant in higher education

---

school.[5] To be a contender for these students, institutional marketing efforts must have an impact before this narrowing occurs, particularly if an institution is considering programs beyond its traditional mission. Finally, student selection of college by reputation is a well-documented pattern determined largely by SAT scores and place of residence and by parents' income and educational levels.[6] Each of these factors must be weighed carefully in assessing the time and expense required for an institution to reposition itself or enter new markets.

Beyond student preferences, effective marketing plans also incorporate communication with support persons—parents, opinion leaders, teachers, guidance counselors, independent counselors, talent search agencies, international student brokers, and coaches, for example.[7] In planning, the enrollment management team may use data available from the Enrollment Planning Service of the College Board and various census and marketing research databases, but the provost or academic vice president, as well as senior admissions officers, must be able to interpret that data in light of an institution's history, current competition, and aspirations.

Periodically, it may be wise to engage the services of an external research firm with expertise in higher education market strategies. These firms can monitor the institution's position in the marketplace and identify the major factors driving recruitment of new students and the attrition of those presently enrolled. Following a collaborative selection process for such a consultant, the resultant report, and particularly its external context, can serve as a common reference point for those proposing improvements to the enrollment potential of the institution. However, campus planners should note that this process will require expertise in research analysis, team building, and the new technologies necessary to deliver messages effectively using various media. Smaller institutions will quickly discover that the expenses involved can be formidable and constitute an entry barrier in some particularly competitive markets.

Finally, the importance of parents in the college admissions process must be recognized, as they increasingly view higher education as an investment decision. Individually and in groups they seek comprehensive information concerning outcomes, indicators of the likely return on their investment, and advice in financing that investment. Most important, they need advice from appropriate institutional representatives to provide the confidence that they are capable of assuming the financial burden of their child's undergraduate degree. No longer clear is the line where the role of the admissions counselor ends and that of the financial aid officer begins. This reality must be reflected in both staff straining and organizational structure. Each admissions counselor will need to become thoroughly familiar with and articulately communicate the data gathered by the college or university on graduate placement rates, career paths, and pertinent statistics on personal and financial success.

The Changing Financial Aid Office

Since World War II, financial aid has basically served as a mechanism to ensure access and choice, enabling students to select the institutions best suited to their goals for educational advancement without regard to cost of attendance. An ideal only partially realized, today that view has been discarded. Financial aid is now a system of differential pricing and discounting, with institutions tailoring price points to different market segments in order to achieve enrollment and revenue targets while shaping the "quality profile" of the entering class. The "financial aid" office is a misnomer for a function designed to help families find ways to meet expenses regardless of whether they receive institutional support or show need.

For most of the 1990s, there has been little in the management of financial aid that is simple or straightforward, aside from a basic belief in equity as a principle and in the primacy of program over price in the final choice of college. However, in daily practice, those values are increasingly difficult to abide by, as colleges stretch limited funds to draw top students regardless of their ability to pay while simultaneously meeting the needs of students who could not otherwise afford to attend an institution of choice. At most schools, resources are insufficient to accomplish both purposes, so a precarious balance has been struck. Merit awards reward the best talent an institution can attract while need-based grants make the institution more accessible to those for whom price is the impediment to attendance.

The allocation of financial aid funds is a powerful tool in shaping entering classes and influencing retention consistent with the strategic objectives of the institution.[8] Research shows differences among population segments in the strength of their interest in the institution and their sensitivity to price. A strong physical therapy program may be able to matriculate highly talented students with less financial aid than a less-renowned program in English, for example. Similarly, a program with no local competitors may find it easier to enroll students with only limited support. Careful analysis across several recruiting cycles is necessary to identify relatively stable relationships among the variables of student choice on which to target aid awards. Key student characteristics to consider will be major program of study, level of academic achievement, level of need, geographic location, and the nature and quality of the other institutions to which the student is seeking admission. A chief academic officer, working in collaboration with the enrollment management team, can develop sophisticated mathematical models that allow the college or university to estimate the effect financial aid will have in achieving its goal to attract the strongest class academically. From an institutional perspective, these models will incorporate the perceived strength of the academic program, the minimum enrollment levels, and the academic caliber of students the institution wishes to enroll.

As a member of the institutional leadership team, the academic vice president will need to consider the significance of financial aid as a factor in the larger revenue streams of the college or university. Aid awards leverage the remainder of the attendance costs that a student must pay, and the ease with which a student can access those funds as well as the speed with which they become available to the institution will be decisive factors in overall cash flow management. These considerations, as well as the potential for improved service to students, make it advisable for the provost or academic vice president to develop formal working relationships with banks and financial services providers to facilitate loan processing via electronic application and fund transfer. As direct lending expands and consortia arrangements among banks and financial institutions proliferate, it will be increasingly important to pursue the kinds of financial arrangements that both serve students well and enhance the revenue stream, while at the same time minimizing the liability and expense to the university.

Service to families wrestling with the complexity of financial aid applications, negotiating loans, and selecting payment plans is an important dimension of the institution's financial aid program. The challenge confronting most families, regardless of need, is to assess the maze of loan programs and payment plans, as well as institutional grants and government aid, in order to create an individualized package enabling them to cover four or even five years of degree expenses within their monthly budgets. Several chief academic officers note that a proactive counseling approach that provides unsolicited assistance in selecting payment and loan programs often enables students to attend an institution that they initially believed was cost prohibitive. In other cases, by guiding them toward less expensive alternatives, enrollment managers have helped families avoid financial overcommitment. In turn, this helps reduce future attrition attributed to financial hardship.

The Bursar and the Registrar: Overlooked Resources

These two offices, traditionally as labor intensive as any on the campus, no matter what its size, have experienced major transformations since the 1980s and have been increasingly integrated into the institution's financial aid function. Demands for convenient service and immediate access to information have driven this change, and computer hardware and software advances have made it possible to respond positively to these expectations while reducing operational expenses in the process.

For a chief academic officer, these changes constitute an opportunity as well as a threat. Automation must be shaped if it is to serve rather than undermine academic procedures. Telephone registration is a convenience that eliminates lines and waiting time, and an on-line database can provide real-time tracking of course section demand; however, if staff are not trained or simply if no one pays attention, callers are closed out of courses instantly, minus the counseling-oriented student, staff, faculty interactions that could identify potential problem situations. When connected to degree audit software, automated registration can now strengthen the advising process by quickly providing students and advisors a common reference point for discussion unfettered by the mechanics of analyzing progress to date.

As the processes of scheduling classes, recording grades, and producing transcripts each become automated, opportunities for office consolidation and staff reallocation arise. A model advocated by chief academic officers on numerous campuses consolidates the registrar's, financial aid, and bursar's functions into a new extension of the institution's "academic offices," affording students the highly requested convenience of handling all transactions in a single location. When supported by an integrated database and management team, this model also facilitates production of reports that highlight issues requiring attention. Reengineering these processes constitutes a major undertaking for a provost or academic vice president already coordinating curriculum revisions and tenure reviews, but the long-term savings and improvements in service to students will more than justify the time and expense involved.

Rapidly advancing developments in information technology now make it possible to provide these services via World Wide Web or with voice response systems to users anywhere in the world at their convenience. Integrated with electronic mail, the student information systems also facilitate immediate, asynchronous consultation among students, faculty, and staff about services, actions, or other aspects of their work together at the institution. There is significant potential in this technology, which is just beginning to be explored, for gains in both productivity and in the timeliness and richness of exchange that are important for instruction as well as for administration.

Increasingly, the creation and administration of payment plans and billing cycles will become integrated with the development of aid packages and fund transfer mechanisms and the planning and management of these activities will become less cumbersome. Significant gains will also be achieved as staff members working on collections better understand the arrangements made in advance and incorporate these considerations into the processes they implement.

Enrollment Management and Academic Leadership

Improvements in quality and responsiveness have been easiest to accomplish in the administrative units for which service has traditionally been the primary office function. However, despite this progress, on many college and university campuses, processes continue to be more responsive to staff convenience and bureaucratic procedures than to the needs and lifestyles of contemporary students. Thus, it is necessary to

---

Best Practices in Enrollment Management

- Make retention and enrollment management an institution-wide commitment expressed by the chief executive, academic, and financial leadership of the institution; support the rhetoric with a system to monitor and fund retention activities
- Appoint an enrollment management working group to involve key faculty and staff across the campus in design and implementation of recruitment and retention initiatives
- Consolidate admission, financial aid, registrar, and bursar functions in a unified management structure with formal communication channels to the academic affairs units
- Systematically gather customer satisfaction data in key areas and establish staff teams to share and evaluate feedback and act on emerging issues
- Orchestrate award of financial aid and construction of payment plans and billing cycles to support retention and recruitment objectives
- Expand the function of the financial aid office to assist all families in configuring payment plans and loan programs that minimize the stress of meeting costs of attendance
- Use emerging information technology such as the World Wide Web, e-mail, and voice response systems to provide information and service to constituents at their convenience wherever they are located and to facilitate immediate, asynchronous communication among students, faculty, and staff

---

include both resident and commuting undergraduates in the design of new systems that claim to reflect their preferences and concerns.

As the requirements of some disciplines and degree programs have recently been claimed to be compromised by attention to new student "consumer needs," the strength of tradition—and resistance to change—in American higher education will challenge a chief academic officer's leadership abilities and personal courage as the institution adapts to shifting economic and demographic forces as well as societal expectations. This leadership will be particularly important in addressing retention issues. Some academic mid-managers now fear that retention implies doing whatever is necessary to keep a student at the institution without regard to standards of quality or behavior. Acknowledging that definitions of "student-centeredness" have become subject to wider debate, these individuals may still need to be reminded by the institution's provost or academic vice president that the most effective retention programs are characterized by educational rigor, superior performance, and a supportive environment that legitimately meets the needs of shifting, sometimes conflicting cohorts of students.

As noted earlier, a successful approach to both retention and recruitment cannot be accomplished without the informed involvement, and leadership, of multiple campus constituencies, some of which rarely interact, much less collaborate, within higher education organizations. The members of the governing board must play an increasingly central role in enrollment management strategic planning, and the chief executive officer will often delegate the intricacies of achieving this involvement to the academic vice president. A well-informed board assumes a vital role in setting and communicating institutional enrollment priorities. However, trustees must be regularly advised of emerging threats and opportunities confronting the institution. In order to accomplish this, the chief academic officer must dedicate ample time to meet individually with board members to increase their understanding of the campus culture and shape their participation in its governance.

Reviewing decisions and activities across reporting lines within the institution is now essential, and coordinating initiatives and decisions across student affairs, academic affairs, faculty, physical plant, financial affairs and even the governing board is an undertaking that may necessitate the creation of more flexible administrative structures enabling both senior and new professionals to integrate their efforts more collaboratively.

The faculty and the enrollment management team will need to interact on a regular, even scheduled basis, and trust must be developed between the faculty leadership and key enrollment managers. On most campuses, the chief academic officer will be responsible for the accomplishment of this objective. Absent a critical level of professional trust, the faculty will not hear the potential impact of programmatic changes they are discussing, and absent a clear understanding of academic programs, enrollment managers will not understand the directions faculty wish to move in or why.

The coordinator of the enrollment management effort will need academic credentials sufficient for credibility with the faculty, and, as significantly, a broad understanding of retention research and the dynamics of higher education. This individual must also possess the skills to foster open discussion and a sense of shared commitment among the campus community, including students, to promote change when necessary, even if unpopular.

The institution's basic premise should be that in subtle but powerful ways each member of the faculty and staff conveys to every student the regard in which he or she is held. A successful result will be each student's sense of being valued as an individual by that institution. Employees may not believe this is their individual responsibility; however, the contemporary dynamics of retention are such that *every* member of a college or university community plays a role in the process, and the more dissonance that is conveyed through individual attitudes, the less effective the overall program will be.

Building Quality and Service into Enrollment Management: A Case Study

The undergraduate student population of New Southern University, a tuition-dependent private institution, had been growing for well over two decades. Each year's new freshman class brought in an abundance of students. The university was located in the center of a large metropolitan area, with poorly supported public institutions. The administration had become lax in its responsiveness to student inquiries. An attitude of "provide it and they will come" permeated the institution from administration to faculty.

While there was an awareness of the predictions of a decline in the number of available eighteen-year-olds, there was also an understandable complacency given the history of the institution. That complacency was shattered with no warning when in the fall of 1990, New Southern was faced with an enrolled freshman class less than three-quarters the size of the class the previous year.

A rapid analysis of the offices key to enrollment in the university led to a complete reassessment of the way the university would have to do business. Both policy and administrative decisions were made within a few months. The policy decisions were to recruit a somewhat smaller freshman class (and to "rightsize" the faculty and administration) and to communicate the desire of the faculty and the institution to increase the preparedness of the student body it accepted. The faculty were recruited to play a major role in communicating with students being recruited for the next fall.

More important, some long-term administrative changes were made. First, a decision was made to combine the admissions office, financial aid, and the registrar into one reporting unit, headed by a senior administrative officer for enrollment management. The enrollment management officer undertook, with the help of consultants, a study of the campus. A second study was undertaken to gather information about the image of the campus held by important external constituents, including potential students and their parents, guidance counselors, as well as students that were enrolled at both the institution and its competitors. Utilizing this information, the campus overhauled its publications to present an attractive and honest image of both what the campus was and its realistic aspirations.

The enrollment management office simultaneously gathered and configured existing institutional data to devise a financial aid strategy that would enroll a class of the size necessary to meet budget with a quality profile appropriate to the demands of the curriculum. Maintaining an eye for the pragmatic, the institution did not try to leap up several notches, but rather began to make efforts to ratchet upwards both class standing and SAT scores of the students it would accept.

Individuals and offices that had not previously worked together, and in many cases had not had a service orientation, were persuaded to adopt a team approach *and* to pay attention to the needs and desires of potential students and their families.

Inquiries by phone or mail were met with rapid and courteous responses. Visitors to campus were shown an enhanced physical environment by well-trained student guides. The admissions office coordinated its efforts with financial aid and with the office of residential life and housing. The bursar's office and the financial aid office formed teams of financial service personnel that provided families with information about university and federal aid as well as possible loans and payment plans. They worked closely to make sure families understood the costs of an education and also understood the variety of ways in which those costs might be met.

Over a period of three years, the number of inquiries at the institution doubled. The proportion of applications that received acceptances decreased from 94 percent to 74 percent, a level approximating the national average. The preparedness of the incoming freshman class also improved. High school class standing rose nearly a decile and SAT composite rose 80 points to a level 70 points above the national average.

This case study is true. While all of the details cannot be provided in such a brief synopsis, it represents a case where the morale of the staff and faculty moved from depression to true excitement about the institution. It became clear that what could have been an educational and financial disaster was converted into a thriving institution with a student body, a faculty, and a staff that felt a commitment to the institution and to building it into a stronger institution than it had ever been.

The Connection between Enrollment Management and Institutional Type

Several factors limit every institution's ability to manage enrollment. Some institutional definitions cannot be changed: publicly supported, religiously affiliated, or independent, for example. Small enrollments, a comprehensive mission, and a conservative approach to new program development constitute other critical enrollment-related characteristics. In fact, most institutions maintain a carefully nurtured image to attract students. Rapid programmatic changes may dramatically change the market "niche" an institution has worked decades to develop.

Many public institutions have generally exercised greater flexibility in making policy changes as their economic base is unlikely to change dramatically in a short period. Yet these same institutions are unlikely to receive significant growth funds during the remainder of this century.

While some states use enrollment formulas to fund their public colleges, community colleges, and universities, these formulas have been based on long-term trends or rolling averages and not on specific, annual changes. Thus, if a public institution decides to move toward greater access but is not able to attract the customers anticipated within a year or two, the public system may be much more forgiving than the budget managers at an independent institution. Public institutions are likely to have time to correct a failed strategy without suffering major economic damage.

Conversely, public colleges and universities located in geographic areas experiencing steady population growth may be subject to rapid enrollment increases without additional revenues, or they may face declining resources at a point of critical expansion. An independent higher education institution, particularly one that is heavily tuition-dependent as most have come to be, has greater flexibility in making these decisions, yet the financial impact of changes that impact enrollment may be more risky in this tuition-driven context and should be even more carefully planned. The consequences of an error in judgment can translate immediately into reduced revenues if anticipated enrollments do not materialize. Thus, those whose primary responsibilities lie in this area should remain aware of the personal consequences, political as well as educational, of offering advice without conducting market studies.

Effective enrollment management carries simultaneous programmatic and financial implications for an institution. As a university-wide function, it demands the oversight of a senior administrator who has facility with academic policy, financial marketing, and student services. Except in smaller institutions, it is now a function most likely demanding more attention than a chief academic officer can individually provide; thus, a provost or academic vice president will be well advised to put in place an individual focusing exclusively on this set of priorities.

Conclusion: The Role of the Chief Academic Officer in Enrollment Management

What roles should the chief academic officer play in enrollment management? Most importantly, he or she must define policy and recommend institutional direction to the chief executive officer. This function cannot be delegated, and it must be decided in collaboration with academic deans and the faculty leadership. Recommendations regarding institutional direction should include precise information on future student markets and assess how new academic and student service programs will impact the attractiveness of the college or university to prospective entering classes.

On many campuses, aside from the chief academic officer and president, the senior enrollment management officer must demonstrate the broadest grasp of critical campus issues as his or her work will impact the institution's finances, student body, curriculum, and alumni more than that of any other office.

The enrollment management officer must maintain an awareness of what is happening in student affairs locally and nationally in order to provide early warnings to those developing new curricular initiatives and to assess the resources offered to students at competing institutions. Special-interest residence halls, extensive internship programs, formal mentoring systems, and innovative class scheduling make sense to increasing numbers of educational "customers," and it is the joint responsibility of the senior enrollment and academic officers to shape the appropriate balance of resources to keep programs viable, retain high-achieving students, and provide the institution with fiscal strength and vitality.

In this context, the chief academic officer must develop an open, trusting relationship with the chief enrollment manager and the members of the enrollment team. This is based on regular communication and the sharing of candid information, especially if it is negative or critical. In this process, he or she must also acknowledge that the relationship between institutional mission and enrollment management has assumed unprecedented academic significance on all campuses, no matter what their heritage or structure, and that the challenge will be to design new models of effective leadership and collaborative action.

CHAPTER EIGHT

Financial Management and Budget Planning: A Primer for Chief Academic Officers

Michael C. Gallagher

The need for careful financial management and budget planning has never been greater on the nation's more than thirty-five hundred campuses. Daily, America's postsecondary institutions are confronted with news of increased prices for goods, equipment, and services as well as increased costs caused by new mandates from the federal government, state regulatory agencies, and activist boards of trustees. Mid-year budget cuts in 1993–94, although down from previous years, continued to plague both private and public institutions in every region of the country, as state support for higher education continued to decline from 56.6 percent of the institution's budget being supplied by state funds in 1988–89 to 50.6 percent in 1993–94.[1]

Either factor, increased costs or declining revenues, taken alone produces an environment in which almost every American college or university finds it difficult, if not impossible, to accomplish the short- and long-term goals it needs to achieve. However, when their operating cost increases are coupled with declining revenues, many schools are faced by a financial situation that prevents them from being able to support programs they have *already* implemented. Regardless of the type or size of institution, activities will continue to become more costly as organizations evolve to meet the needs of multiple student constituencies. Careful budget planning and financial management can enhance the ability of these institutions to satisfy constituent needs, and their chief academic officers increasingly find themselves responsible for major aspects of this process.

The Present Financial Environment for Higher Education: Implications for Chief Academic Officers

Any serious effort to address the roles of the chief academic officer in higher education financial management and budgeting must begin with an awareness of how colleges and university systems relate to the economy as a whole. In studying this relationship, three major issues emerge: economic strength and support for higher education, increasing public expectation, and enrollment-driven versus priority-driven funding mechanisms.

Between 1969 and 1989, state support for higher education increased in states with strong economies and declined where economies where not strong.[2] During this time of general economic prosperity, however, periods of high inflation reduced the real impact of increased dollar support. As salary dollars increased, real faculty salaries as measured by purchasing power increased less, remained static, and even declined in some states. During the early 1990s, even though inflation rates declined, a general economic downturn caused state support also to decline. These low inflation rates brought lower interest rates as well as lower returns on endowments and giving.

Declining Resources

Struggling with declining resources in higher education can be devastating. Specific legislative measures like Proposition 13 in California and Measure 5 in Oregon, which resulted in four consecutive years of higher education budget cuts, have caused the elimination of literally hundreds of academic programs. Long-term effects of these budget problems cited in a recent study by administrators at public institutions include increased teaching load and class size, outdated laboratories and teaching equipment, deterioration of physical plants, reallocation of resources, more revenue-generating programs, and more state control.[3]

In the private sector, competition for students and resultant tuition discounting have affected the financial vitality of an increasing number of institutions. Tuition dependence and reduced dollar yield also has caused organizations like Moody's and Standard & Poors to downgrade debt ratings, which results in increased capital costs. Further, as tuition yield and state allocations have receded, federal and private funds have become more scarce and more competitive. From the perspective of academic budget managers, the current era of fiscal conservatism both in state legislatures and in Congress is likely to continue well into the next century. Many chief financial officers hold the view that it is unlikely higher education will ever return to the era when each year brought significantly larger private revenues and state appropriations to the institution. In fact, most forecasts indicate that enhanced productivity, shared resources, administrative downsizing, and other cost-efficient strategies must be developed and immediately implemented in order to restore public confidence in the utilization of available funds and halt further revenue declines.

Increased Expectations

At the same time that consumers have become critical of the efficiency of higher education systems, they are also demanding more services from those systems. Specialized academic advising, financial aid, economic development assistance, research assistance, library and database access, self-paced degree programs, remediation, health care, and childcare are just several of the demands that have increased since the 1980s. The complete list is much longer, and challenging, than this one. These increased demands further strain financial resources as they require new or modified facilities, more human resources, and expensive, state-of-the-art information and computer technologies. Outside of the higher education community, this craving for additional services has also increased demand for state and federal funding among agencies that compete with colleges and universities for grants and contracts.

New Funding Mechanisms

For almost a century, broad access at low cost has been the hallmark of the U.S. higher education system. Traditionally, college and university operating budgets have been tied to student enrollments, with allocations increasing as enrollments have also increased. During the 1980s, as many state postsecondary systems experienced declining enrollments, public higher education found it more difficult to obtain the appropriation levels they sought. Conversely, states that experienced increasing enrollments and participation rates found it more difficult to maintain appropriations per FTE student. The common response to bridge this gap between requests and appropriations was to increase student tuition and required fees. Between 1983 and 1993, tuition as a percent of unrestricted higher education revenue grew nationally from 24 percent to 31 percent, outpacing inflation, disposable personal income, and the growth in financial aid.[4] However, continued reliance on tuition revenues to balance budgets will negatively impact student access and affordability, thus limiting opportunities for a majority of Americans who seek a college education.

As we enter the next century, traditional enrollment-based funding mechanisms are not likely to be able to keep pace with growth in demand. By the year 2009, it is projected that 3.1 million students will graduate from our nation's public high schools, exceeding the 1979 peak of 2.8 million students.[5] With new workforce requirements, increasing enrollments, and competing demands for state services, it will become more difficult to maintain current levels of state appropriation per FTE student. States are becoming, as one source puts it, "purchasers of services rather than supporters of institutions."[6] Therefore, new funding mechanisms that relate more directly to levels of service will need to be developed if institutions are going to continue to improve quality and access.

Traditional Roles of the Chief Financial Officer

"He or she who has the gold, makes the rules," is a popular modification of the Golden Rule. This expression illustrates the problem of financial control when taken to an extreme. Some chief financial officers view their role as that of key vote in all college or university decisions. They attempt to set academic priorities and may even determine specific expenditures based on their own set of values. Individuals who work with financial data sometimes appear to believe that their sense of reality is superior to that of others, whether on a campus or in a corporation. Most business officers who act in this manner do not survive, however, unless the chief academic and other senior administrators abdicate their ongoing responsibilities in financial decision making. The appropriate role of the chief financial officer in setting institutional priorities is to provide assistance in maximizing resources available to accomplish objectives and to outline the financial outcomes of various alternatives. Specialized assistance and advice rather than domination are ways to succeed in this new role. Most successful business officers clearly recognize this strategy and become vanguards of service in areas like accounting, performance audits, federal compliance, benchmarking, restructuring, risk management, and investments. Additionally, they provide data, ask difficult questions, and help maintain focus on the big picture. Though their staff, they provide invaluable information, methods, and tools for analysis and budget management.

The Role of the Chief Academic Officer in Setting Budgetary Priorities

The chief academic officer holds central responsibility to lead the development of academic priorities on college and university campuses. Institutions have developed a multitude of models that enable academic leaders to work directly with faculty, students, administrators, and ex-

---

Emerging Financial Trends

- The current era of financial conservatism exhibited by state legislatures and the U.S. Congress represents a permanent shift which will constrain traditional higher education funding sources into the twenty-first century
- Efforts to enhance relationships between institutions of higher education and traditional funding constituent groups are increasing; partnerships and connections to new groups are expanding
- Tuition and financial assistance policies are being studied and developed which more closely relate to consumer-marketing concepts like product bundling, finance programs, and differential pricing
- Enhanced productivity, shared resources, administrative downsizing, and other cost efficient strategies applied in business organizations are being implemented in higher education institutions in an effort to restore public confidence in the utilization of available funds
- Reductions in traditional higher education–based research funding are being accompanied by a greater focus on applied research and research accountability

---

ternal information sources to clarify, implement, and periodically review academic goals.

Academic priorities promote institutional role and mission while providing direction for financial planning through the identification of time and magnitude parameters. Short-run goals are usually determined in one- and two-year cycles and constitute the basis for the annual budget projections required to support them. Once appropriate priorities have been developed, detailed budgets of income and expenditures at unit levels can be established. In this regard, the primary responsibility of the chief academic officer is to establish academic priorities that lead, not follow, the budgeting process.

The Budget Planning Process

The budget planning process includes four major stages:

1. a review of priorities

2. an estimation of income

3. an estimation of expenditures

4. finalization of the budget

On most campuses, budget officers provide annual general income projections to organizational unit heads. These unit heads typically have much less input into income projection than into estimating and categorizing expenditures, thus explaining why many deans, directors, and department heads initially prefer to view budget difficulties as a problem of resource acquisition rather than resource utilization.

Academic unit leaders must participate in the development and prioritization of goals, as the absence of key-leader support for such goals will inevitably undermine their achievement. Although the goals themselves are not likely financial, the ability to achieve most of them depends on available levels of financial support. Therefore, the absence of either adequate leadership or financial support will divert energy from goal achievement potential. Similarly, an institution's effectiveness in reaching its short-run goals will significantly affect its ability to achieve longer-term objectives.

The institutional budget officer will provide preliminary income estimates or expenditure targets as the first step in the budget preparation process after he or she has made adjustments to the previous year's base budget. At this point, academic managers should ask for income estimates so that projected expenditures can be budgeted in light of projected resource levels and remain consistent with established goals. Significant reductions in income or increased expenditures should be viewed within the context of institutional and unit priorities.

The estimation of expenditures is principally accomplished by reviewing actual expenditures from the previous year. This estimate is then modified by using a "needs approach" procedure to adjust budget categories. In order for the budget to be finalized, income estimates must equal or exceed expenditures for the year; and to budget effectively, the cost of achieving goals, the income available, and the priority of particular activities should be weighed carefully by the chief academic officer at this point in the process. Budget approval follows as the formal process of budget finalization. However, even with an approved, balanced budget, regular budget analysis and revision exercises will be required throughout the year.

Resource Allocation Strategies

On many campuses, members of different subgroups will have educational interests and preferences that may conflict during the annual budgetary process. In fact, developing the budget can accentuate difficult behaviors since many view the process as a "winning or losing" proposition. General mission and goal statements may be supported by nearly everyone at the institution, but as the budget process advances, specific differences of interpretation and opinion, often the result of historical compromises, will inevitably emerge and become magnified.

One chief financial officer humorously observed that budgeting is really quite simple, "Give them 97 percent of what they need and then make them live within their budget." An academic dean proposes a solution of simply asking for more money than was needed last year. The problem with both approaches, of course, is determining, and justifying, the true level of an institution's needs. A number of approaches are used to justify "needed" funding. Some of the more common ones include the following:

The *maintenance of quality* approach is one of justifying generous funding with high quality. Maintaining quality quickly becomes the sacred cow of a college or university faced with continuing financial cuts. Similarly, "If our budget is cut, quality will decline," is a common cry heard in many candid internal budget discussions. Other potential outcomes are relegated to a secondary position in the name of quality. No one in higher education has ever been approached by a departmental faculty with the idea of doing away with the departmental major so that the quality of the institution's general education goals would be enhanced. Still, decisions that clearly improve quality are among the easiest of all since, as a value, no participant needs to be convinced of its importance.

Two related approaches are the *stability justification* and *false crisis* strategies. Both employ the rationale that, "If we do not receive the needed level of funding the college will collapse, or worse." The stability strategy is different from the game of creating a false sense of crisis because individuals making this request honestly believe that the consequence of not receiving the requested funding will be a lack of stability and institutional reputation. Real threats to stability and real crises do occur; however, the danger of pushing either of these justifications too far is the elimination of various lower priority activities and possible personnel changes as a consequence.

Relative or proportional comparisons are used as the methodology of the *relative comparison* approach to budget justification An example would be, "Unit A received $10,000 in this category, we have twice as many majors so we should get $20,000." Few allocation decisions are ever this simple.

Similar to this model is the *recognition funding* procedure. From the perspective of the individual making the request, this is the funding needed to provide the "proper" level of recognition. Managers of primary mission units and high institutional priority activities sometimes make a "crucial" appeal within the budgeting process for funds that would allow them to become "nationally recognized." These entreaties should be followed by a candid discussion between the chief financial officer and the academic vice president so that a collaborative decision can be reached before the remainder of the process becomes unduly affected.

The use of *leverage* is another strategy. The justification in this instance is: "With this needed funding, we will be able to obtain additional funds or other assets." A slight variation to leverage is the *investment* strategy, with the major difference between the two being timing, as leverage pays off in the short-run, while investment usually takes longer. In actuality, the results of these justifications can be extremely rewarding to an institution if the activity fits within the range of its institutional priorities.

Piggybacking is a common approach used in appeals. In this instance, requests that support activities that have high institutional priority may include other related or nonrelated items. This method is used in an attempt to elevate requests that may have high unit priority but low institutional priority.

A similar strategy is *ratio justification*, in which a doubling of enrollments in one year produces a request for twice as much office personnel the next. This approach often ignores the concept of productivity, however, which is both difficult to apply in higher education, and, since there have been few traditional rewards for productivity, carries no natural internal constituency.

Another popular form of ratio justification is the *criteria*, or rational, approach. Enrollment as an allocation criteria was discussed earlier in the context of the general institution. Similar criteria such as the numbers of majors, degrees awarded, credit hours produced, grants received, programs offered, and other numerical comparisons can also be used internally to justify allocations and budget requests.

What the Chief Academic Officer Should Know about Budgeting Basics

Academic deans and vice presidents should understand that the budget is a communication tool that provides information to a multitude of interested parties, even on smaller campuses. Initially, funds are provided to institutions based on broad objectives that legislators or boards expect to see addressed and with some understanding as to how they will be spent. These understandings can be quite formal, but sometimes are also quite informal, focusing on the spirit, rather than the letter, of the terms under which the funding was made available. These mutual understandings define parameters within which allocations can be made. If these terms are formal, their communication usually is quite clear. During budget development, these terms should be communicated in the form of guidelines, instructions, and discussion to all persons involved in the budget development process. When the process is complete, it provides the impetus to inform interested parties within and outside the institution about major features of the budget plan, including resource availability, problems addressed, shifts in allocations, services to be provided, and new directions.

Within higher education institutions, the budget is primarily a structural plan used to allocate resources and should be developed to assist academic administrators. In this context, the first thing which must be grasped about budgets by academic officers and faculty is that they are developed throughout the entire year and simply refined during the budget process. At the moment a new budget takes effect, it is out of date and adjustments must begin to be made. New structural units and accounts will be created, accounts will be consolidated, and funds will be transferred between accounts. These changes will not only impact the current base figures but also influence the development of the following year's budget, as well. Therefore, to shape important events, provosts and academic vice presidents must pay close attention to financial and budget activities throughout every segment of the fiscal year.

A simple way for the chief academic officer to keep track of financial changes is to make appropriate notes in the margin of the current budget book. More detailed information can be stapled directly to related pages. In addition to providing an efficient method of tracking specific changes, these notes will easily identify the number and magnitude of the changes. Even a cursory glance through this modified budget book will allow identification of problem areas that have emerged through the course of the year.

From an academic management perspective, budget-formation has become a focused responsibility for chief academic officers specifically in the areas of planning, coordination, direction, and control.[7] Budgets force academic managers and faculty to develop program goals and to assign funds associated with these goals. Therefore, the annual process becomes the principle financial means by which senior administrators can express and formalize plans. This process provides a common denominator—dollars—for diverse activities and actions; and when priorities "lead" budget allocations, it can be viewed as a strength. However, if dollars are budgeted to an activity without reviewing priorities, or additional dollars can be raised through increased fees or gifts, it may not follow that a budget "weeding" process will occur, as few decision makers are willing to give up what they have accumulated, which leads many mid-level managers to believe that the only way to control costs is to control income. Actually, the pressure to clarify and refine priorities as a prerequisite to the budgetary process may be its greatest contribution to controlling costs.

The budget process can also be used as an instrument to coordinate the activities of the various schools, institutes, and departments within the institution. Figures that support the activities of separate departments will need to be weighed for mutual consistency, financial feasibility, and to confirm that their combined results support broader institutional objectives. In this manner, the budget process can be utilized as a mission review system for subunits of the college or university.

Budgets also direct professional behavior. Interactions required in the development process help define and integrate expectations of administrators and subordinates. By specifying the category and amount of resources to be utilized, budgets clarify and direct achievement of the subgoals required to implement broader institutional objectives as well as contribute data to the annual evaluations of those charged with these responsibilities.

From a purely financial perspective, the annual budget process also serves as a fiscal control device. By comparing predetermined criteria with actual results, fiscal performance can be monitored and common comparisons can be made between current and previous periods and between actual and projected activity. Variations can be shown in both absolute and percentage terms to allow easy analysis. However, academic managers can be held responsible for program and fiscal integrity issues in their units only if they have ongoing access to accurate and timely information from the chief academic and chief financial officers. This information should be available using data, records, and systems already in existence and, if so, should become a standard for appraising current operating results and a mechanism for periodic organizational analysis.

The various budget characteristics discussed above guide and evaluate performance and represent rational forms of control, yet motivation must also be considered as a sometimes hidden factor within the annual budgeting process. Motivation, as a behavioral aspect of this activity, represents the human side of the control issues being discussed, and it reveals the emotional aspects of an organization. The more overlap that occurs between personal and organizational values, often shaped through the supervision of a dean or provost, the less need there will be to rely on formal aspects of control. If financial standards, information, and evaluation are structured and managed with this behavioral aspect in mind, they become less coercive to non–financially trained professionals.[8]

Perhaps the most important reason for academic managers to understand financial information is because virtually every decision on a college or university campus now carries financial consequences, and a familiarity, even confidence, with these consequences helps department heads and teaching faculty prepare for them proactively.

Sources of Funds

As colleges and universities do not maintain a system of "bottom line" profits to drive decisions, it is harder to understand how many are financed. In business, the relationship between income and expenditures is very clear; however, in the "business" of higher education, the financial goal is to maintain an adequate quantity of resources to support academic excellence in all programs and activities. The relationship over time of income received to expenses paid will determine the level of available educational resources and, over time, the larger issue of institutional quality.

Where revenues come from, how they are produced, and in what amounts is a mystery to a large percentage of the academic administrators on most American campuses. While some prefer it that way, the chief academic officer must become fully knowledgeable about income sources. Five basic categories of institutional income must be managed: subsidies, fee income, grants and gifts, sales and service income, and other income.

Subsidies

Appropriations from state, church, or other centralized agencies, such as tax districts for community colleges, can represent one of the largest sources of institutional income. Most subsidies are tied to formula or other defined distribution schemes and represent a large dependency on a single source of income. Enrollment and credit-hour production, often weighted by level and discipline, play an important role in many of these schemes. This especially is true in state-supported institutions. Some states also are beginning to employ performance indicators, which may also affect future appropriations.

Fee Income

Tuition and required fees represent a second dominant source of funding for institutions. For independent institutions, this usually is the single largest source. Under various budgeting and traditional accounting arrangements, fee income usually is pooled with subsidies to supply the major income source of the general fund. Other fees related to such services as health and computing; special programs such as law, pharmacy, medicine; or specific pedagogies such as music and science laboratories normally are attributed to the specific unit providing the service, program, or course. Administrative fees like application fees, late fees, transcript fees, and special examination fees are commonly designated to the unit providing the direct service to pay for personnel and materials.

Gifts and Grants

Income from gifts and direct grants is normally directed to a particular unit on whose behalf the award was made. Unspecified awards go into a general institutional fund, with endowment income included in this category. Schools typically exercise a range of policies regarding the attribution of interest income accrued on gift and grant funds with the number, size, and origin of funds being important variables to be considered in analyzing additional gift and grant income potential.

Sales and Service Income

Auxiliary service fees, rental income, clinic patient fees, and other fees charged by a college or university's local and business enterprises generate valuable income. In addition to traditional housing, food service, and bookstore operations, some more entrepreneurial institutions have implemented a broad variety of activities, including hospitals, shopping centers, graphic design centers, and childcare facilities. This income area has seen significant growth during the 1990s as numerous institutions have developed new sources of annual revenue. At the same time, sales and service income have also become a source of major controversies within the town-gown relationships of many universities and their local towns or cities. Recent changes in unrelated-business income tax require educational institutions to be taxed more directly on many business activities associated with, and run by, the institution. Additionally, complaints of unfair competition have been lodged by competing private business and service providers against some state-supported institutions engaged in a variety of entrepreneurial services.

Other Income Sources

The federal government is the most significant source of other income. Direct and indirect costs associated with federal contracts or sponsored research and services are reimbursed to the institution. Grant-related income occurs as colleges and universities are compensated for administering federal student financial assistance programs such as Pell

Grants, College Work Study support, Supplemental Education Opportunity Grants, and Perkins Funds. Additional nonfederal sources include income from activities ranging from royalty income to the disposal of assets no longer needed.

All income received by an institution will be either unrestricted or restricted. Restricted funds come with externally established stipulations or limitations on their use, while unrestricted funds generally are divided into three categories: general, designated, and auxiliary. Other than defining design, these terms are not important with one exception. Designated funds represent internal allocation decisions that are self-imposed and usually made by the institution's administration or governing board.

The Application of Funds

Somewhat surprisingly, the utilization of financial resources is often an overlooked means of achieving new efficiencies in higher education. How chief academic and chief financial officers manage institutional funds during a period of declining resources are sure to be subjects of even more vigorous campus debate in the future as colleges and universities search for adequate resources to accomplish institutional objectives.

Typically, three types of costs are associated with higher education activities: fixed, semivariable, and variable. *Fixed costs* continue and remain constant no matter what level of service activity is provided. Facility operation and maintenance, insurance, and administration are examples. *Semi-variable costs* remain constant at one level until additional, usually significant, levels of service are provided. They then become constant at a new level of expenditure. Utilities, faculty, and equipment costs are examples of semivariable costs. As an example, custodial costs for a set of buildings will generally remain constant until service level is increased, such as by extending classes to a weekend program. In that instance, costs will escalate and plateau at that new level. Similarly, in a dental laboratory that carries relatively strict student-to-faculty ratios due to accreditation standards, the marginal addition of one student can necessitate an additional clinical faculty member. When added, however, additional students can be accommodated with the slack provided within that ratio.

Variable costs are those that vary directly with increases in service. Disposable laboratory materials, admission forms, and other consumable goods are examples. Matching each of these cost categories with income sources requires different income and budget strategies. Additionally, understanding the relationship of these costs to total costs helps explain the budget implications of enrollment changes within an institution. In general, increases in enrollment increase variable, semivariable, and total costs while reducing fixed or overhead costs per student.

Another way to categorize expenditures is as direct and indirect costs. *Direct costs* are those required to acquire and use goods and services. Traditionally, the management of expenditures at the unit level is limited to direct costs. *Indirect costs*, such as those associated with academic support areas and physical plant costs, usually appear either as accounting assessments that are allocated by formulas, for example, physical plant cost based on space occupied, or as direct charges for specific services, such as telephones, provided to institutional units. Indirect costs assessments to auxiliary units form a "tax" assessed for being part of the organization and do not involve choice. Direct charges for services by support areas are limited only to services actually used, and involve some degree of choice by faculty members and mid-level academic budget managers.

The term "indirect" cost can create confusion on some campuses as most contracts and grants in higher education utilize this terminology, and many persons will hear this term within a reimbursement context rather than a cost context. Grant and contract rules allow direct expenditures to be reimbursed to institutions at cost and provide an additional amount, usually a percentage of direct cost, to cover indirect expenditures. Indirect cost, when viewed in this context, actually constitutes a form of income to most academic budget units since they receive all or part of the indirect costs received from grants and contracts as revenue.

Academic budget managers must guard against making decisions on the basis of what is spent for a product or service at the time it is acquired without considering other, indirect costs associated with that action. An example of such a decision might be the purchase of solvents for use in a particular laboratory at a quantity discount, thus reducing direct cost per gallon. However, when the additional solvent is not needed, disposing of the chemical by the environmental unit (an indirect cost) can dramatically increase the total cost to the institution. Additionally, the potential for fines resulting from possible improper storage and disposal of the excess solvent increases financial risk.

Expenditures

Chief financial officers utilize major expenditure categories to classify and summarize the use of funds. A detailed discussion of classification, category, and subcategory can be found in a source commonly used by business officers known as the *Financial Accounting and Reporting Manual for Higher Education.*[9]

Expenditures and transfers are organized on a functional basis to recognize their purpose or contribution toward general institutional objectives:

1. *Instruction*. Expenditures associated with the institution's credit and noncredit offerings in academic, vocational, extension, special, and remedial areas.

2. *Research*. Activities specifically organized to support research, including research centers, institutes, and project research funded from institutional resources.

3. *Public service*. Institutional funds that support noninstructional activities that serve groups external to the institution.

4. *Academic support*. Funds for activities that support the primary institutional objectives of instruction, research, and public service. Library, academic computing, media services, curriculum development, academic administration, museums, and galleries are subcategory examples.

5. *Student services*. Funds expended for enrollment management, admission, registration, records, and a broad array of activities that contribute to the physical, emotional, cultural, and social development of students. Subcategories include financial aid, counseling, student services administration, and intercollegiate athletics and the student health center unless the latter two are run as self-supporting operations.

6. *Institutional support*. Expenditures for central executive-level activities that provide institutional management and logistics. Institution-wide executives, fiscal operations, general administration, public relations, development, and administrative computing are subcategories.

7. *Operation and plant maintenance*. Current operating expenditures associated with the operation and maintenance of campus facilities and grounds, as well as maintenance and administration, renovations, insurance, custodial services, and utilities.

8. *Scholarships and fellowships*. Financial grants provided to students that have resulted from selection by the institution or an entitlement program; staff tuition benefits or other remission of fees are also included in this category.

9. *Auxiliary enterprises*. Activities managed as self-supporting operations, including residence halls, arenas, food service, bookstore, and staff parking, as examples. The intercollegiate athletics program and student health center belong in this category if they are self-supporting.

Transfers and Deductions

Transfers are funds moved between fund groups to promote the objectives of the receiving activity. Some transfers will be mandatory, such as income from student fees designated to retire a student center bond obligation, and others will be voluntary. These nonmandatory transfers usually occur as institutional priorities or obligations evolve and are made at the discretion of senior administrators and the members of the governing board. Deductions occur when current fund balances are reduced by legislated mandatory deductions, "hold-back," or refunds.

The Importance of Financial Information to the Chief Academic Officer: A Case Study

The preceding list constitutes what most campus leaders would consider "the budget," and it is imperative for chief academic officers to be able to interpret and manage it in a knowledgeable way. Failure to understand financial data and its implications can easily cause daily decisions and personnel situations to become needlessly complex.

Many institutions employ at least one Professor Jones, a tenured faculty member, accomplished teacher, and researcher, who has overspent one of his research-support accounts. Pragmatically, most financial staffers understand that Professor Jones sees his financial statements as a nuisance. They not only recognize this but understand their need to assist him in managing the activities associated with the high-priority research he conducts, which brings additional prominence to the institution.

Since Professor Jones's laboratory account has a negative balance, in the absence of other information, questions might also be raised concerning the quality of his professional research, yet the performance of his research laboratory is reflected only indirectly in institutional budget figures. Since financial information is quantitative, it may appear to some to be more accurate. This phenomenon, plus availability and ease of observation of this data, heightens the potential for decision makers to rely on single, quantitative financial measures rather than probing the realities behind those numbers. Of greater importance in the case of Professor Jones, however, may be the service he performs to the overall mission of the institution. For instance, he could be in complete budget compliance but fulfilling his role to enhance institutional mission poorly or not at all.

For observant provosts and academic vice presidents, financial data will reflect symptoms as well as problems. The deficit in Professor Jones's account may be due to the timing of the budget reporting system rather than a problem within the financial allocation. If a problem does arise, it may be that a more strategic budget reporting model for research grants is needed, rather than any change of significance to Professor Jones's research activity.

Chief academic officers gradually learn the unalterable fact that financial data is not innovative, discriminating, nor questioning, in and of itself. When budgets are prepared mechanistically by staff members in a budget office removed from the academic governance structure and with little thought given to long-term academic need, form usually triumphs over substance. Academic managers can improve this aspect of the budget process by involving faculty members who have better information, and, according to research, who become more personally committed to the achievement of goals if they are involved in the process.[10] Additionally, research confirms a significant link between job satisfaction and budget participation for line managers.[11]

Poor budget data always drives out good budget data, and inaccurate information and unreliable measurements will gradually produce tensions between financial and nonfinancial managers at various points in this process. Also, experienced managers acknowledge that the basic simplicity of budget numbers invites arbitrary actions by inexperienced planners. Most financial decisions are multidimensional and cannot be made with rigid formulas in an administrative vacuum, rather, best practices will be based in shared information, collegial decision making, and a willingness to consider thoughtful exceptions to any rule.

Linking Academic Responsibility with Financial Authority: Decentralized Decision Making

Financially speaking, wise chief academic officers never act alone. Once educational goals have been clarified and budgets approved, the academic vice president can delegate to deans, department chairs, and directors the responsibility to accomplish these plans. In fact, from this point, the primary role of the chief academic officer should be one of assisting other academic managers to accomplish the plans established for their units.

Each time responsibility is delegated to a subordinate, managers will be concerned with control and knowing whether the work will be performed satisfactorily and on time, thus, measures and techniques that conform to the responsibilities delegated should be incorporated into the system in order to facilitate assessment. This may be accomplished in two ways: periodic written or oral reports, and information supplied on an exceptional basis when deviations from normal operations occur.

Another form of control is self-control by mid-managers. Provosts may be vitally concerned that appropriate reviews take place within an operation but still take no personal role in their execution. Knowledge that documentation of such reviews is available if a problem develops will be sufficient. Still, for delegation to succeed, personnel must be sufficiently trained in technical skills, standards of performance must be clearly understood, and chief academic officers must trust those to whom responsibilities have been assigned.

Ultimately, the effectiveness of delegation will be evaluated through individual and program performance review. While most administrators in higher education assume this to be true, too often annual evaluations occur without the recommended changes taking place. While this may be status quo on some campuses in an area like curriculum planning, in the case of financial reviews, more pressing action will often be necessary. If income is outstripping expenditures, it will be necessary to transfer appropriate fund balances to other priorities immediately, for example.

Living with the outcomes of financial decisions may be stressful, but it is one of the best tools for the chief academic officer to assure responsible behavior. Dealing with year-end balances serves as an example to illustrate this point: In organizations that do not allow carryover of positive balances, there will be less incentive to act responsibility. In such an environment, often no incentive exists beyond sense of community to cut expenditures or maximize revenue when surpluses are collected at the end of a year for use in other areas of the institution. In their defense, some budget managers believe the most responsible action is to spend surplus funds for future goods and services wherever possible. In universities where policy prevents carryover, the end-of-year buying binge can become a tradition. Also, the resulting investment in inventory and space necessary to store purchased items creates a less efficient use of resources.

Where policy does not allow carryover, the chief academic officer can encourage frugality and avoid end-of-year buying binges by offering to recapture surplus funds. Those funds can then be pooled to purchase computers or other items budgeted to be purchased in the next fiscal year. Finally, the savings to that subsequent year can be used to return to units the surplus funds previously captured by the chief academic officer.

If end-of-year carryover is allowed, negative as well as positive balances should be retained by the units incurring them. Many provosts are sympathetic to those academic managers whose departments find themselves in end-of-year deficit situations. Yet, if chairs and directors do not have to live with the consequences of their decisions, chief academic and financial officers cannot ask them to serve as responsible budget planners, much less educational leaders, in complex and difficult situations.

Budget flexibility impacts financial responsibility. Some funds will be received as restricted line items, carrying specific amounts for designated purposes. This type of allocation limits responsibility for budgetary and accounting obligations by removing management choice, whereas lump-sum allocations require detailed choices regarding their utilization. Through the distribution of these funds, academic managers can direct resources specifically toward the accomplishment of mission-related goals and objectives; as acknowledged "owners" of the educational enterprise, department chairs and division directors will more readily assume responsibility for decreasing unnecessary costs and enhancing the amount of annual institutional revenues.

Best Practices in the Development of Academic Financial Policies

Different academic managers will employ different strategies to cope with a supervisor's budgetary leadership style and the interpersonal stress associated with the budgeting process. Four budgetary "gameplay" patterns have been identified and studied: devious, economic, incremental, and time pattern.[12] The *devious* model, as the name implies, involves less than forthright behavior on the part of the budget planner. Managers employing this approach inflate costs, attach sacrificial lambs to budget requests, create false senses of crisis, and finally rely on connections with someone holding higher authority to achieve their objectives. *Economic* games include the presentation of rational, budget-related "facts," demonstrations of how requests can pay for themselves, and invitations to superiors to "come and see for themselves."

Budget managers utilizing the *incremental* strategy base their requests on amounts from the previous year, conservatively defending the need only for existing levels, and seeking only incremental increases in their annual requests. *Timing* is the major determinate of the fourth strategy. Managers who practice this strategy look for the "right time" to make budgetary requests. They may lack confidence in their ability or distrust their supervisor's judgment, waiting for particular circumstances to serve as their ally. As a best practice, many chairs and directors with budget authority will effectively combine the economic, incremental, and timing strategies, while avoiding the devious model. According to this research, they also report reduced levels of stress in working with financial and budget data over the course of an academic year.

In a classic study of the impact of the budgeting process on personnel completed almost forty years ago, stress was identified as a core management issue.[13] This study also revealed various attitudes that prevailed at that time regarding budgets and financial planning, including the per-

---

Financial Best Practices

- Establish academic priorities that lead, not follow, the budget process
- Use priorities to control costs
- Use budgets to express and formalize plans; budgets can inform interested parties within and outside the institution about resource availability, new directions, shifts in allocation, problems to be addressed, and services to be provided
- Clarify roles and working relationships between academic and non-financial managers
- Expect financial responsibility

---

ceptions that pressure was the best way to improve productivity and financial managers should hold authority over other academic officers in budget-building activities. Clearly, attitudes have shifted from the time this study was completed, as many proactive senior officers now collaborate to avoid placing subordinates in financial positions that produce success at the expense of others. Similarly, nonfinancial academic managers must grasp that their willingness and ability to learn from budget officers will be a determining factor in the quality of the support they receive.

Pressures to cut costs and reduce budgets will challenge chairs and directors to reduce trivial budget amounts first. This is a standard mistake made by inexperienced managers, as the number of cuts being made can produce the illusion that real cost-cutting and budget reduction have occurred. However, reductions of this size rarely save significant funds and, more often, cause pervasive reductions in staff morale. As a general rule for academic managers, it requires many small cuts to equal one large one, and the more operational areas that are affected, the larger the number of employees who may turn against the process. In this sense, budget "cuts" involve a great deal more than simply reducing monetary amounts; consequences almost immediately translate into personnel and curricular issues.

In 1960, the concept of *suboptimization* was introduced in another classic study on budgeting.[14] According to this study, the combined effort of individual departments concentrating on the optimization of departmental budget goals will not lead to the best possible performance at broader organizational levels. From the organizational perspective, *suboptimization* is a negative concept that describes the subunit activity of optimizing a goal within that unit to the extent that the net effect damages broader organizational objectives. A classic example involves the patient who dies of a heart attack on the stretcher in an admitting room while the admission staff search for proof of insurance. The subgoal, that is, ability to pay, of the admitting unit was optimized to the detriment of the hospital's objective, that is, patient care, and ultimately the demise of the patient. Similar, but thankfully less dramatic, events reflecting suboptimization occur on most campuses daily as various departmental objectives, which may be contrary to the larger institutional goals, are promoted. The departmental and discipline-based nature of colleges and universities contribute to the problem of suboptimization and accentuate the need for coordinated budgets, information, and activities.

The Role of the Chief Academic Officer in Financing Academic Support: Who's Minding the Commons?

The historical concept of the "commons" derives from a track of land owned or used jointly by members of a community to be "shared by all." A similar concept applies to areas within a college that provide services to support and promote the institution's educational mission. Most "services" provided by the administration, libraries, graduate programs, computer and media centers, outcomes assessment offices, athletic facilities, and student service operations fall into a "public good" category and are provided without charge to students, faculty, and friends of the institution. Some other services may not be offered for free, however, and charges will be assessed when specific users can be easily identified and are willing to pay for access due to popularity or scarcity.

New information and computer technologies have also changed the complexion of campus "services" and the budget processes that support them. In the learning resource center, as an example, the power of data manipulation tools has increased the number and sophistication of services available, as well as their cost, to unprecedented levels. Many of these more sophisticated services are viewed as outside the traditional "commons" and, as such, are prime candidates for utilization fees. The impact of new technologies has also blurred the lines between access to those printed materials that have traditionally been free and hard copies for which fees have always been charged.

As institutional, as well as departmental, appetites grow, the tendency to create additional fees for service will also increase. On some campuses, various internal offices and departments have become targets of increased fees from their own support units. Areas such as communication, computing, and renovation services are particularly prone to these "unit-to-unit" charges, as overall student affordability issues have limited the steady growth of fees at hundreds of mid-range institutions. As described earlier, students already have seen an expansion of new fees into such areas as technology and health with the rationale for escalating fees often linked to fund growth rather than increases in real costs or improved quality of service.

Academic vice presidents increasingly hold the responsibility to evaluate fee requests and assess their appropriateness, fairness, and consistency. Many exercise this authority realizing that once established, fees are seldom reviewed and rarely discontinued. Therefore, institutions should develop an operating policy that distinguishes between services that promote the public good and those that are to be rationed by market factors. Consideration should also be given to the establishment, within this policy, of growth rate guidelines for fees that are not linked to costs. With these academic safeguards, each time a fee request is received it can be readily assessed according to the institution's fee policy and overall objectives.

Conclusion: Paying for the Ivory Tower

Since the early 1980s, greater attention has been paid by policy shapers in the higher education community to resource acquisition than resource utilization, yet utilization remains the more complex issue, particularly for chief academic and chief financial officers. Approximately 80 percent of most college and university operating budgets consists of salaries, leaving the cumulative cost of books, computers, and *all* other instructional materials to the remaining 20 percent. Critics of this situation are quick to point out that average faculty teaching loads as high as fifteen semester hours only twenty years or so ago have declined to nine hours or less at many institutions. These same individuals question productivity and efficiency with the clear implication that if faculty would teach as much as they used to, many nonpersonnel resource constraints would somehow disappear. Others believe that productivity will increase as the result of new technologies and by restructuring the role of faculty.[15]

As we move into the next century, chief academic officers will be challenged to exercise new levels of institutional leadership in addressing higher education's growing financial challenges through innovative curriculum development, flexible personnel policies, imaginative course scheduling, productive workloads, and more judicious use of available resources. In the area of curriculum, primary responsibility will remain with the faculty, and if the campus culture is one in which departments still jealously guard course inventories, prerequisites, and majors, significant curriculum reform will not be accomplished and the chief academic officer will be both compromised and increasingly perceived as an ineffective outsider among colleagues.

The rising cost of staff has caused more reliance on part-time and temporary faculty to implement complicated degree programs. With 40 percent of the nation's 825,000 faculty members employed as part-time teachers, and 40 percent of the remaining full-time instructors holding the rank of assistant professor or less, three out of every five of the classroom teachers charged with preparing "knowledge workers" for the high-technology workplace of the future live with little or no job security and even less authority to shape their professional futures.[16] These data indicate a need for provosts and deans to develop solutions which carefully balance financial, curricular, and faculty personnel considerations.

Class schedules will need to be coordinated to reflect program demand and to maximize the use of available space. Innovative, even contrarian, approaches that redesign periods of demand and require premiums for popular programs will also need to be investigated to overcome the most intractable problems related to facilities and workload. Flexible faculty contracts that reward specific skills and distinguished professional "citizenship," among other contributions, will become a strategic option.

The chief academic officer will also need to design cocurricular forums that bring students and faculty together in more collaborative formats, allowing them to develop a new, stronger sense of community beyond the prerogatives of single programs and departments. Broad recognition that resources are becoming more limited and must be allocated on the basis of inter-related priorities will be necessary, and student councils and faculty senates will need to join agendas to evaluate the potential feasibility of any institutional initiative carrying significant fiscal implications.

The primary financial responsibility for the chief academic officer in this process will be to develop and maintain budgetary, personnel, and educational systems that support the academic priorities which make the institution vital and progressive. Effectively managing the college or university's financial systems will enable the academic vice president to design and implement academic best practices. Failure to fulfill this mandate will ultimately jeopardize institutional democracy and the ability to provide educational excellence to future entering classes.

III

The Extended Community

CHAPTER NINE

Managing a Cross-Cultural Experience: Grants and Contracts

Jon M. Strolle and Ruth Larimer

Almost every American college and university is experiencing the need to find ways to support its teaching mission with revenues other than tuition, to compensate for decreased funding from traditional state and public sources, and to compete more effectively for private-sector assistance. For chief academic officers, this need to find grants and contracts has multiple repercussions. The revenue goal is attractive, but there are cautions. Between the development and execution of these projects, faculty and support staff may find their time seriously drained from core functions as classroom teachers, researchers, and members of the larger institutional community. Even the excitement of a successful proposal can be overwhelmed by the realization of responsibilities not fulfilled and institutional commitments placed on hold until this assignment can be completed.

The first step in matching current institutional interests with long-term opportunities is to conduct a campus inventory of capacity, expertise, interest, and readiness. Some disciplines have an ingrained culture of grant support, such as the research sciences, medicine, engineering, and fields directly related to federal projects in defense, health, security and other nationally established needs. The social sciences have client-provider relationships that rise and fall with the political status of concerns about education, children's welfare, and various economic policies, for example. In this context, the chief academic officer benefits his or her institution by conducting regular assessments to make certain that institutional focus is coherent and the management of ongoing projects is coordinated with the introduction of new proposals. Researching opportunities has become more efficient as guides such as the *Federal Register* and the *Commerce Business Daily* have become available from

---

Emerging Trends in Academic Grants and Contracts

- Fewer federal resources must be compensated by greater opportunities from state, local, and nongovernmental sources
- Increased competition is occurring within the profession from individual researchers who may in the future "sell" their experience and talent to new institutions and create their own projects
- Projects that can be completed on electronic networks may no longer require academic institutional settings, and the highest cost of projects may be abandoned altogether
- International needs will present new opportunities for strategic alliances, consortia, and other partnerships that can compensate for domestic reductions
- The multiple risks of global competition—culture, language different institutional structures—are real but surmountable

---

the Government Printing Office in both hard copy and electronic form.[1] This information is an appropriate starting point for identifying coincidences of interest between grantors and the institution.

Chief Academic Officers and the Management of Grants and Contracts: A Leadership Challenge

The well-known bane of many contract and grant offices is the unfocused enthusiasm of an individual faculty scholar who has discovered what appears to be a program to fund exactly what he or she is researching. By the time the proposal is refined to a point of likely consideration, the process of educating the individual to the language and stipulations of the grantor will have consumed considerable energy and time. Rather than stifling creative impulses, the chief academic officer can encourage them through leadership that provides an ongoing forum for the combination of ideas, resources, and personnel into quality proposals to appropriate agencies and foundations.

Strategic information can be gathered by the provost through careful monitoring of grant and contract opportunities from federal, state, and local agencies. The closer the communication between the chief academic officer and the members of the grant-writing team, the more comprehensive their final proposals will be, particularly with regard to identifying new sources of funding and imaginative approaches to them.

While a degree of creativity will be needed between the experts on both sides of grant and contract-making, a special level of fiscal expertise will be of equal value to sustain long-term success. When government agencies are involved, reporting requirements may be diametrically different from the open style a private foundation requires. In either instance, experienced financial management must support the grant's fiscal structure as much as disciplinary expertise has shaped its academic substance.

While some grants may engender constant fine-tuning to achieve required outcomes, once an initial agreement has been made, it is wise to prepare the leadership team for negotiations with contractors who may, and often will, interpret conditions and outcomes differently from the understandings of those executing the grant. Typically, completing the contract will prove second only to the initial securing of the agreement in difficulty. At this phase, excellent record-keeping and extensive notes on all conversations and meetings, reviewed and initialed by everyone, will eliminate accidental misunderstandings and help bring a closure satisfactory to all parties.

Prospects and Cautions for Academic Grant-Writing

The elections of the 1990s and their long-term consequences on legislation have noticeably diminished traditional sources of academic contracts. The Department of Defense has been spared, relatively, but the competition has become significantly more intense for the opportunities that remain, and the degree of specialization and expertise required has eliminated all but a few highly concentrated providers. Other traditional funding agencies have been faced with resource cuts causing their disappearance through consolidation with related offices and operations. This realignment process has increasingly returned the responsibility for resources to state and regional authorities, which must meet those research needs previously assumed by the federal government. As a result, more and smaller projects will gradually distribute contract and grant money across a narrower range of institutions. Skills and techniques that succeeded on the national level can be applied by analogy, as a knowledge of one's local and regional contexts becomes increasingly valuable.

While new interest in regional, state, and local funding sources will be a predictable response to the reduced federal resource environment, even small and medium-sized institutions should not hesitate to explore overlooked opportunities now emerging in the international domain.[2] Some countries which have for decades tied their capital resources very closely to their national economies are beginning to release funds through contract and grant-making to those colleges and universities demonstrating the greatest amount of innovative programming and relevant expertise. Korea, Taiwan, and China have been the most aggressive in pursuing new projects in the 1990s, often collaborating initially with an academic partner from within the home country's educational community. Success, or failure, in one international agreement can challenge an institution to develop a capacity to work across multiple cultures and expand global awareness and involvement. Chief academic officers should assume their own ignorance in cross-cultural communication and grant development and pledge to re-learn the basics and to develop organizational practices sensitive to the realities of the society and institution where the project will be completed.

To make these considerable investments of human and fiscal capital worthwhile, provosts and academic vice presidents can increase the likelihood of institutional success in three ways.

1. *Learn all communication requirements.* In essence, do we speak the same "language"? As higher education administrators increase their professional interactions with those in the government and private sector, both philanthropic or for-profit, they quickly discover that many years inside the academy may have separated their discourse from that of peers off the campus. This adjustment can be jarring professionally, and it is also necessary to realize that while a research scholar may need only to understand these distinctions, a successful grant or contract writer must incorporate them successfully into practice.

2. *Learn the cultural "signs."* Chief academic officers must educate their grant-writing teams to the value in learning the differences of expectation and procedure of nonacademic institutions. The requirements of laboratories in the private sector may look identical to those of an academic institution. However, once outside the frameworks of higher education, communicating to specialized groups that are not part of the academic world most likely will require a study of different methods of approach and perception. If the contract seeker does not acknowledge these differences, however slight, it is possible that the nonacademic party may perceive condescension rather than ignorance.

3. *Learn the calendar.* Carefully considering the exact requirements of requests for information, draft submissions, and final proposals is the first step to bridging communication and cultural differences. The provost or academic vice president and the members of the proposal team must analyze the grant-maker's calendar in order to identify integral aspects of the overall process. For instance, is there a legal requirement to observe the exact time for submissions, or is the agency or foundation

somewhat more liberal regarding schedules and guidelines? Developing answers to these and other questions will be useful in shaping the work of the grant-writing team, and in helping them to make the final document timely and compelling.

Future Revenues and Future Litigation: A Primer on Patents and Copyright

In this section, and the concluding case study, chief academic officers are challenged to implement best practices against a series of powerful, sometimes negative, trends.

In conversations with provosts from several regions whose institutions maintain extensive technical research contracts resulting in commercial processes and products, the subject of patents and copyright produces uniform expressions of caution, frustration, and fear. In this area, most frequently, the prospect of litigation should never be minimized. Yet, it is within this same confluence of ideas, documentation, and resources that the greatest potential for undeveloped revenues now exists for many modestly endowed higher education institutions.

In the mid-1980s, U.S. government contracts were changed to allow the contractee to retain patent rights. Even with this development, however, two institutions with similar amounts under contract may maintain vastly different numbers of patents. The research culture of the college or university will ultimately determine this number. As there will also exist "cultural" differences among the many granting agencies, assigning a staff or faculty member to monitor these idiosyncrasies, along with the evolving body of laws pertaining to these initiatives, will form a vital complement to the work completed by those in the laboratory. Even with early and appropriate disclosure, however, the process of reducing solid prospects to marketable products suggests a ratio of one hundred disclosures to ten ideas worth patents to one project finally funded for commercial purposes.[3]

Whatever the tradition at one's institution, the chief academic officer is responsible for creating and maintaining a "culture of invention" among senior professors as well as untenured beginners through professional development and resource incentive programs. This influence eventually shapes the content and individual research of every project supported by the college or university, from that of a student whose degree is deferred for a year because his or her research connects to a patent under preparation to that of a team of senior clinicians undertaking a multipart project years, even decades, from completion. In these instances, an academic vice president must demonstrate leadership skills not found in a classroom or committee meeting to fulfill this aspect of the organization's educational mission.

Negotiating a Federal Contract: The Development of an Armenian Course—A Case Study

Although the process of obtaining a grant or contract usually begins with a series of exploratory visits to funding agencies or a perusal of journals and registers, this one began with a phone call from a colleague who had been invited to submit a proposal for a large contract with a government agency. She needed the sponsorship of an accredited institution to obtain the contract, and an agreement was reached to partner in this venture. Soon, however, for various reasons, she had to withdraw, and the dean found herself responsible for writing a proposal to obtain half a million dollars to develop a curriculum to teach an exotic language.

As an administrator and professor of applied linguistics, she believed that bringing this grant to the Monterey Institute of International Studies Graduate School of Language and Educational Linguistics would benefit our students and that the Institute had the expertise to implement a successful project over the long-term. The guarantee of a contract, however, had its advantages and disadvantages. Our leadership team realized that if they could complete a thorough proposal, we would receive the contract, yet, we had missed the first informational workshop and initial filing deadline. There was also the challenge to reorganize staff members on very short notice to manage additional areas of responsibility. Almost immediately, the members of our project leadership team found themselves in negotiations with the federal agency established to administer funds to improve language instruction in the government services, the Center for the Advancement of Language Learning (CALL). Our main contact for substantive issues, the project officer at CALL, was a former German professor highly knowledgeable about language curriculum. We also began to work directly with government financial advisors assigned to the negotiation and approval of our budget.

Contract Implementation

As an initial requirement, a professional with government grant experience was hired to train the members of the business office in appropriate financial practices.

Setting the Overhead Rate

Although the Institute had completed many previous projects funded by grants, we had no experience with federal contracts and had to begin

---

Best Practices Regarding Grants and Contracts

- *People:* Personnel choices drive contracts and grants. A conscious policy to seek appropriate talent will prove worthwhile if the individuals chosen are matched precisely to the demands of the grant and contract environment.
- *Policy:* Recognizable rewards for the contributions of faculty researchers must be clear. The institution's and the individual's investments must be placed in a coordinated relationship over the long term.
- *Place:* The distinctiveness of the institution and the depth of its expertise must sustain the contract or grant process. Knowing and building on true strengths will provide chief academic officers with a necessary reserve of institutional resources.
- *Performance:* Outcomes are the benchmarks on which all else will be judged. The chief academic officer must weigh effort required against investment made to determine the ultimate value of these projects for institutional mission. In so doing, he or she should balance current needs against future goals in the contexts of curricular depth, faculty development, and financial resources.

---

by negotiating a federal overhead rate, a daunting task which many larger institutions will have already established. Items to be provided by the participating institution within the overhead also had to be negotiated with the contracting office. As an example, it was our responsibility to provide both a working space and furniture. If we chose to purchase hardware, such as computers, scanners, videotaping equipment, and various upgrades, ownership would remain with our institution at the close of the project. Conversely, if these items were purchased on budget lines in the contract, they would belong to the government but could revert to the Institute if not recalled. We also included supplies in the overhead, as we were advised in a curriculum development project that they often constitute a significant and overlooked expense.

Staff Planning

Funding staff support constituted the least flexible element of the project's financial agreement. Although we were permitted to move funds among most of the budget lines, staff support had to be hired at previous salary levels and could not be given raises during the course of the contract. In addition, if someone's skills were determined to be different from what was expected, it was equally difficult to secure a "raise." After extended negotiation, this issue was resolved with the help of a cooperative government budget office by creating new positions for individuals in question. Alternatively, all contracts could be designed for six- or nine-month periods so that the entire work team can be readjusted with a minimum of disruption.

As we were a small institution, we were aided in budgeting and billing from the outset by our chief financial officer and controller. As the contract progressed, it became evident that the government expected someone to be at the other end of a phone whenever an official called to discuss contractual changes or to request current financial information. Fortunately, midway through the project, the Institute hired a government contracts officer, which removed a significant burden from project staff and the business office. Team members agreed it would be difficult, if not impossible, to complete another contract without the involvement of an individual who could provide precise financial management data as well as identify funding procedures that might trigger "red flags" for the government.

Hospitality

Unlike practices sometimes used in higher education, the government allows no hospitality charges on a federal contract. This can become a problem working over an extended period with a group of Middle Eastern employees, for instance, who are used to giving and receiving food and gifts on important occasions. Hospitality expenses will need to be borne by the university.

Process

After the preliminary budget was submitted, a meeting in Washington was required to discuss substantive and financial issues before proceeding to full contractual agreement. A group of government contract specialists reviewed our plan to clarify the final agreement, recommending several changes in method as well as wording. The overall budget was also examined to ensure that the Institution had requested enough to cover the necessary expenses of traveling to Armenia to collect authentic video, audio, and textual materials. In the process, numerous purchasing requirements, even specific product types, were identified and had to be negotiated before incorporating them in project procedures.

At its maximum, the project's staff included: a principal investigator who also served as the main methodological consultant; an office manager who coordinated equipment requests and employee requests and retained responsibility for quality control of the final product; two Armenian curriculum writers who were experts in the field, one in the language itself and the other in language teaching; a transcriber/translator who was bilingual in Armenian and provided us with the background documentation for the video, film, and audiotaped tasks we needed to complete; and two part-time American graduate students who revised and formatted the actual lessons, scanned pictures, and performed editing on the English instructions and translations. In the second year, we also employed a three-quarter time video editor who contributed valuable desktop publishing skills in addition to working with the video clips. At various stages, several part-time staff members were hired for single tasks requiring specific skills not available elsewhere.

One of the most important lessons we learned in this process was the benefit in hiring a consulting media specialist before acquiring any equipment. Project members quickly discovered that the campus computer person did not possess the requisite professional experience and that someone who had completed this kind of specific project would be necessary to its success. Finally, even experienced institutions should prepare for the fact that government reviewers may require a very different kind of "product" than that with which even experienced university researchers are familiar.

For the chief academic officer, the single greatest challenge in meeting the specifications of a federal government contract is acknowledging that the funding agency will not necessarily provide the institution with freedom to produce the product its project team believes appropriate; rather, the government agency will simply demand the fulfillment of its exact specifications even while some within that agency may disagree on best methods. In the case of a curriculum project of this nature, after commissioning the project team, the first objective will be to form a comprehensive plan to collect authentic text materials and to prepare a prototype unit for the reviewing team to assess and approve.

Experience in writing language teaching textbooks has shown that the development of a prototype chapter may require as much as half of the total project time. In the case of reviewers representing multiple interests (in our case, four different government language schools), the process inevitably becomes complex and protracted. The diplomacy and patience of the project manager may be severely tested, and this should be weighed in selecting the team's principal researchers.

Additionally, reviewers should be asked to present the institution with *examples*, not descriptions, of the kind of products they want to see developed. While this sounds elementary, in our case it was crucial finally to realize we were not speaking the same language as our reviewers. In fact, both parties became increasingly frustrated when the initial product did not meet their specifications.

One of largest obstacles inherent in this particular project was obtaining permission to reprint copyrighted materials. This involved working with international copyright law in the context of one country of the former Soviet Union. That country's law experts, including government attorneys and a local university attorney, had some difficulties interpreting the copyright laws. As a result, we determined we needed to secure permissions, if possible, from all publishers and authors who could be contacted. This task was made more difficult because of the severe economic conditions in Armenia, causing many of its publishers to close without forwarding addresses. In addition, near the conclusion of the project, an Armenian Ministry of Justice and Copyright Office was established. That Office believed it held some form of responsibility over requests for permission to reprint but was unable, finally, to clarify what that should be. Ultimately, most permissions were obtained from publishers or authors, and a few selections had to be deleted.

Completion of the Project

As the contract period approached its conclusion, we realized that the agreed-upon work product could not be completed within the established time frame. Over the same period, our project managers had conserved resources and produced an unexpected budget excess. After reasonably negotiating with the government's budget advisors, who were unprepared for a budget surplus, the members of our project team agreed to reduce the scope of the final product slightly and to extend the agreement for two months at no extra cost to the government. At this point, the contract officer became invaluable, as she was able to compute a "burn rate" for the project, dependably informing us every two or three days how many more people we could still afford to pay. Without these detailed financial projections, it would not have been possible to complete the project on its revised schedule. Although the nature of the product is negotiable to a point, completing the contract once it has been agreed on is the burden of the college or university.

Conclusions: Academic Leadership and the Speed of Change

Having assessed the demanding work schedule of its project development team along with the complex negotiations by administrative and financial managers, would our institution seek another contract such as this? The answer is, unanimously, yes. Regarding our initial effort, there is little question that the Institute produced a quality product: a five hundred–hour language course based on professional-quality, almost entirely authentic video materials incorporating the only pedagogical grammar of Eastern Armenian in existence. Regarding a future contract, we now believe that we could be both far more efficient in managing project time and more skillful in negotiating financial support.

Although there is not great commercial demand for the course, the Institute has benefitted from greatly increased visibility both in government and language teaching circles. We have also professionalized our contracts office and broadened its experience in curriculum development, a field central to the mission of an international institute. Finally, we have moved the institution several steps ahead technologically. In particular, a cohort of individuals knows considerably more about professional video editing and desktop publishing, and this will be central to the success of some grants and contracts in the future.

Provosts either shudder or exult at the mention of grants and contracts and the qualities of leadership required to bring a research concept to final funding. However, only at the level of chief academic officer can the overview of mission, curriculum, budget, and professional development effectively be articulated for the institutional community overall. Finally, it is imperative for the college or university's academic managers to remain flexible and ready to learn new methods to meet the changing, sometimes contradictory, requirements of future contracts and grants. The accelerating speed of change and its accompanying call for accurate and comprehensive data suggest that chief academic officers, most of all, will need to demonstrate these qualities in an increasing number of settings in the next century.

External Relations and Institutional Advancement: Building Bridges, Seeking Friends

Georgia E. Lesh-Laurie

External relations encompasses those activities that ensure that a college or university maintains respected citizenship in its various "communities." On an increasing number of campuses, chief academic officers now play a major role both in accomplishing this and managing the benefits realized from the process. As current provosts and academic deans identify new friends of the institution, these interactions introduce them to a wider range of publics, as well as a larger role in financial planning and the design of campuswide development projects, than the academic officers of prior decades.

Historically, fund-raising has been the responsibility of college and university advancement officers. While this activity may have been accomplished in concert with the institution's academic offices, the academic vice president served primarily as a resource person or a coordinator of the priority-setting process. This chapter identifies the best practices which place chief academic officers at the center of the institutional advancement and external relations agendas of an institution and which demand new and sometimes unfamiliar areas of responsibility and competence.[1]

As academic "effectiveness" has become increasingly viewed in entrepreneurial terms, external relations activities are excellent opportunities for a vice president for academic affairs to assess his or her ability to perform various aspects of these responsibilities. A successful self-assessment will require frank consultation with colleagues, both faculty and administrative, as well as a decision to assume responsibilities beyond those of a traditional academic officer to enhance the college or university's educational mission. The process begins simply through attendance at and participation in a wider range of campus events. This extends be-

172

Emerging Trends in External Relations and Institutional Advancement

- External relations is an arena in which future chief academic officers will be expected to operate with effectiveness
- Diminished public resources will force each institution to examine dispassionately current practices to determine if it can continue to perform all of the activities in which it has previously engaged
- Public calls for institutions to become more productive will force an examination of faculty workloads
- As lifelong learning and older students become realities on every campus, student life functions will need to change to be attuned to these students' needs and wishes
- Fewer corporations are interviewing annually on campuses, hence it becomes increasingly important to provide students real-world experience through, for example, internships and cooperative education programs

---

yond mere cameo appearances; rather, an academic vice president should actively participate in events for which one's presence is not expected as an academic officer, including athletic events, campus art gallery openings, employer fairs designed by the career services office, and student advisory committees.

Chief academic officers are now becoming involved in new areas of responsibility, including: fund-raising, external relations, and institutional development. Successful initiatives involving external advisory committees, new forms of community outreach, and alumni development programs, several involving students as institutional ambassadors, are described below.

The Value of External Advisory Committees

External advisory committees are a key to success in these new areas. Chief academic officers should carefully build external advisory committees to include individuals who comprehend the changing nature of both academic leadership and institutional needs and who can make specific contributions to the college and university. An academic vice president must also be aware that an advisory committee is both difficult to form and difficult to keep functioning. For these reasons, he or she should monitor its activities, using whatever mechanisms may be most appropriate, and meet formally with the group on a regular schedule. Advisory committees may also serve as a means to cultivating and assessing potential trustee candidates. As each institution seeks its committee's advice on specific topics, the quality of that advice can be enhanced through forms of socialization beyond traditional meeting times and agendas. As an example, a provost might invite committee members to an athletic competition or student concert as guests of the college apart from whether that event relates specifically to the committee's area of responsibility.

To maintain a sense of momentum, committee agendas should be designed by the chair, and they should include at least two action items. At a growing number of colleges and universities, external advisory committees have identified research-related objectives as a primary focus. In some instances, committee members have served as resources themselves to secure much-needed equipment for science, art, and health-related programs by providing a percentage of the funding through incentive grants. At larger universities, especially, committees have increased the role research plays at all levels of the curriculum by providing partnership opportunities for faculty and students with industrial colleagues. Proactive committees also provide contacts for seed money to begin these projects and establish internship and cooperative education opportunities at nationally recognized corporations and state and federal agencies.

New Strategies for Community Outreach

Advisory committees can help shape their institutions through the design of outreach initiatives to address evolving community needs. In order to accomplish this, chief academic officers and directors of external relations should pose these questions to the committee: Is our institution customer-oriented? Is our institution essentially proactive or reactive? Has our institution identified a realistic number of mission-related goals on which to concentrate? However, even well-established committees should not undertake too many initiatives in a single planning year.

To begin, colleges might consider innovative certificate programs offered through the continuing education division; degree-completion programs unique to their state or local area; or developing programs in emerging areas of academic and external interest, such as leadership and community service. In this example, local community and corporate leaders might participate in the selection of promising students for internship programs as well as contribute scholarship support over the period of a multiyear agreement.

Initiatives such as these can draw a wide range of institutional constituencies together in mission-complementary pursuits while creating a new external profile for the institution as a caring, outward-focused enterprise.[2] One noteworthy example has been the plan by Portland State

---

Building Effective External Advisory Committees

Formation

- Focus on areas in which the institution has an internal infrastructure and which will help it achieve mission

- Give specific charge to each committee and make the charges relevant

Structure

- Select membership carefully
- Include people who can, and will, make specific suggestions for the improvement of the campus
- Ask the committee chair to begin the model for meetings and agenda setting

Meeting Format

- Plan two meetings in advance
- Issue agendas one week prior to each meeting
- Allow sufficient discussion time, but also permit the group to reach conclusions
- Include at least two action items at each meeting
- Distribute notes or actual minutes from each meeting no matter how rudimentary

Impact on Institutional Quality of Life

- Seed funding for educational research projects
- Matching money for equipment purchases
- Internships and cooperative education experiences for students
- Community support for activities

University to employ community service as a guiding principle in its internal restructuring process. PSU will use community-based measures of success to assess its performance and has defined its academic agenda in collaboration with its local community.

An increasing number of colleges and universities have launched entrepreneurial centers to serve as incubators for new business ventures and to provide specific academic programs for students interested in these areas of professional development. At Brown University and the University of Colorado at Denver, environmental studies/sciences programs focus on community-defined problems, with students collaborating with local activists and politicians as well as nationally recognized scholars to address these concerns. The success of each community-related initiative will depend, in part, on how well the institution markets these opportunities. The chief academic officer holds the authority to commission the advertising strategy, to identify its potential audiences, and to evaluate its effectiveness.

Utilizing Alumni in Development Initiatives

Effective colleges and universities produce alumni who comprehend their institution's overall academic programs, are proud of their educations, and will work at length without recognition or compensation to achieve educational objectives. The role of an effective chief academic officer is to serve as a conduit between each new class and the ongoing mission of the college or university. Many liberal arts colleges and research universities already maintain active, involved alumni organizations, and academic vice presidents quickly come to appreciate how significant the contributions of alumni can be to the academic mission and advancement of an institution. With this in mind, chief academic officers will be well-served by scheduling time each month to accompany the alumni director on visits to local and regional chapters.

The chief academic officer can serve as the link between specific academic units and their alumni. The campus alumni director can assist the chief academic officer by developing comprehensive lists of activities in which each academic unit can become involved. While an academic vice president can serve as facilitator for alumni activities for the campus as a whole, each academic department or division can best form the connecting point between its programs and alumni. Many of these goals may be achieved by making good use of the focused publications that most alumni offices fund in their annual budgets.

For a new chief academic officer, working with alumni on a regular basis can serve as an entree to some of the most influential members of the institution's external community. Yet, if the provost or academic vice president agrees to serve as a conduit between alumni and the campus, procedures for efficient follow through will be critical. Those procedures will be similar to the guidelines for external advisory boards detailed above. The University of Colorado at Denver has designed a computer network, Together Net, that links alumni of the Education Program from their workplaces back to the university. With relative ease, alumni can continue to direct questions to former instructors, while faculty can follow the professional development of former advisees.

Positive publicity is an integral aspect of effective alumni development. The institution's public relations office should be directed to place at least one article per week highlighting a new program or project in local print media. In addition, the chief academic officer should also be introduced to all local news media, as free "spots" are generally available on television stations, often at attractive time periods, and constitute a potent opportunity to introduce the institution along with some of its most successful graduates to wider audiences.

Academic Programming and Institutional Advancement

Chief academic officers are coming to view "academic outreach" as one process through which academic programs are legitimately transformed into symbols and products that shape institutional image. In this context, the academic vice president must assess degree programs against new kinds of criteria and by asking new kinds of questions. For example, what programs are particularly attractive to the campus's external constituencies? Do these programs provide students with highly sought internships and opportunities for volunteer community service? Are the majority of academic programs sensitive to the professional goals and needs of the employees of the institution?

Modes of course delivery must be monitored continually for relevance and effectiveness, and the institution's senior academic officer will need to determine whether the college or university has thoroughly considered models such as weekend degrees, bulletin board courses, and distance education programs. An institution's willingness to provide programs in alternative teaching formats can open new student markets, which rapidly become mainstream markets. Modern technology now makes it possible for students to complete continuing education courses, certificate programs, and even baccalaureate degrees, from their homes and offices. In an increasing number of communities, local cable television systems donate free educational air time, for example.

Another method for universities to reach new publics is to teach existing degree programs on the premises of local businesses. Courses can be offered in self-paced learning models that will assist the company and yet not compromise on-campus schedules or syllabi. In the process, these programs may produce beneficial funding arrangements for the institution while providing faculty with supplemental earnings. Some have noted that these degree programs typically have a lifetime of two to five years, during which time the institution gains value-added publicity for demonstrating heightened sensitivity to the needs of its external environment.

Finally, academic outreach can be characterized by basic, ongoing institutional innovation, such as an accelerated baccalaureate degree program in cooperation with a local K-12 system. By registering high school students for college courses in their junior year, participants are not forced to compromise the time they spend in high school or the time necessary to complete a traditional baccalaureate degree, and a significant amount of tuition can be saved in the process. While implementing such a program can be a complex and time-consuming project, it is one of most effective methods to build an institutional reputation as a caring, sensitive community, willing to accommodate both the financial as well as academic needs of prospective students.[3]

The University of Colorado at Denver has established an accelerated baccalaureate degree program, CU-SUCCEED, based on a partnership initiated with the local secondary school system in 1990. The partnership was developed in response to concerns that the University was not attracting the level of minority student enrollment it might have with more aggressive planning. As the case study below illustrates, the program has been judged a success over its first six years. For example, it offers qualified high school teachers positions as adjunct university faculty members and provides weekend college courses and "interims," that is, courses during vacation breaks, when the university's physical plant is unused, for example.

Institutional Advancement and the Chief Academic Officer: Three Case Studies

The following three case studies detail best practices for chief academic officers from the perspectives of external relations and institutional advancement.

CU-SUCCEED, An Academic Partnership between a University and Its Local High Schools: Case Study 1

The CU-SUCCEED program is an academic partnership developed between the University of Colorado at Denver (CU-Denver) and high schools in that city. It has three related purposes:

1. to increase the attendance rate of students with academic potential, especially minority students, who may not consider college a primary option after high school

2. to enhance the curriculum in the high schools and provide students with skills, knowledge, and information to aid their success in college

3. to ease the transition from high school to college for students and to afford them the opportunity to earn college credits while in high school

---

Best Practices in External Relations and Institutional Advancement

- Establish and effectively utilize external advisory committees
- The chief academic officer should establish an external relations function, whether one exists and whether it is a part of one's job description
- Obtain grants; they free the institution from the constraints imposed by limited internal funding
- Make deans and department chairs clearly accountable for their budgets
- Re-examine one's reward systems to be certain that they reflect the increasing emphasis being placed on teaching and public service

---

CU-SUCCEED provides the university with an excellent opportunity to combine faculty professional development and curricular innovation with a high-profile strategy for community outreach and institutional advancement.

Through the CU-SUCCEED program, high school juniors and seniors have the opportunity to test their academic skills in a university course offered in the familiar setting of their own school. In addition to earning semester hours of university credit, students receive information about applying for admission and financial aid from CU-Denver student services personnel.

The CU-SUCCEED program's curriculum consists of lower-division offerings from various departments of the College of Liberal Arts and Sciences. The courses are co-taught by a CU-Denver full- or part-time faculty member and a master teacher from the host high school. Generally, CU-SUCCEED courses are taught during one of the school's regularly scheduled periods and meet five days per week. Students spend three days with the CU-Denver instructor and two with the cooperating teacher. This schedule makes it possible for students to earn both university and high school credits, which most often also satisfy high school graduation requirements.

Students in CU-SUCCEED courses are typically recommended by teachers and counselors of the host school. Approximately two-thirds of the program's enrollment is comprised of minority students. Some of these students are at risk academically, and many are unsure or apprehensive about attending college. The remaining one-third of the enrollment consists of average-to-high achievers whose enrollment is encouraged for the purpose of creating, in each class, the diversity and heterogeneity that students will encounter on a college campus.

The CU-SUCCEED program began in 1990 with one communication class for twenty-four students, most of whom had no intention of proceeding to college after high school. The experience of taking a university class in a nonthreatening and supportive environment with peers proved very beneficial to the majority of this group. In the fall semester following their graduation from high school, seventeen of the twenty-four students matriculated in an institution of higher education, five of them at CU-Denver.

Encouraged by the success of the pilot project, the program obtained private funds to initiate courses in other schools. In the six years since its inception, CU-SUCCEED has grown at a consistent and rapid rate. In the 1994–95 academic year, the program offered twenty-two courses in sixteen high schools; it enrolled almost four hundred students.

The CU-SUCCEED program has enjoyed success, as evidenced by the program's steady growth and by the college attendance and success rates of the program's participants. Approximately 75 percent of the program's participants enroll in college after high school graduation. A total of fifty-one students have enrolled in the CU system, forty-eight at CU-Denver. The group finished the fall 1993 semester with a mean cumulative grade point average of 2.47.

Presently, CU-SUCCEED is a major component of CU-Denver's Accelerated Baccalaureate Program and has expanded to allow students more freedom to enroll in these courses if their parents wish them to do so. The program continues to require substantial institutional support, yet it seems clear that in Colorado, CU-Denver's dual academic and community outreach strategy has achieved a public relations triumph with the image of a national university vesting interest in its local community and demonstrating a willingness to make a considerable effort to encourage and then support enrollment by local minority students and, more-generally, by high school students whose background does not include the cultural tradition of college.

"A Celebration of Baseball" for a City and University:
Case Study 2

In 1991, Cleveland State University created a "Celebration of Baseball." Designed as a multidisciplinary event, this celebration allowed the campus and the community to explore the experience of baseball through art, science, history, literature, film, memorabilia, and statistics. The institution collaborated with the Cleveland Indians Baseball Club, the Society for American Baseball Research, a cable television system, and several local businesses to design a multipart program that incorporated as many aspects of university life as possible. From the perspectives of academic affairs and external relations, the "celebration" was judged a significant success in community outreach. Several program components were also scheduled to coincide with the university's twenty-fifth anniversary, reinforcing the essential educational nature of the enterprise.

Highlights of the event included the presentation of papers by baseball historians; the premier of a cable television program on League Park, the original home of the Cleveland Indians; an illustrated lecture on baseball and art; and a conversation between Herb Score and Ernie Harwell, two of the best-known figures in Cleveland baseball, on the subject of broadcasting games. Additional sessions focused on baseball and physics, the Negro Leagues, baseball and literature, and classic films on the sport. The institution was also able to attract nationally known authors W. P. Kinsella, Donald Hall, and George Bowering to give public readings from their work. A "Celebration of Baseball" achieved national and international publicity for the University.

The Institute for Sacred Landmarks Research, A Collaboration between Cleveland State University and the City of Cleveland: Case Study 3

The Sacred Landmarks Research Group at Cleveland State University (CSU) provides an innovative vehicle to integrate the university and its external community through a combination of continuing education, regular college-level courses, tours, research projects, video productions, and photographic catalogs. Ongoing fund-raising is necessary to achieve the goals of the Sacred Landmarks Research Group, and local Cleveland foundations and individual patrons have contributed significantly to this third example of joint-academic and community outreach.

For more than ten years, members of the Sacred Landmarks Research Group (SLRG) of Cleveland State University have dedicated themselves to helping the city recognize and understand the heritage of its religious structures.[4] The group's members—scholars, writers, and other interested citizen—have completed a study of selected places of worship in the city and have made the results of this study available to CSU students and the Cleveland-area public through a variety of print and electronic media. The project educates students and the interested public regarding the diversity and importance of the historical, architectural, artistic, and cultural resources embodied by these structures and their archives. Other projects completed by members of the SLRG during its first decade include:

1. A special issue of the regional journal, the *Gamut,* focusing on local churches and synagogues and describing their history and significance. More than six thousand copies of this issue were distributed, locally and nationally.

2. An exhibition of photographs and artifacts entitled, "Cleveland's Sacred Landmarks 1830–1930" in the CSU art gallery.

3. A book entitled, *A Guide to Cleveland's Sacred Landmarks,* published by Kent State University Press in 1992, which received published critical praise and sold more than one thousand copies.

4. A series of videotapes researched and written by SLRG members and produced and televised by cable television stations in greater Cleveland. Topics included neighborhood history, building preservation, adaptive reuse, ecclesiastical stained glass, and seasonal music. A half-hour documentary, *A Survivor Threatened,* detailed the story of the now-destroyed St. Joseph's Franciscan Church; it was nominated for an Emmy Award.

5. Several public education projects completed by SLRG members, including a continuing education course, "Inside Cleveland's Sacred Landmarks," and the establishment of a successful collaboration with the Cleveland Restoration Society to sponsor educational tours and musical concerts.

Planning has also involved the development of an upper division undergraduate/graduate course examining Cleveland's sacred landmarks and a guidebook to the stained glass windows of the Episcopal cathedral located on campus. The ongoing goals of the SLRG including advising student research; collaborating with organizations such as the Cleveland Restoration Society and local congregations on community-based projects; providing community education to the citizens of greater Cleveland; and disseminating books, guidebooks, and conference papers. Clearly, research concerning sacred landmarks has proven to be an appealing and durable opportunity for a university and a major city to collaborate on a series of projects incorporating academic value and broad popular attraction.

Advancing the Institution in a Global Marketplace: New Roles for the Chief Academic Officer

The global economy of the year 2000 will offer numerous opportunities to enhance external relations on campuses. Chief academic officers hold a central responsibility to draw together individuals from the

---

Criteria for Successful Academic Outreach

Philosophy

- Academic programs are an institution's best "products" in terms of external relations and institutional advancement

Output Criteria

- Determine whether the campus operates degree programs with specific outcomes attractive to external constituencies

Delivery Mode

- Utilize alternative delivery modes and new technologies, such as distance learning and bulletin board courses, as well as alternative formats, such as weekend courses and contracts with local industries

Innovative Characteristics

- Accelerated baccalaureate degree
- Weekend college
- Celebration of a sporting event
- Uniqueness of location

---

international community to serve as members of strategic external advisory committees. Cooperative education and internships can produce numerous opportunities to advance institutions by introducing colleges and universities to companies that may be located at significant distances from the campus. Training activities can provide not only potential future employment for students but also lasting relationships with both major corporations and international education organizations in terms of faculty development research grants, on-site training programs, and technology transfers.

Expanding computer networks, campus centers, and international institutes will provide more effective communication with foreign countries as grants from local corporations maintaining international offices will support short and medium-length training programs for students in appropriate majors as well as travel-study grants and scholar exchanges across the curriculum.

Beyond this, provosts and academic vice presidents need to consider the unusual academic opportunities that can only emerge from long-term relationships with foreign countries. By assessing those areas in which the college or university currently excels and determining which countries currently have needs for this training and expertise, institutions can develop proactive partnerships to export their educational missions. Traditional liberal arts training and business administration curricula, for example, are easily transportable and in high demand. Because some U.S. colleges and universities are apt to extend themselves beyond their capacities in such a competitive environment, there are two guidelines for all institutional commitments: maintain a high level of quality and ensure that all programs provide mutual benefit to all participants.

In conclusion, external relations and institutional advancement represent areas of institutional responsibility for which many chief academic officers continue to feel inexperienced and ill-prepared, yet these same functions provide unprecedented opportunities for an academic manager to develop new skills as an educational entrepreneur and institutional ambassador. Although academic vice presidents are rarely trained in this cluster of organizational operations, numerous constituencies are now calling for higher education institutions to act more responsively to the political, cultural, and financial environments in which they are located. External relations and institutional advancement offer senior academic officers a direct and immediate agenda to fulfill these new obligations.

CHAPTER ELEVEN

College Legal Counsel and the Chief Academic Officer: Changing Times, Changing Law, and Changing Challenges

James E. Samels and James Martin

In less litigious times, chief academic officers rarely consulted directly with legal counsel. When academic managers and attorneys did confer, it was usually to focus on standard cases of involuntary withdrawal, contested tenure, or student plagiarism. However, since the 1980s, academic vice presidents and campus counsel have been forced to address a far wider range of academic policy and administrative issues, including educational malpractice, truth in advertising, faculty-student consensual relationships, Americans with Disabilities Act accessibility implications, and fieldwork liability waivers, to name only several. While the need for legal counsel on campus may still seem unnecessary to some administrators, the above-mentioned challenges have reshaped the nation's college and university classrooms over the past decade—as well as the role of chief academic officers in relation to them.

The Emergence of Contemporary College Counsel

Until the 1970s, attorneys were typically engaged and retained on a special or limited basis by universities to defend their institutions in the few lawsuits that occurred. In their most serious form, these legal conflicts threatened to interfere materially with the ongoing operation of campuses and to infringe on their traditional concepts of collegial self-governance. Academic administrators responded to this increasingly rigorous judicial scrutiny with mixed strategies, hurriedly adopting what they hoped would be judicially appropriate rules for program standards, peer review procedures, and codes of discipline for staff as well as students. Driven by concern and legal necessity, trustees, presidents, and chief academic officers began to seek the services of private, general practice attorneys to address this institutional unrest and restore campus order and self-governance. It is this most recent transition that has principally shaped the roles and functions of contemporary institutional legal counsel.

Gradually, federal and state appellate courts have articulated a set of commonly understood judicial guideposts that clarify the numerous legal inter-relationships structuring the modern campus. In the process, a common body of law specifically dedicated to higher education has taken its place along with other specialty areas of law, as increased government regulation and litigation have impelled institutions to devise strategies to deal proactively with unprecedented legal challenges. In response, a choice of delivery models has emerged: full-time campus-based counsel, outside counsel, specialty counsel, faculty-campus counsel, and attorney-trustee counsel. Successful approaches share at least one of these common features: centralized coordination of legal defense, service delivery, policy making, and preventive planning. Whether staffed by full-time in-house legal counsel, outside retained counsel, or a combination of the two, a coordinated campuswide system now constitutes the single most significant factor in effective higher education legal services, characterized by a principal institutional legal representative working in partnership with the chief executive, academic, and student affairs officers, most importantly.

As a senior advisor and member of the president's cabinet, campus counsel now oversees all campus legal services, often in consultation with the academic vice president or the dean of faculty. In this capacity, counsel no longer dispenses curative advice from an outsider's point of view. Rather, he or she serves as a focused "legal administrator," preserving academic freedoms, preventing litigation, and identifying liability exposure through ongoing legal audits and reviews of evolving state and federal case decisions.

In this centrally coordinated system, diagnostic skills are continuously sharpened through a working familiarity with the institution's legal history, the interdisciplinary perceptions of colleagues, recent audit outcomes, and litigation log results. In collaboration with trustees, the president, and the chief academic officer, college counsel can then more efficiently coordinate the monitoring and treatment of each institutional legal challenge within an increasingly litigious national environment.

A Preventive Legal Audit for Chief Academic Officers

As the practice of preventive law has become more widespread within higher education, American colleges have discovered the advantages of eliminating incipient legal problems before they create troublesome liability, claims litigation, and financial exposure. At the core of

---

Emerging Legal Trends in Higher Education

The most significant legal trends in higher education in the 1990s have occurred in the following areas:

- Academic standards
- Academic honesty
- Academic labor law
- Equal academic employment opportunity and academic affirmative action
- Sexual harassment
- Pregnancy and age discrimination
- Educational consumer rights
- Academic freedom
- Privacy and confidentiality rights
- Academic fraud
- Academic disabilities
- Intellectual property rights (copyright, trademark, and technology transfer)
- Licensure
- Accreditation
- Regulatory oversight

One need consider only briefly the spectrum of newly defined educational issues to grasp the future legal context for chief academic officers: political correctness and hate speech, faculty-student consensual relationships, AIDS in the classroom, and the elimination of race-based scholarships, to name just a few. In this era of close governmental scrutiny, an experienced provost will consult with legal counsel before initiating policies that may in the future become targets of litigation or regulatory enforcement action.

---

this approach to modern higher education legal practice lies the "institutional legal audit," an aggressive process that identifies recurring legal problems not readily apparent even to experienced campus leaders. If capably performed, the audit will serve as a practical, useful tool to avoid unnecessary legal claims and their associated costs while allowing chief academic officers to relinquish their role as campus legal "firefighters," running from one academic conflagration to another.

Avoiding Legal Pitfalls in Academic Personnel Management

For most academic managers, personnel administration has emerged as the most daunting challenge in the workplace. Faculty appointments and nonrenewals, tenure- and nontenure-track policies, peer reviews,

Preventive Legal Audit for Chief Academic Officers

- *Preaudit briefing sessions* conducted by chief academic officer and chief legal counsel with key academic managers explain the vision, purposes, methods, and expected outcomes of the legal audit, in particular to ensure compliance of the institution's academic policies, standards, and practices with applicable law
- *General orientation sessions* for senior academic managers review the purposes and scope of the audit, the interview schedule, document requests, the form of findings, recommendations, and postaudit implementation priorities.
- *Each academic manager assembles information* in his or her areas of functional responsibility. This information may pertain to any number of the following: organizational hierarchy; strategic plans; academic programs and policies; inventory of pending educational consumer and other academically related claims and litigation logs; standard form documents; promotional literature, recruitment brochures, catalogs, faculty and student handbooks; faculty collective bargaining agreements; admissions applications; procurement forms; personnel evaluation forms; research or service contracts, licenses, leases, regulatory filings, and related campus legal documentation.
- *Designate senior academic officer as audit contact person* responsible for overseeing accuracy, comprehensiveness, and currency of documentation.
- *Develop a questionnaire by legal counsel in consultation with senior managers* to address areas such as updating of academic policies, standards, and procedures in compliance with current legal developments; clarification of lines of authority; development or revision of general grievance procedures as well as grievance procedures to be initiated under specific policies such as nondiscrimination and sexual harassment; and exploration of preventative strategies for any significant or recurring issues arising since the last audit.
- *Complete questionnaire,* aggregate results, interview with key managers, and distill interview and questionnaire information into compendium.
- *Integrate questionnaire results by legal audit practitioner,* including review of all documentation and findings to develop recommendations aimed at reducing liability exposure, taking corrective actions, and implementing an ongoing system to check the legal health of each department, division, or other functional unit.
- *Conduct exit conference with institution's executive leadership and academic management* in the form of a roundtable discussion ensuring that key campus leaders understand the context in which the audit was conducted and how to implement a systematic method to address its recommendations.

student advising, and classroom evaluations of teaching effectiveness are among the thorny personnel issues that confront provosts and academic vice presidents. An effective academic administrator must be able to provide legal counsel with an accurate and up-to-date list of the rules and processes governing that institution's work force. Historically, American colleges and universities have placed the focus of control over academic personnel with the chief academic officer. Over the past two decades, academic managers have gradually been influenced in their formulation of policy by the American corporate model.

In the early 1970s, faculty union organizing efforts, collective bargaining demands, and concerted work actions, strikes, and boycotts exacerbated campus tensions beyond the point where they could be resolved informally and collegially. In the area of employment agreements, claims were typically based on constitutional grounds of substantive and procedural due process, with faculty suits seeking contract-based monetary remedies beyond reinstatement, back pay, and claims for defamation and consequential damages. By the 1980s, college campuses—which had long been considered bastions of social and economic opportunity—were confronted by demands for equal educational and employment opportunity by members of minority groups, women, disabled veterans, and other disadvantaged students, faculty, and staff members. In the wake of these legal challenges, affirmative action plans and minority hiring goals were redefined by judicial interpretation and quasi-judicial adjudication, as chief academic officers were increasingly forced into the role of conflict resolution mediator.

In a predictable response to the concentration of managerial authority in the academic vice president, faculty associations began to develop policy statements aimed at revitalizing collective faculty responsibility for academic governance. In the name of individual academic freedom, and later through the spread of faculty unionization, these associations gathered numerous campus faculties together to represent a collective view in negotiations over wages and terms and conditions of employment. Following recognition by the National Labor Relations Board acting pursuant to federal labor legislation, a number of state legislatures—first in Michigan, then in New York under the Taylor Law, then later in Massachusetts and a group of other states—enacted enabling statutes granting bargaining rights to faculty unions to organize and represent their membership for these essential purposes. Through much of this period, faculty unionization flourished, as bargaining units arose across the nation at multiple public and private institutions.

The rise of faculty unions constituted one of several major signals indicating a significantly changed legal environment in American higher education, yet the legislative, executive, and judicial branches of government have remained reluctant to interpose themselves in the academic governance and administration of postsecondary institutions. Until the mid-1960s, in fact, American colleges and universities were considered sanctuaries, largely immune from private litigation and public legislation. Judicial intrusion at any level was perceived as being incompatible with academic freedom and institutional self-governance. For most of the postwar period, society has viewed the campus environment as being governed by faculty in loco parentis to the student body, and clear deference has been made to the judgment of campus leaders regarding standards of faculty scholarship and student life. This circumstance resulted in significant autonomy and collegial self-governance at the campus level combined with an inclination toward nonintervention within the judicial and executive branches of government.

The Changing Legal Environment for Academic Governance

In this context, the college's chief academic officer was the individual most often called upon to render informed professional judgments based on the community's commonly held educational values and ethical standards. As a matter of regulatory policy, courts and government licensing agencies were disinclined to disrupt the day-to-day operations of academic life or the broader policies governing standard educational decision making.

Yeshiva, a landmark faculty governance decision rendered by the U.S. Supreme Court in 1980, signaled to provosts and deans a metamorphosis in campus labor relations and the beginning of the contemporary era in higher education law. *NLRB v. Yeshiva University*, 100 S.Ct. 856 (1980), now known simply as "the Yeshiva Decision," created an exclusion for managers in mature "Yeshiva-like" university settings. This model does not, however, extend to less mature faculty governance situations, which can be paternalistic in substance although their processes may be documented in comprehensive detail.

By its ruling in the case of *Yeshiva*, the Court reasoned that an employer is entitled to the undivided loyalty of its faculty representatives who, due to the nature and weight accorded their authority and decisions in academic areas such as curriculum, teaching methods, grading policies, and admissions standards, are regarded as "managerial" employees. Yeshiva's faculty members even participated in financial management decisions covering tuition increases, course loads, and the budget allocation process. As with any appellate decision of potentially far-reaching application, the Court limited its findings based on the specific factual circumstances at Yeshiva in recognition of the faculty's influence in academic governance matters. This dominant faculty role in the administration of the university was apparent by virtue of the fact that the faculty's recommendations to the academic dean in nearly every one of its cases of hiring, tenure, sabbaticals, termination, and promotion has been upheld.

On campuses where faculty members might otherwise be considered "managers," institutions may still voluntarily choose to bargain with the faculty union under *Yeshiva*. Experience dictates, however, that faculty unions insist on the best of both governance worlds—a stronger voice in core academic and administrative governance decisions including hiring, admissions, and workload, and a "Yeshiva-type" bar that prohibits management from seeking exclusion of the bargaining unit based on Yeshiva principles. As the campus's chief academic officer, a provost or vice president for instruction is often trapped between unpopular positions in this situation. One successful strategy has been proactively to invite faculty involvement in the academic governance process while resisting faculty pressure for primacy in core academic policy decisions and personnel actions.

For public colleges and universities, *Yeshiva* has no binding effect since the Supreme Court decision interprets the National Labor Relations Act and not state labor law legislation. Nevertheless, state labor relations commissions tend to follow the guidepost of *Yeshiva* in deciding cases involving managerial exclusions. By way of example, in 1979, the Massachusetts Labor Relations Commission excluded community college division chairs based on the administration's systematic deference to faculty recommendations in academic personnel matters. Taking a broader view of post-*Yeshiva* decisions, an administration's, and chief academic officer's, consistent adherence to faculty wishes weighs as the primary criteria labor boards will consider in determining the managerial status of faculty. Labor tribunals will seriously review the role of academic deans and department chairs in following faculty recommendations or, conversely, in modifying such recommendations before transmitting them to higher levels. Several state labor boards ostensibly have been persuaded by policy provisions contained in employment contracts, faculty handbooks, or collective bargaining agreements which stipulate the faculty's central role in the governance process. However, unless the factual record of faculty involvement actually comports with the empowering provisions contained in the contract, handbook, or collective bargaining agreement, labor boards will most likely be more impressed with the facts of governance than the written word.

Labor relations commentators have widely noted the tendency of the post-*Yeshiva* courts to focus on the long-term factual record of meaningful faculty involvement on a campus, rather than on policies and procedures specifically designed to provide faculty with a voice in personnel decisions. In fact, both the NLRB and the courts have been reluctant to find an exclusion of faculty where the circumstances surrounding personnel actions did not comport with the contractually stipulated role of faculty in developing recommendations for these decisions. Unhappily, NLRB rulings since the *Yeshiva* decision have produced anomalous results on similar factual records. For example, faculty were found to be managerial by the various Circuit Courts of Appeals in Boston University and Lewis University in 265 NLRB 1239 (1982). For its part, the National Labor Relations Board has been sympathetic to the faculty union viewpoint in certain instances, Loretta Heights College in *Loretta Heights College v. NLRB*, 742 F.2d 1245 (10th Cir. 1984), Cooper Union in New York, and Florida Memorial College; in other instances, it has even reached down to find managerial exclusion at the junior college level at Dean Junior College in Massachusetts.

Leadership Lessons for Chief Academic Officers from the *Yeshiva* Decision

For a growing number of colleges and universities, campus consensus has disappeared into a widening chasm of labor relations rhetoric. Without meaningful faculty involvement in the academic policy-making process, a campus may gradually break down into disparate instructional and research units incapable of forming the critical mass of focused scholarship essential to the academic enterprise. However, through skillful consensus-building with proactive campus counsel, chief academic officers can implement a leadership model that incorporates faculty members into all levels of academic policy formation and budget development. Still, sharing power via faculty governance continues to provoke controversy at many institutions. Faculty union activists assert that shared governance simply provides a license for timid administrators to blame faculty for unpopular decisions or to permit the institution's executive leadership to escape responsibility for the nonrealization of strategic objectives. Conversely, some executive officers display a persistent distrust of faculty leaders who seek a meaningful voice in the broader governance of the institution.

In retrospect, faculty involvement in campus governance has experienced three critical transitions since 1960. That decade will be remembered for activism and genuine participation, while much of the 1970s will be remembered for the organization and advancement of faculty labor movements seeking to arbitrate, litigate, and legislate the faculty's collective way into the decision-making process. However, the 1980

U.S. Supreme Court decision involving Yeshiva sent these new messages to the chief academic officer as well as college counsel:

1. *Faculty must hold meaningful involvement in campus decision-making processes.* When managerial exclusion is predicated on transparent processes that result in dead ends for meaningful participation, faculty labor unions should and will prevail.

2. *Faculty unions must accept the full measure of institutional governance responsibility.* Were it otherwise, faculty union leaders could claim a rightful stake in educational policy and resource allocation decisions while disclaiming with impunity any responsibility for student learning outcomes.

3. *Faculty must exercise meaningful authority in the institutional strategic planning process.* Colleges and universities must prepare for a changed educational "marketplace" in which student "consumers" exert growing influence and administrators depend on the innovations of classroom teachers to achieve necessary student recruitment and retention goals.

4. *Campuses must address the rising sentiment within the national accreditation community for increased faculty participation in the governance process.* This new model of governance calls for trustees, presidents, chief academic officers, and faculty leaders to communicate more extensively while sharing greater levels of authority in broader institutional decision making.

5. *Chief executive and chief academic officers must expand faculty involvement in institutional stewardship.* Going beyond the traditional levels of faculty involvement in curriculum development, academic vice presidents should also prepare for enhanced participation by all levels of the professoriate in annual budget planning.

Legal Best Practices for Chief Academic Officers

On balance, the chief academic officer holds the greatest responsibility to identify and avoid the primary liability pitfalls in managing the campus. With this in mind, seven legal "best practices" have been developed as guidelines for the accomplishment of that goal.

Educate

Inform both oneself and the members of one's academic management team regarding the current applicability and effect of all policies, standards and procedures. In the process, make it a priority to educate the entire campus academic workforce, particularly deans, department chairs, and senior faculty members, concerning the parameters of these same policies, standards, and procedures. Finally, be certain that all academic policies and expectations are clearly published in catalogs, student handbooks, and course syllabi, thus forming the basis of the institution's compact with the educational consumer.

Regulate

In emergent areas with legal implications, such as AIDS policies, nonfraternization guidelines, and academic grade inflation, regulate with predictability by promulgating judicially tested academic procedures and standards to reduce liability exposure.

Enforce

Be certain that once the academic management team and student body are made aware of academic policies and standards that critical documents are uniformly distributed and updated according to a regular schedule. Courts remain loathe to interpose their judgments except on infrequent occasions when an administrator has acted arbitrarily or capriciously.

Document

Whether the case implicates academic management decisions or faculty evaluations, an effective academic vice president comprehensively and contemporaneously documents its factual events and circumstances. Academic managers should also state clearly their performance expectations in multiple institutional publications, as faculty and staff members are entitled to written fair warning that their productivity is inadequate along with recommendations for improvement and the consequences of failure.

Be Proactive

Only an untested chief academic officer will now wait for a discontented parent or student to complain about a lack of instructional effectiveness, program relevance, or academic remediation. Experienced managers design and implement proactive monitoring systems to evaluate teaching and learning outcomes, thus providing early warning of residual liability and related educational consumer litigation.

Mediate, Arbitrate, and Resolve

Alternative dispute resolution identifies potential controversies early in the governance or management process and diffuses them before they escalate and require litigation. Chief academic officers should mediate these differences or, failing a mutually agreed upon course of action, arbitrate by reviewing the evidence, applying established academic standards, and resolving the matter without deferral. While remaining sensitive to both student and faculty privacy, an academic vice president should not be afraid to review in detail faculty personnel files or student educational records when this serves a legitimate academic management or educational policy objective.

When in Doubt: Call Counsel

In matters with potential liability exposure that lack applicable guidelines, best practice suggests that academic managers contact campus counsel immediately to settle disputes that might otherwise have been resolved through early intervention and mediation.

Recent Developments in Disabilities Law

Another substantive area of increasing importance for chief academic officers is the need to provide necessary services and accommodations for students and faculty with disabilities. A common misperception has been that with the passage of the Americans with Disabilities Act (ADA) in 1990 drastic new requirements were leveled on college and universities to serve the needs of individuals with disabilities. However, Section 504 of the Rehabilitation Act of 1973 (29 U.S. Code section 794) (hereinafter Section 504) had already imposed on those same colleges and universities receiving federal funds most of the requirements that the ADA imposes. Theoretically, the ADA derives much of its substantive framework from Section 504, making the ADA's language very familiar to the institutions that receive federal financial assistance. Section 504 and its regulations demand that colleges and universities make their facilities accessible to students, faculty and staff with disabilities. Thus, it would appear that universities would not need to make drastic changes if they already comply with section 504.[1]

Section 504 and applicable federal regulations prohibit discrimination against otherwise qualified students on the basis of handicap in programs which receive federal financial assistance. With respect to postsecondary education, a handicapped person is qualified if he or she "meets the academic and technical standards requisite to admission or participation in the recipient's education program or activity" (34 C.F.R. s. 104.3 [k][3]).

Although programs are required to make "reasonable accommodation" for qualified handicapped students, programs are not required to modify academic requirements that are essential to the program of in-

---

Best Practices Regarding the Needs of Individuals with Disabilities

- Do not make preadmissions inquiries regarding whether individuals have a disability, unless such inquiry is for the purpose of taking remedial action to correct the effects of past discrimination
- Once individuals have been admitted, encourage them to voluntarily disclose what types of reasonable accommodation they require to succeed at the institution
- Always consider the individual merits and factual circumstances of each and every case including but not limited to the nature and extent of the disability, skills and requirements for specific programs, the types of accommodation requested, the types of accommodation the institution can offer, and any new technological developments that will make a program more accessible
- If the institution is unable to offer a specific accommodation requested by the student, explore alternatives that would be effective in achieving accessibility
- If an institution does not have the financial resources to provide a needed accommodation, assist the individual in pursuing government and private funding sources

---

struction being pursued or to any directly related licensing requirements (34 C.F.R. s. 104.44 [a]). For example, under appropriate circumstances, a student with a diagnosed learning disability may be allowed extra time on tests and a student with a visual impairment may be allowed to take an oral examination. However, it would not require that an institution waive a required nursing course for a disabled student if such course is a prerequisite to sitting for the state licensing examination.

Title III of the ADA extends Section 504 prohibitions of discrimination to privately operated public accommodations and commercial facilities. In the case of higher education, private institutions of higher education who were not recipients of federal funding were not subject to the prohibitions against discrimination contained in Section 504; however, such institutions would now be subject to the prohibitions against discrimination of the ADA.

Perhaps one of the most significant distinctions between Section 504 and the ADA for educational institutions is in the area of whether those institutions may use cost as a grounds for refusing to supply a requested auxiliary aid. In this regard, Section 504 appears to make greater demands on institutions than the ADA. With respect to Section 504, the position of the Office of Civil Rights appears to be that an educational institution has the right to select the accommodation it will provide, as long as such accommodation is effective, but may not use cost to exclude categorically particular types of auxiliary aids from consideration. With respect to the ADA, the implementing regulations specifically state that an institution may be excused from "any action that it can demonstrate would result in . . . undue financial and administrative burdens (35 C.F.R. s. 164).

The issue of cost comes up frequently with respect to individuals with hearing impairments, since many state rehabilitation agencies are no longer able to provide funding for such students and the cost of providing a qualified interpreter for all classes may be in the five-figure range. In cases where an institution does not have the funding to provide the necessary hours of interpreter services, it is recommended that the institution assist the student in pursuing government and private funding. In addition, it is recommended that the institution explore with the student other types of accommodation such as note-takers, preferred seating for a student with lip-reading abilities, and the use of technological devices such as an FM monitor.

Conclusion

The moment has arrived for chief academic officers to accept greater levels of legal accountability in the management of their campuses. As trustees, business officers, and alumni must operate within a newly litigious environment, so, too, must senior academic managers acknowledge that educational policies and practices may now be placed under a legal microscope without warning or regard to prior assumptions. No longer able to claim immunity, provosts must become familiar with emergent case law, statutory changes, and regulatory requirements governing life on and off campus, and, in light of the growth of distance education, internationally. Within this tumultuous, unpredictable legal environment, the chief academic officer can and should leverage the power of new partnerships with college counsel to advance more effectively the institution's educational agenda.

CHAPTER TWELVE

Conclusion: The Disappearing Chief Academic Officer

James Martin and James E. Samels

As the preceding chapters collectively attest, chief academic officers now face a more complex and intractable set of challenges than at any time during this century. Yet, confronted by a need for transformational leadership and vision, these same individuals have practically disappeared on many of their campuses. What forces have caused this growing "invisibility"?

At the executive level, a group of high-profile, nationally recognized presidents has transformed that office into a glamorous, celebrity function comparable to that of professional athletes and major artists. Simultaneously, vice presidents for institutional advancement have staked powerful claims to campus influence and media attention with hundred million–dollar capital campaigns enlisting famous alumni from motion pictures, television, and the national style pages.

As even vice presidents for student affairs use local news to announce controversial policies on sexual harassment, domestic abuse, and student lifestyle issues, provosts and academic vice presidents have increasingly found themselves lost in the campus shuffle, internally and externally, while being assailed by unemployed graduates demanding tuitions back for degrees that did not meet personal "quality standards," by accrediting agencies requiring highly sophisticated "assessment instruments" for even minor procedures, and by aggressive trustees and presidents calling for new forms of institutional "accountability." In this chapter, we examine the developments that have turned chief academic officers into invisible figures on their own campuses along with strategies to halt this academic "drift."

Federal cutbacks, declining student skill levels, graying faculty members, new measures of "value" and "quality," and a corrosive loss of public confidence in higher education systems, to name just a few trends, have placed higher education on the defensive with little relief in sight. As students and parents hold out hope that a baccalaureate degree still means job security, 450,000 American workers were terminated, and twenty-nine companies eliminated at least five thousand positions *each* over the 1993–94 period, according to data reported to the Association of Governing Boards.[1] The *New York Times* describes it as "The Rise of the Losing Class," in which "For the first time in 50 years, we are recording a decline in people's expectations," according to Richard T. Curtain, director of the University of Michigan's Consumer Surveys.[2] Even more strikingly, according to another poll, a significant percentage of Americans apparently believe "in their hearts" that these layoffs are justified: "They work longer hours and take more home, without letting the boss know, to give the impression that they can do difficult tasks quickly," yet there remains "a sense among people that [as employers] we are inefficient and bloated."[3]

Aside from the turbulence of the late 1960s, faculty members have been the dominant shapers of campus life for the past fifty years or more,[4] with chief academic officers left to the roles of advocate, clerk, colleague, and servant. During the 1990s, however, influences on and off the campus have redesigned the American "college experience," as older students have become more empowered and older faculty have become more hesitant. Amid rising levels of education and ethnic identity in our overall population, powerful demographic trends have provoked deep resistance to change on the part of many longstanding campus leaders. As K. Scott Hughes, author of an essay entitled "Transforming Academic Institutions," observes, "the second trait slowing substantive change is the historic reticence on the part of academic leadership and faculty to recognize the importance of undergraduate students as the primary customers of most of this country's academic institutions."[5]

Whether as supported learners, discriminating consumers, or political force, students now dominate campus life. Confronted by self-paced degree programs, virtual classrooms, and the "malling" of institutional services, career academicians must manage a complex and unfamiliar educational agenda with no training and little help. Whether the mandate is to downsize, restructure, benchmark, or reengineer, the provost is increasingly responsible to acquire resources and mobilize personnel for campuses whose missions have changed dramatically since he or she started as an untenured scholar. To compound these difficulties, a sense also prevails at many institutions that since the 1950s something significant has been lost from the framework of shared values defining the national higher education system, such that, "if colleges and universities are more inclusive, they, like the rest of society, are also more fractious, given to divisive quarrels and uncivil behavior."[6]

Halting the Drift: New Leadership Roles

At the center of these challenges and uncertainties sits a largely untutored chief academic officer who must reshape her or his campus into a more proactive, efficient, and responsive enterprise. Leaner, more flexible reporting structures will be necessary in "flattened" organizations of the future, as academic vice presidents explore cyberspace rather than faculty governance systems for the organizational models to meet their needs. In the view of one university vice president for administration:

> Higher education organizations have become complex business enterprises, measuring their size against Fortune 500 companies. Colleges and universities are in the education, research, public service, health care, economic development and entertainment businesses. All of these business enterprises spawn subsidiaries such as research parks, sports complexes, performing arts centers, and hospitals. The traditional higher education organizational structure is not capable of dealing with such a complex business enterprise.[7]

Higher education's "rigid" culture has created a fragmented administrative structure that stifles entrepreneurship, duplicates work, and diminishes teaching excellence. In Bruegman's opinion, colleges and universities have become cumbersome business conglomerates that, by adopting the concept of "a chief executive officer [the president] and a chief operating officer [the provost], would clearly define the lines of responsibility and authority. . . . [by] patterning the higher education organization after a corporate model."[8]

Still, at many higher education institutions, the "corporate model" remains anathema, diametrically opposed to even the most bureaucratic tendencies of the "collegium" that has become synonymous with institutional culture. However, even conservative provosts must now acknowledge new ways are needed to balance the "academic" budget and achieve greater quality with fewer resources. Future chief academic officers will need to explore far more innovative management models than their predecessors, including the possibility of outsourcing health care, research, advancement, auxiliary enterprises, and communications technology, as examples, each to be privatized and managed as an independent business entity with performance incentives built into that agreement.[9]

In this unsettling environment, classroom teachers and research scholars who have left tenured positions to serve as dean or provost rightfully ask what kind of leadership skills will be necessary to ensure that their institution remains academically vital and competitive. Having watched some colleagues invest large sums in Total Quality Management programs and then, like half of the institutions involved in one follow-up study twelve months later, no longer pursue it,[10] and others spend dangerously high levels on computer hardware only to discover the institution's needs in this area were, finally, more "organizational, or sociological . . . than technical,"[11] many inexperienced academic managers learn the vocabularies of productivity and assessment but remain paralyzed when the moment arrives to write a crucial grant or initiate a much-needed program. Caught between friends on the faculty who silently "satisfice" their teaching by reaching a quality threshold and turning their full attention to research[12] and needy students in all age and skill categories who demonstrate through achievement that sustained interaction with their professors directly correlates with positive academic outcomes, it is little wonder that these administrators register for professional development seminars in greater and greater numbers.

As Robert Hahn, president of Johnson State College, explains, "We need to deal with the fact that our *concept of leadership success* is unclear, beclouded as it is by paradox, accident, and aberration. . . . In thinking about leadership, we are too ready to traffic in imagery, to take appearance for reality."[13] If chief academic officers are to develop a coherent vision on their campuses not only for the faculty and curriculum but also for less familiar functions such as advancement, alumni relations, and government contracts, they will need to do so by distinguishing the subtle but critical differences among competence, excellence and leadership. The distinctions among these three categories must not be "just a matter of same or better of the same. New and distinct abilities and achievements are involved, and explicit statements of standards should make this clear."[14] Whether it is in the classroom or the boardroom, the greatest leadership challenge for provosts in the next generation will *not* be to identify and correct incompetence. Rather, it will be to overcome those campus forces that simply accept things as they are—and have been—in the face of declining resources, student skills, and public confidence. In the present environment, to accept things as they are academically is to move closer to extinction at the hands of institutional competitors aggressively seeking one's student "market-share."

Implementing Best Practices across the Institution: Four Recommendations

The following initiatives can establish institutional momentum and provide chief academic officers with the resources necessary to enhance

---

Implementing Best Practices across the Institution: Recommendations

- Create think tanks and regional networks of chief academic officers
- Establish strategic alliances and institutional collaborations on and beyond the campus
- Use advisory boards to help develop links with local businesses, corporations, and nonprofit organizations
- Implement a national computer database for chief academic officers

---

the student learning process while improving overall institutional performance in the universe of areas discussed in previous chapters.

Create Think Tanks and Regional Networks of Chief Academic Officers

On a daily basis, chief academic officers are inundated by tasks and crises requiring immediate action. As forces beyond their campuses impose new requirements on educational accountability and productivity, they will need to shape a collective response via organized initiatives such as formal networks and think tanks.

Removed from the daily pressures of departments, committees, and classrooms where the perceived need to act often takes precedence over informed decision making, provosts can collaboratively develop initiatives extending beyond their own campuses, even their own regions, while enhancing academic leadership in the process. Having established these formal networks, academic officers can then share the results of their deliberations through local and national policy recommendations based on data systematically gathered and assessed for its implications regarding both student learning and institutional management.

Establish Strategic Alliances and Institutional Collaborations on and Beyond the Campus

The benefits in developing strategic alliances, affiliations, and even mergers between and among colleges and universities have been increasingly documented through the 1990s.[15] As scarce resources and the burgeoning power of the Internet have drawn even competitive colleges and universities into greater cooperation and consolidation, this trend has moved beyond the stage of "innovative partnerships in higher education" to that of a global phenomenon, as postsecondary institutions in countries such as Australia, England, Japan, and the United Arab Emirates have explored leveraging their current resources and long histories in new forms of collaboration.

Beyond the documented advantages of stabilized enrollment, enriched faculty, and deepened alumni support, the academic benefits to students in these alliances have also been recorded, whether through expanded course catalogs or team approaches to complex subject matter. As Zelda Gamson, the author of "Collaborative Learning Comes of Age," notes:

> One challenge, then . . . is to increase its institutional effects beyond the classroom by actively sponsoring campus discussions about teaching in general and collaboration in particular . . . in other words . . . to deliberately create a collaborative teaching community.
>
> The fragmentation of colleges and universities can be overcome by integrative structures that cross the usual boundaries . . . [such as] offices that combine student affairs and academic affairs, freshman year programs that encompass most aspects of first-year students' lives . . . and learning communities.[16]

Whether in the classrooms on one's campus or across a regional network incorporating dozens of institutions and thousands of learners, strategic alliances and their new models of cooperation can provide provosts with powerful resource combinations to achieve expanded educational objectives.

Develop External Linkages through the Use of Advisory Boards to Assess Institutional Effectiveness

The academy still has a great deal to learn from the corporate and business communities regarding accurate measurements of performance and effectiveness. Competition and profit have spurred corporate trainers to develop practices that can assess the distinctions among competence, excellence, and leadership mentioned previously. The more that academic vice presidents learn of the specific factors that create quality in these external enterprises, the greater the opportunities to implement appropriate counterparts in classrooms, committee meetings, and strategic planning exercises. Developing campus assessment instruments that thoughtfully integrate concepts of worker productivity, market forces, and product development techniques can provide faculty leaders as well as chief academic officers with a wider selection of instruments to accomplish the learning objectives of future, rather than former, students.

As institutions in all classification categories move from the traditional, faculty-centered "instruction paradigm" of the past fifty years to a broader "learning paradigm," the programs and services of an entire college or university become responsible for success in the student learning process. George R. Boggs believes that "everyone at the institution should be evaluated based on contributions to student learning, and the focus should be on continuous, improvement of the environment for learning."[17] In this environment, every institutional office, no matter how peripheral, is implicated in achieving goals to improve student learning outcomes. The use of college, department, and program advisory boards composed of local business leaders, alumni, and specialists in the discipline has been shown to enhance this process. The perspectives of professional practitioners on emerging trends and best practices, not to mention the creation of internships and community service experiences, can ensure both curricular depth and expanded employment opportunities for graduates.

Chief academic officers can function most effectively as conveners of these discussions and by holding deans and department chairs responsible to focus each agenda on the core connection between student success and institutional effectiveness, as higher education institutions increasingly address the need to meet "corporate" calls for accountability.

Implement a National Computer Database for Chief Academic Officers

For too long, senior academic officers have managed in an information vacuum, on campus and within their regions, as a natural web of integrated resources and technologies has been forming around, but just beyond, their grasps. Experienced provosts realize how much they can benefit by learning what colleagues at similar institutions have attempted regarding general education requirements, accreditation expectations, or budgeting models, for example. Telephone conversations, facsimile transfers, and attendance at national conferences may provide informal reinforcement for a pressing decision, but most chief academic officers acknowledge that more formal data sharing is now necessary to meet the challenge of demonstrating visionary institutional leadership while simultaneously exercising efficient academic management.

The establishment of a comprehensive computer network and database among chief academic officers is a necessary extension of institutional collaboration. While the deans of poorly endowed colleges will testify that they would be happy with a single e-mail account, and vice presidents at research universities will respond that assistants manage their technologies for them, the concept of an easily accessible, multipurpose database created by and for chief academic officers will gradually become a working reality within the next generation of academic leadership.

This study of the roles and responsibilities of the chief academic officer, along with emerging trends and best practices that will shape the position in the next century, began with a concern that individuals currently in the position lacked the essential guidelines and shared understandings necessary to shape educational policy and implement even basic operational decisions. These chapters conclude with the concern that during the past several years of research this lack of basic resource materials has continued, contributing in its own way to the disappearance of academic leadership on many campuses. As we approach the close of the century, a new cohort of professionals is redefining the position of chief academic officer. This volume represents the integrated vision of several who are dedicated to collaborating with them in that effort.

Notes

Chapter 1. First among Equals

1. Charles William Eliot, *University Administration* (Boston: Houghton Mifflin, 1908), 242–43, 241.

2. Ibid., 243–44.

3. William C. DeVane, "The Role of the Dean of the College," in *The Academic Deanship in American Colleges and Universities*, ed. Arthur J. Dibden (Carbondale: Southern Illinois University Press, 1968), 252. See also Clyde A. Milner, *The Dean of the Small College* (Boston: Christopher Publishing House, 1936); Herbert Hawkes and Anna Rose, *Through a Dean's Open Door* (New York: McGraw-Hill, 1945); F. A. McGinnis, "The Dean and His Duties," *Journal of Higher Education* 4 (1933), 191–96; Ruth L. Higgins, "The Functions of the Academic Dean," *Association of American Colleges Bulletin* 33 (1947), 393–99.

4. Harold Enarson, "The Academic Vice President or Dean," in *The Academic Deanship in American Colleges and Universities*, ed. Arthur J. Dibden (Carbondale: Southern Illinois University Press, 1968), 252.

5. George B. Vaughan, *Pathway to the Presidency: Community College Deans of Instruction* (Washington, D.C.: Community College Press and American Association of Community and Junior Colleges, 1990), 6.

6. Jonathan Fife and Eric Goodchild, eds., *Administration as a Profession*, New Directions for Higher Education, no. 76 (San Francisco: Jossey-Bass, 1991), 1–3.

7. Statistics provided in the first portion of this section are drawn from John W. Gould, "The Academic Deanship: A Summary and Perspective," in *The Academic Deanship in American Colleges and Universities*, ed. Arthur J. Dibden (Carbondale: Southern Illinois University Press, 1968), 252.

8. Theodore Marchese, "The Chief Academic Officer: An Interview with Richard J. Miller," *AAHE* [American Association for Higher Education] *Bulletin* 41, no. 6 (1989), 3. Gerald E. Dupont, "The Dean and His Office," in *The Academic Deanship in American Colleges and Universities*, ed. Arthur J. Dibden (Carbondale: Southern Illinois University Press, 1968), 9. Also, see page 8, where Dupont states that a "prefect of studies" was described in the earliest Jesuit rule, the *Ordo Studiorum* of

1565, which directed the government of the newly founded Roman College. Dupont confirms that these rules are still the basis of Jesuit educational practice. Fordham University named a Prefect of Studies at its founding in 1841 and later changed the title to dean in 1919. Thus, in some Catholic colleges and universities, the precedent can be seen of an early version of the chief academic officer. As Dupont explains, "therefore, the deanship seems to be of older tradition in Catholic colleges of the Jesuit type than in secular institutions."

9. Barbara K. Townsend and Michael D. Wiese, "The Higher Education Doctorate as a Passport to Higher Education Administration," in *Administration as a Profession*, New Directions for Higher Education, ed. Jonathan D. Fife and Lester F. Goodchild, no. 76 (San Francisco: Jossey-Bass, 1991), 81.

10. Statistics on common areas of operation and time on task for the new model of chief academic officer are drawn from Marchese, "Chief Academic Officer," 3–6.

11. The New England Resource Center for Higher Education, based at the John W. McCormack Institute at the University of Massachusetts, Boston, works to bring attention to educational policy issues and to build understanding between higher education and government, industry, and nonprofit organizations. The Chief Academic Officers Think Tank, founded in 1987, is a group of chief academic officers that meets four times each year in retreat format to address critical questions facing provosts, academic vice presidents, and deans on New England campuses. Membership for the 1994–95 academic year included representatives from the following institutions: Bennington College, Berklee College of Music, Bradford College, Brandeis University, Bunker Hill Community College, Central Connecticut State University, Clark University, Community College of Rhode Island, Community College of Vermont, Eastern Nazarene College, Endicott College, Keene State College, Maine College of Art, Massasoit Community College, Middlebury College, Mount Ida College, New England Association for Schools and Colleges, New England Resource Center for Higher Education, North Adams State College, Northeastern University, Norwalk Community Technical College, Quinebaug Valley Community College, University of Hartford, University of Maine at Farmington, University of Massachusetts at Boston, University of New Hampshire, Wesleyan University, Westfield State College, and Wheaton College.

12. Estela M. Bensimon, Anna Neumann, and Robert Birnbaum, *Making Sense of Administrative Leadership: The "L" Word in Higher Education*, ASHE-ERIC Higher Education Report, no. 1 (Washington, D.C.: George Washington University, 1989), 80.

13. Association of Governing Boards of Universities and Colleges, *Trustees and Troubled Times in Higher Education* (Washington, D.C.: Association of Governing Boards of Universities and Colleges, 1992), 9–10.

14. Pew Higher Education Roundtable, "To Dance with Change," *Policy Perspectives* 5, no. 3 (1994), 1A–2A.

15. Robert C. Hetrick Jr., "Technological Change and Higher Education Policy," *Priorities* [Association of Governing Boards of Universities and Colleges] 1 (1994), 1.

16. Douglas Lederman, "Survey of Campus Crime Reports," *Chronicle of Higher Education*, January 20, 1993, A32.

17. "Price of Higher Education Becomes Even Dearer," *New York Times*, September 28, 1994, B8.

18. David DiSalvo, "Reflections on the Revolution in Telecommunications: An Interview with George Gilder," *Campus* 5, no. 2 (1994), 8.

19. Zelda F. Gamson, "Collaborative Learning Comes of Age," *Change* 26, no. 5 (1994), 49.

20. Pew Higher Education Roundtable, "To Dance with Change," 2A.

21. Kenneth E. Eble, *The Art of Administration* (San Francisco: Jossey-Bass, 1981), 10.

22. Jeanne Neff, "The New American College," unpublished position paper developed for "The New American College" study group, August 21, 1992, 12.

23. Arthur Levine, "Student Expectations of College," *Change* 25, no. 5 (1993), 4.

24. The 1964 survey is discussed in Gould, "The Academic Deanship," 41–51; the 1988 survey is discussed in Marchese, "Chief Academic Officer," 3–6.

25. Edwin L. Lyle, "Should the Dean Teach?" *Liberal Education* 44 (1963), 381.

26. Allan Tucker and Robert A. Bryan, *The Academic Dean: Dove, Dragon, Diplomat*, 2d ed. (New York: American Council on Education and Macmillan, 1991), 266.

27. Ibid., 6.

28. DiSalvo, "Reflections on the Revolution in Telecommunications," 8.

29. Suzanne S. Brown, "Strengthening Ties to Academic Affairs," in *New Futures for Student Affairs*, by Margaret J. Barr, M. Lee Upcraft, and associates (San Francisco: Jossey-Bass, 1990), 245–46, 248–53.

30. Pew Higher Education Roundtable, "To Dance with Change," 8A.

31. Janny Scott, "Journeys from Ivory Tower: Public Intellectual Is Reborn," *New York Times*, August 9, 1994, B4.

32. The authors acknowledge special contributions by the following individuals to the section on characteristics of the new chief academic officer: Michael A. Baer, provost, Northeastern University; James R. Coffman, provost, Kansas State University; Michael C. Gallagher, president, Mesa State College; Alice Bourke Hayes, president, University of San Diego; Georgia E. Lesh-Laurie, interim chancellor, University of Colorado at Denver; and Jeanne Neff, president, The Sage Colleges.

Chapter 2. Faculty Relations and Professional Development

1. William H. Bergquist, *The Four Cultures of the Academy: Insights and Strategies for Improving Leadership in Collegiate Organizations* (San Francisco: Jossey-Bass, 1992), 44.

2. Bergquist, *The Four Cultures of the Academy*, 47.

3. See *Policy Perspectives*, published by the Pew Higher Education Roundtable, especially, "Cross Currents," "A Calling to Account," and "Double Agent." Referring to the demographic changes affecting higher education, Arthur Levine predicts, "These realities point to a period of adversity for colleges and universities as bad as any in the memory of those living today." *Shaping Higher Education's Future: Demographic Realities and Opportunities, 1990–2000* (San Francisco: Jossey-Bass, 1989), 170.

4. "The Lattice and the Ratchet," *Policy Perspectives* 2, no. 4 (1990), 5–8.

5. *Colloquy for the Year 2000: A Report Submitted by the President, Edward A. Malloy, C.F.C., to the Trustees of the University of Notre Dame*, May 7, 1993.

6. "Lilly Fellows Program in Humanities and the Arts," *Cresset* 59, no. 6 (1996), 42–43.

7. Robert Boice, *The New Faculty Member: Supporting and Fostering Faculty Development* (San Francisco: Jossey-Bass, 1992), 209–19.

8. Parker Palmer, *To Know as We Are Known* (New York: Harper and Row, 1983); Robert Bellah, *Habits of the Heart: Individualism and Commitment in American Life* (Berkeley: University of California Press, 1985); Ernest L. Boyer, *Campus Life: In Search of Community* (Princeton: Carnegie Foundation for the Advancement of Teaching, 1990).

9. Ernest L. Boyer, *College: The Undergraduate Experience in America* (Princeton: Carnegie Foundation for the Advancement of Teaching, 1987), 41.

10. Boyer, *Campus Life*, 7.

11. For an excellent set of guidelines on new faculty orientation, including a model schedule, see Boice, *The New Faculty Member*, 220–30.

12. Gerald W. Gibson, *Good Start: A Guidebook for New Faculty in Liberal Arts Colleges* (Bolton, Mass.: Anker, 1992).

13. Gibson, *Good Start*, 6.

14. For a thorough review of the literature on faculty development, see Carole Bland and Constance C. Schmitz, "Faculty Vitality on Review: Retrospect and Prospect," *Journal of Higher Education* 59, no. 2 (1988), 190–224.

15. Madeleine J. Goodman, "The Review of Tenured Faculty: A Collegial Model," *Journal of Higher Education* 61, no. 4 (1990), 408–24.

16. Bergquist, *The Four Cultures of the Academy*, 29.

17. For a recent defense of the importance of research in the university, see Jaroslav Pelikan, *The Idea of the University: A Reexamination* (New Haven: Yale University Press, 1992), 78–88. The case for the view that research is not necessary in higher education is made by Ronald Barnett, "Linking Teaching and Research: A Critical Inquiry," *Journal of Higher Education* 63, no. 6 (1992), 619–36.

18. Ernest L. Boyer, *Scholarship Reconsidered: Priorities of the Professoriate* (Princeton: Carnegie Foundation for the Advancement of Teaching, 1990).

19. Ibid., 75.

20. R. Eugene Rice, "Making a Place for the New American Scholar," draft of a discussion paper, American Association for Higher Education Conference on Faculty Roles and Rewards, Atlanta, Ga., January 20, 1996.

21. Trudy W. Banta and associates, *Making a Difference: Outcomes of a Decade of Assessment in Higher Education* (San Francisco: Jossey-Bass, 1993).

22. Elaine El-Khawas, *1993 Campus Trends Survey* (Washington, D.C.: American Council on Education, 1993).

23. G. Bruce Dearing, "The Relation of the Dean to the Faculty," *Journal of General Education* 15 (1963), 191, reprinted in *The Academic Deanship in American Colleges and Universities*, ed. Arthur J. Dibden (Carbondale: Southern Illinois University Press, 1968), 120.

24. Bergquist, *The Four Cultures of the Academy*, 65.

25. Donald C. Bruegman, "A Organizational Model for the 21st Century: Adopting the Corporate Model for Higher Education," *NACUBO Business Officer* 29, no. 5 (1995), 28–31.

26. William M. Plater, "The Future of Tenure: Rotten with Perfection," paper presented at the annual meeting of the American Conference of Academic Deans, Washington, D.C., January 13, 1996.

27. For a description of the post-tenure review system that has been implemented

at the University of Hawaii, see Goodman, "The Review of Tenured Faculty," 410–23.

28. Plater, "The Future of Tenure," 3.

29. Goodman, "The Review of Tenured Faculty," 423.

30. Rice, "Making a Place for the New American Scholar," 1.

31. William M. Plater, "Future Work: Faculty Time in the 21st Century," *Change* 27, no. 3 (1995), 223–33.

32. Rice, "Making a Place for the New American Scholar," 21.

33. Ibid., 22–31.

34. George D. Kuh, "Guiding Principles for Creating Seamless Learning Environments for Undergraduates," *Journal of College Student Development* 37, no. 2 (1996), 135–48.

35. Ernest L. Boyer, "The New American College," *Perspectives* 24, nos. 1 and 2 (1994), 6–11.

36. Carol Everly Floyd, *Faculty Participation in Decision Making*, ERIC Clearinghouse on Higher Education (Washington, D.C.: George Washington University, 1986).

37. Kent John Chabotar, "Managing Participative Budgeting in Higher Education," *Change* 27, no. 5 (1995), 21.

38. Ibid., 23–29.

39. Institute for Research on Higher Education at the University of Pennsylvania, "Leaving Hats at the Door: Themes from the Pew Campus Roundtables," *Change* 28, no. 3 (1996), 51–52.

40. Ibid., 52.

41. Joseph Katz and Mildred Henry, *Turning Professors into Teachers: A New Approach to Faculty Development and Student Learning*, American Council on Education Series on Higher Education, 2d ed. (Phoenix: Oryx Press, 1993), esp. 6–9.

42. Jane Kendall, *Combining Service and Learning* (Raleigh, N.C.: National Society for Experiential Education, 1990).

43. Boyer, *College*, 218.

44. Assistance in establishing service learning programs may be obtained from Campus Compact: The Project for Public and Community Service at Brown University.

Chapter 3. Leveraging Resources to Enhance Quality

1. Gordon Winston, "The Decline in Undergraduate Teaching," *Change* 26, no. 5 (1994), 8–15.

2. Martin Anderson, *Imposters in the Temple* (New York: Simon and Schuster, 1992), 31–38.

3. Michael J. Albright and David L. Graf, *Teaching in the Information Age: The Role of Educational Technology*, in New Directions for Teaching and Learning, no. 51 (San Francisco: Jossey-Bass, 1992), 7–15; and Ernest Boyer, *Scholarship Reconsidered: Priorities of the Professoriate* (Princeton: Carnegie Foundation for the Advancement of Teaching, 1990), 15–25.

4. Harold L. Hodgkinson, *A Demographic Look at Tomorrow* (Washington, D.C.: Institute for Education Leadership, 1992), 10–11.

5. Ibid., 14.

6. Anderson, *Imposters in the Temple*, 38–42.

7. Boyer, *Scholarship Reconsidered*. For contextual thinking as to attaching value to the diverse work of the university, including teaching, learning, and curriculum design, the entire book is essential.

8. Pew Higher Education Research Program, "Keeping the Promise," *Policy Perspectives* 4, no. 4 (1992): 1A–8A. This article should be read in its entirety.

9. Alan E. Guskin, "Reducing Student Costs and Enhancing Student Learning: Part 2, Restructuring the Role of the Faculty," *Change* 26, no. 5 (1994), 16–25.

10. Carol A. Twigg, "The Need for a National Learning Infrastructure," *EDUCOM Review* 29, no. 5 (1994), 16–20.

11. Christopher Knapper, "Large Classes and Learning," in *Teaching Large Classes Well*, in New Directions for Teaching and Learning, ed. Maryellen Gleason Weimer, no. 32 (San Francisco: Jossey-Bass, 1987), 5–15.

12. Peter J. Frederick, "Student Involvement: Active Learning in Large Classes," in *Teaching Large Classes Well*, New Directions for Teaching and Learning, ed. Maryellen Gleason Weimer, no. 32 (San Francisco: Jossey-Bass, 1987), 45–56.

13. Ibid.

14. Jane Mouton and Robert Blake, *Synergogy* (San Francisco: Jossey-Bass, 1984), 144–59.

15. Pew Higher Education Research Program, "Keeping the Promise."

16. Winston, "The Decline in Undergraduate Teaching," 8–15.

17. Ibid.

18. Thomas H. Jackson, "The Complicated Balance between Teaching and Research at Universities" (excerpt), *Policy Perspectives* 4, no. 4 (1993), 1B–2B.

19. Winston, "The Decline in Undergraduate Teaching," 8–15; Russell Edgerton, "A National Market for Excellence in Teaching," *Change* 26, no. 5 (1994), 4–5.

20. William Geoghegan, "Stuck at the Barricades," *AAHE* [American Association for Higher Education] *Bulletin* 47, no. 1 (1994), 13–15.

21. Judith V. Boettcher, ed. *101 Success Stories of Information Technology in Higher Education: The Joe Wyatt Challenge* (New York: McGraw-Hill, 1993). The entire book provides splendid examples from which to draw.

Chapter 4. Academic Governance

1. Robert Birnbaum, *How Colleges Work: The Cybernetics of Academic Organization and Leadership* (San Francisco: Jossey-Bass, 1988), 4.

2. Ibid., 5.

3. Henry Rosovsky, *The University: An Owner's Manual* (New York: W. W. Norton), 243.

4. G. D. Kuh and E. J. Whitt, *The Invisible Tapestry: Culture in American Colleges and Universities*, ASHE-ERIC Higher Education Report, no. 1 (Washington, D.C.: Association for the Study of Higher Education, 1988), 13.

5. W. G. Tierney, "Organizational Culture in Higher Education: Defining the Essentials," *Journal of Higher Education* 59, no. 1 (1988), 5.

6. Rosovsky, *The University*, 245.

7. Birnbaum, *How Colleges Work*, 222–23.

8. Ibid.

9. American Association of University Professors, "Joint Statement on Government of Colleges and Universities," in *AAUP Policy Documents and Reports, 1984 Edition* (Washington, D.C.: American Association of University Professors, 1984).

10. Ibid., 109.

11. Pew Higher Education Roundtable, "To Dance with Change," *Policy Perspectives* 5, no. 3 (1994), A2.

12. Ibid., A1.

13. Pew Higher Education Roundtable, "A Calling to Account," *Policy Perspectives* 6, no. 2 (1995), 5.

14. Alan E. Guskin, "Reducing Student Costs and Enhancing Student Learning: Part 1, The University Challenge of the 1990s," *Change* 26, no. 4 (1994), 28.

15. Alan E. Guskin, "Reducing Students Costs and Enhancing Student Learning: Part 2, Restructuring the Role of the Faculty," *Change* 26, no. 5 (1994), 16, 18.

16. Lee G. Bolman and Terrence Deal, *Reframing Organizations: Artistry, Choice, and Leadership* (San Francisco: Jossey-Bass, 1991), 447.

17. Birnbaum, *How Colleges Work*, 209.

18. William F. Massy, Andrea K. Wilger, and Carol Colbeck, "Overcoming 'Hollowed' Collegiality," *Change* 26, no. 4 (1994), 11–20.

19. Kenneth P. Mortimer and Annette C. Caruse, "The Process of Academic Governance and the Painful Choices of the 1980's," in *Leadership Roles of Chief Academic Officers*, New Directions for Higher Education, ed. David G. Brown, no. 47 (San Francisco: Jossey-Bass, 1984), 45–46.

Chapter 5. Shaping the Leadership Team

1. Robert Birnbaum, *How Academic Leadership Works* (San Francisco: Jossey-Bass, 1992), 38–39.

2. J. J. Lathrop, "Sharing leadership: The Nature of Relationships between Presidents and Chief Academic Officers in Colleges and Universities," Ed.D. diss., Teachers College, Columbia University, 1990; cited in Birnbaum, *How Academic Leadership Works*, 38–39.

3. Cyril O. Houle, *Governing Boards: Their Nature and Nurture* (San Francisco: Jossey-Bass, 1989), 10–11.

4. Patricia Plante and Robert L. Caret, *Myths and Realities of Academic Administration* (New York: American Council on Education and Macmillan, 1990), 139.

5. John A. Witt, *Building a Better Hospital Board* (Ann Arbor, Mich: Health Administration Press and the Foundation of the American College of Healthcare Executives, 1987), 23–24.

6. Jonathan R. Cole, "Balancing Acts: Dilemmas of Choice Facing Research Universities," *Daedalus* 122 (1993): 1–36.

7. Donald Kennedy, "Making Choices in the Research University," *Daedalus* 122 (1993): 127–56.

8. Houle, *Governing Boards*, 95.

9. Barbara E. Taylor, *Working Effectively with Trustees: Building Cooperative Campus Leadership*, ASHE-ERIC Higher Education Reports, no. 2 (Washington, D.C.: Association for the Study of Higher Education, 1987), 3–6.

10. Houle, *Governing Boards*, 112; Taylor, *Working Effectively with Trustees*, 76–77.

11. Peter F. Drucker, "Lessons for Successful Nonprofit Governance," *Nonprofit Management and Leadership* 1 (1990): 7–14.

12. James E. Orlikoff, "Trustee Orientation: The Basic Building Block of Board Effectiveness," *Trustee* (1992), 12–13, 22.

13. Richard J. Mahoney, "Chair of the Department of Junkyard Dog: Can Business Redesign Work for the University?" *Business/Higher Education Forum*, February 11, 1994.

14. American Association of University Professors, "Joint Statement on Government of Colleges and Universities," in *AAUP Policy Documents and Reports, 1984 Edition* (Washington, D.C.: American Association of University Professors, 1984).

15. Jerry N. Boone et al. "University Autonomy: Perceived and Preferred Location of Higher Authority," *Review of Higher Education* 14 (1991): 135–53.

16. Taylor, *Working Effectively with Trustees*, 75.

17. Clark Kerr and Marian L. Gade, *The Guardians: Boards of Trustees of American Colleges and Universities* (Washington, D.C.: Association of Governing Boards of Universities and Colleges, 1989).

18. Ibid.

Chapter 6. Creating Common Ground

1. Allan Bloom, *The Closing of the American Mind* (New York: Simon and Schuster, 1987), 346.

2. Maxine Greene, "Diversity and Inclusion: Toward a Curriculum for Human Beings," *Teachers College Record* 95, no. 2 (1993), 211–21.

3. Alexander Astin, *What Matters in College: Four Critical Years Revisited* (San Francisco: Jossey-Bass, 1993).

4. Richard C. Richardson Jr. and Elizabeth Fisk Skinner, "Adapting to Diversity: Organizational Influences on Student Achievement," *Journal of Higher Education* 61, no. 5 (1990), 485–511.

5. Richard C. Richardson Jr., "Six Ways Universities Can Maintain Quality and Diversity," *Education Digest* 56, no. 5 (1991): 22–25.

6. Richard C. Richardson Jr. and Elizabeth Fisk Skinner, *Achieving Quality and Diversity: Universities in a Multicultural Society* (New York: American Council on Education and Macmillan, 1991).

7. Alexander Astin, *What Matters in College* (San Francisco: Jossey-Bass, 1993), 398.

8. Ibid., 415.

9. Ibid., 398.

10. Ibid., 431.

11. Betty Friedan's book was published in 1963, the same year that a whole generation of middle-class women watched as Jackie Kennedy was suddenly wrenched from her role as the nation's Ideal Wife by her husband's assassination. Soon, she was reduced to being the derided object of tabloid photographers and paparazzi, as though the identity and respect she had earned as First Lady no longer had meaning.

12. Mary Field Belenky, Blythe McVickar Clinchy, Nancy Rule Goldberger, and Jill Mattuck Tarule, *Women's Ways of Knowing: The Development of Self, Voice, and Mind* (New York: Basic Books, 1986), 141.

Chapter 7. Enrollment Management

1. D. Hossler, *Enrollment Management: An Integrated Approach* (New York: College Entrance Examination Board, 1984), 5.

2. P. Kotler and K. Fox, *Strategic Marketing for Educational Institutions* (Englewood Cliffs, N.J.: Prentice Hall, 1985), 7.

3. V. Tinto, *Leaving College: Rethinking the Causes and Cures of Student Attrition* (Chicago: University of Chicago Press, 1987), 91.

4. Coopers and Lybrand L.L.P., *Reinventing the University: Managing and Financing Institutions of Higher Education*, ed. Sandra L. Johnson and Sean C. Rush (New York: John Wiley and Sons, 1995), 105.

5. L. H. Litten, *Ivy Bound: High-Ability Students and College Choice* (New York: College Entrance Examination Board, 1991). This work is a treatment of the college choice process; the entire work is devoted to the point.

6. R. Zemsky and P. Oedel, *The Structure of College Choice* (New York: College Entrance Examination Board, 1983). Zemsky and Oedel provide a historical model; the entire work is devoted to the point.

7. K. Ciompi, *How Colleges Choose Students* (New York: College Entrance Examination Board, 1993), 12–17.

8. J. J. Scannell, *The Effect of Financial Aid Policies on Admission and Enrollment* (New York: College Entrance Examination Board, 1992), 53–65.

Chapter 8. Financial Management and Budget Planning

1. American Council on Education, *Campus Trends 1994* (Washington, D.C.: American Council on Education, 1994), 8.

2. Edward R. Hines, G. Alan Hickrod, and Gwen B. Pruyne, *State Support for Higher Education: From Expansion to Steady State to Decline, 1969–1989*, MacArthur/Spencer Series, no. 9 (Normal, Ill.: Center for Education Finance and Higher Education, 1989).

3. American Council on Education, *Campus Trends 1994*, 10.

4. Western Interstate Commission for Higher Education, *Reports on Higher Education in the West* (Boulder, Colo.: Western Interstate Commission for Higher Education, 1994), 1.

5. Ibid., 2.

6. Pew Higher Education Research Program, "A Call to Meeting," *Policy Perspectives* 6, no. 4 (1993), 6.

7. Robert N. Anthony, John Dearden, and Vijay Govindarajan, *Management Control Systems* (Homewood, Ill.: Richard D. Irwin, 1992), 46.

8. Shahid Ansari and Jan Bell, "Symbolic, Behavioral, and Economic Roles of Control in Organizations and Society," in *Accounting Control Systems: A Technical, Social, and Behavioral Integration*, ed. Jan Bell (New York: Markus Wiener, 1991), 16.

9. National Association of College and University Business Officers, *Financial Accounting and Reporting Manual for Higher Education* (Washington, D.C.: National Association of College and University Business Officers, 1990), 300 ff.

10. Vijay Govindarajan, "Impact of Participation in the Budget Process on Managerial Attitudes and Performance: Universalistic and Contingency Perspectives," *Decision Sciences* 17, no. 4 (1986), 511.

11. Mitzi Leung and Alan S. Dunkl, "The Effects of Managerial Roles on the Relationship between Budgetary Participation and Job Satisfaction," *Accounting and Finance* 32, no. 1 (1992), 9.

12. Frank Collins, Paul Munter, and Don W. Finn, "The Budgeting Games People Play," *Accounting Review* 62, no. 1 (1987), 48–49.

13. Chris Argyris, *The Impact of Budgets on People* (Ithaca, N.Y.: Controllership Foundation, 1952).

14. A. C. Stedry, *Budget Control and Cost Behavior* (Englewood Cliffs, N.J.: Prentice-Hall, 1960).

15. Alan E. Guskin, "Reducing Student Costs and Enhancing Learning: Part 2, Restructuring the Role of Faculty," *Change* 26, no. 5 (1994), 25.

16. Robin Wilson, "Professional Peons," *Crosstalk* [Publication of the California Higher Education Policy Center] 2, no. 3 (1994), 10.

Chapter 9. Managing a Cross-Cultural Experience

1. The best information is available from the U.S. Government Printing Office, Washington, D.C. References can also be found on the Internet at http://marvel.loc.gov.

2. A recent publication by the Institute for Management in Higher Education of the Organization of Economic Cooperation and Development by Hans de Wit, highlights the contrasts between Europe and North America on these issues. See *A Comparative Study of Australia, Canada, Europe, and the United States of America* (Amsterdam: European Association for International Education in cooperation with IMHE-OECD and the Association of International Education Administrators, 1995).

3. Dr. Harrison Shull, former provost of the Naval Postgraduate School and of Rensselaer Polytechnic Institute, in particular, provided useful observations on these topics.

Chapter 10. External Relations and Institutional Advancement

The author wishes to thank David Groth, Barbara Schneider, Edward Nuhfer, and MaryLou Fenili for their critiques of the original manuscript. Thanks are also due to Kristine Zewe for her preparations of the chapter.

1. A helpful resource organization for the issues raised in this chapter is: Council for Advancement and Support of Education, 11 Dupont Circle, Suite 400, Washington, D.C. 20036-1261.

2. Johnetta B. Cole and Roger H. Nozaki, "Out of the Ivory Tower and into the Streets," *Trusteeship* 5 (September/October 1994), 26–29.

3. Lee Teitel, *The Advisory Committee Advantage: Creating an Effective Strategy for Programmatic Improvement*, ASHE-ERIC Higher Education Report, no. 1 (Washington, D.C.: George Washington University, 1994).

4. "Sacred Landmarks of Cleveland," special issue of the *Gamut*, February 1991.

Chapter 11. College Legal Counsel and the Chief Academic Officer

1. Wayne A. Hill Jr., "Americans with Disabilities Act of 1990: Significant Overlap with Section 504 for Colleges and Universities," *Journal of College and University Law* 18, no. 3 (1992): 415.

Chapter 12. Conclusion

1. Richard P. Chait, "The Future of Academic Tenure," *Priorities* [Association of Governing Boards of Universities and Colleges] 3 (1995), 3.

2. Louis Uchitelle, "The Rise of the Losing Class," *New York Times*, November 20, 1994, final edition, sec. 4, p. 1, col. 1.

3. Ibid.

4. "It has been said that, in the eighteenth and for much of the nineteenth centuries, trustees were the dominant force in American higher education, with the latter decades of the nineteenth and the early decades of the twentieth centuries being an era of presidential dominance, which was superseded by the growing triumph of the faculty by midcentury." Joseph F. Kauffman, "Governing Boards," in *Higher Learning in America: 1980–2000*, ed. Arthur Levine (Baltimore: Johns Hopkins University Press, 1983), 223.

5. K. Scott Hughes, "Transforming Academic Institutions: Colleges and Universities Respond to Changes in Society," *NACUBO Business Officer* 29, no. 2 (1995), 23.

6. Pew Higher Education Roundtable, "A Calling to Account," *Policy Perspectives* 6, no. 2, (1995), 4A.

7. Donald C. Bruegman, "An Organizational Model for the 21st Century: Adopting the Corporate Model for Higher Education," *NACUBO Business Officer* 29, no. 5 (1995), 29.

8. Ibid., 28.

9. Ibid.

10. David H. Entin, "A Second Look: TQM in Ten Boston-Area Colleges, One Year Later," *AAHE* [American Association for Higher Education] *Bulletin* 46, no. 9 (1994), 4.

11. Technology and Restructuring Roundtable, *Leveraged Learning: Technology's Role in Restructuring Higher Education* (Stanford, Calif.: Stanford [University] Forum for Higher Education Futures, 1995), 14.

12. William F. Massy and Andrea K. Wilger, "Improving Productivity: What Faculty Think about It—And Its Effect on Quality," *Change* 27, no. 4 (1995), 20.

13. Robert Hahn, "Getting Serious about Presidential Leadership: Our Collective Responsibility," *Change* 27, no. 5 (1995), 14.

14. Graham Gibbs, "Promoting Excellent Teaching Is Harder Than You'd Think: A Note from an Outside Observer of the Roles and Rewards Initiative," *Change* 27, no. 3 (1995), 19.

15. See James Martin, James E. Samels, and associates, *Merging Colleges for Mutual Growth: A New Strategy for Academic Managers* (Baltimore: Johns Hopkins University Press, 1994); Michael Y. Yoshino and U. Srinivasa Rangan, *Strategic Alliances: An Entrepreneurial Approach to Globalization* (Cambridge, Mass.: Harvard Business School Press, 1995); and Robert L. Breuder, "Merger: The Opportunities and Challenges of Institutional Partnership," *Educational Record* 77, no. 1 (1996), 46–52.

16. Zelda Gamson, "Collaborative Learning Comes of Age," *Change* 26, no. 5 (1994), 47, 49.

17. George R. Boggs, "The Learning Paradigm," *Community College Journal* 66, no. 3 (1995–96), 26.

Bibliography

Albright, Michael J., and David L. Graf. *Teaching in the Information Age: The Role of Educational Technology*. New Directions for Teaching and Learning, no. 51. San Francisco: Jossey-Bass, 1992.

American Association of University Professors. "Joint Statement on Government of Colleges and Universities." In *AAUP Policy Documents and Reports, 1984 Edition*. Washington, D.C.: American Association of University Professors, 1984.

American Council on Education. *Campus Trends 1994*. Washington, D.C.: American Council on Education, 1994.

————. "Tuition Increase Rate Continues to Decline." *Higher Education and National Affairs* 43, no. 18 (1994): 2.

Anderson, Martin. *Imposters in the Temple*. New York: Simon and Schuster, 1992.

Anderson, Richard E., and Joel W. Meyerson, eds. *Financial Planning under Economic Uncertainty*. New Directions for Higher Education, no. 69. San Francisco: Jossey-Bass, 1990.

————. *Productivity in Higher Education: Improving the Effectiveness of Faculty, Facilities, and Financial Resources*. Princeton: Peterson's Guides, 1992.

Anthony, Robert N., John Dearden, and Vijay Govindarajan. *Management Control Systems*. Homewood, Ill.: Richard D. Irwin, 1992.

Ansari, Shahid, and Jan Bell. "Symbolic, Behavioral, and Economic Roles of Control in Organizations and Society." In *Accounting Control Systems: A Technical, Social, and Behavioral Integration*, edited by Jan Bell. New York: Markus Wiener, 1991.

Argyris, Chris. *The Impact of Budgets on People*. Ithaca, N.Y.: Controllership Foundation, 1952.

Association of Governing Boards of Universities and Colleges. *Trustees and Troubled Times in Higher Education*. Washington, D.C.: Association of Governing Boards of Universities and Colleges, 1992.

Astin, Alexander W. "Involvement in Learning Revisited: Lessons We Have Learned." *Journal of College Student Development* 37, no. 2 (1996): 123–33.

————. *What Matters in College: Four Critical Years Revisited*. San Francisco: Jossey-Bass, 1993.

219

Austin, Ann E., and Zelda F. Gamson. *Academic Workplace: New Demands, Heightened Tensions*. ASHE-ERIC Higher Education Report, no. 10. Washington, D.C.: George Washington University, 1983.

Balderston, Frederick E. *Managing Today's University*. San Francisco: Jossey-Bass, 1974.

Baldridge, J. Victor, David V. Curtis, George Ecker, and Gary L. Riley. "Alternative Models of Governance in Higher Education." In *Governing Academic Organizations: New Problems, New Perspectives*, edited by Gary L. Riley and J. Victor Baldridge. Berkeley, Calif.: McCutchan, 1977.

Banta, Trudy W., and associates. *Making a Difference: Outcomes of a Decade of Assessment in Higher Education*. San Francisco: Jossey-Bass, 1993.

Barnett, Ronald. "Linking Teaching and Research: A Critical Inquiry." *Journal of Higher Education* 63, no. 6 (1992): 619–36.

Beckham, J. "Reasonable Independence for Public Higher Education: Legal Implications of Constitutionally Autonomous Status." *Journal of Law and Education* 7, no. 2 (1978): 177–92.

Belenky, Mary Field, Blythe McVickar Clinchy, Nancy Rule Goldberger, and Jill Mattuck Tarule. *Women's Ways of Knowing: The Development of Self, Voice, and Mind*. New York: Basic Books, 1986.

Bellah, Robert. *Habits of the Heart: Individualism and Commitment in American Life*. Berkeley: University of California Press, 1985.

Bennett, B. *Risky Business: Risk Management, Loss Prevention, and Insurance Procurement for Colleges and Universities*. Washington, D.C.: National Association of College and University Attorneys, 1990.

Bensimon, Estela M., and Anna Neumann. *Redesigning Collegiate Leadership: Teams and Teamwork in Higher Education*. Baltimore: Johns Hopkins University Press, 1993.

Bensimon, Estela M., Anna Neumann, and Robert Birnbaum. *Making Sense of Administrative Leadership: The "L" Word in Higher Education*. ASHE-ERIC Higher Education Report, no. 1. Washington, D.C.: George Washington University, 1989.

Bergquist, William H. *The Four Cultures of the Academy: Insights and Strategies for Improving Leadership in Collegiate Organizations*. San Francisco: Jossey-Bass, 1992.

Bess, James L. *Collegiality and Bureaucracy in the Modern University: The Influence of Information and Power on Decision-making Structures*. New York: Teachers College Press, 1988.

Birnbaum, Robert. *How Academic Leadership Works*. San Francisco: Jossey-Bass, 1992.

———. *How Colleges Work: The Cybernetics of Academic Organization and Leadership*. San Francisco: Jossey-Bass, 1988.

Bland, Carole, and Constance C. Schmitz. "Faculty Vitality on Review: Retrospect and Prospect." *Journal of Higher Education* 59, no. 2 (1988): 190–224.

Bloom, Allen. *The Closing of the American Mind*. New York: Simon and Schuster, 1987.

Boettcher, Judith V., ed. *101 Success Stories of Information Technology in Higher Education: The Joe Wyatt Challenge*. New York: McGraw-Hill, 1993.

Boggs, George R. "The Learning Paradigm." *Community College Journal* 66, no. 3 (1995–96): 24–27.

Bogue, E. Grady. *Leadership by Design: Strengthening Integrity in Higher Education.* San Francisco: Jossey-Bass, 1994.

Boice, Robert. *The New Faculty Member: Supporting and Fostering Faculty Development.* San Francisco: Jossey-Bass, 1992.

Bolman, Lee G., and Terrence E. Deal. *Reframing Organizations: Artistry, Choice, and Leadership.* San Francisco: Jossey-Bass, 1991.

Boone, Jerry N., et al. "University Autonomy: Perceived and Preferred Location of Higher Authority." *Review of Higher Education* 14 (1991): 135–53.

Boyer, Ernest L. *Campus Life: In Search of Community.* Princeton: Carnegie Foundation for the Advancement of Teaching, 1990.

———. *College: The Undergraduate Experience in America.* Princeton: Carnegie Foundation for the Advancement of Teaching, 1987.

———. "The New American College." *Perspectives* 24, nos. 1 and 2 (1994): 6–11.

———. *Scholarship Reconsidered: Priorities of the Professoriate.* Princeton: Carnegie Foundation for the Advancement of Teaching, 1990.

Breuder, Robert L. "Merger: The Opportunities and Challenges of Institutional Partnership." *Educational Record* 77, no. 1 (1996): 46–52.

Brewster, Kingman, Jr. "Politics of Academia." In *Power and Authority: Transformation of Campus Governance,* edited by Harold L. Hodgkinson and L. Richard Meeth. San Francisco: Jossey-Bass, 1976.

Brown, David G., ed. *Leadership Roles of Chief Academic Officers.* New Directions for Higher Education, ed. Martin Kramer, no. 47. San Francisco: Jossey-Bass, 1984.

Brown, Louis M. "Introducing a Legal Audit Manual: Procedure and Substance, Part One." *Preventive Law Reporter* 2, no. 6 (1984): 162–68.

———. "Legal Checkup, Legal Audit, and Bankruptcy." *Preventive Law Reporter* 4, no. 2 (1985): 42–45.

———. *Preventive Law Manual for Periodic Legal Checkup.* N.p.: PL Publishers, 1983.

Brown, Louis M., and E. Dauer. *Planning by Lawyers: Materials on a Nonadversarial Legal Process.* Mineola, N.Y.: Foundation Press, 1978.

Brown, Suzanne S. "Strengthening Ties to Academic Affairs." In *New Futures for Student Affairs,* by Margaret J. Barr, M. Lee Upcraft, and associates, 239–69. San Francisco: Jossey-Bass, 1990.

Bruegman, Donald C. "An Organizational Model for the 21st Century: Adopting the Corporate Model for Higher Education." *NACUBO Business Officer* 29, no. 5 (1995): 28–31.

Bruffee, Kenneth A. *Collaborative Learning: Higher Education, Interdependence, and the Authority of Knowledge.* Baltimore: Johns Hopkins University Press, 1993.

Burns, Gerald P., ed. *Administrators in Higher Education: Their Functions and Coordination.* New York: Harper and Brothers, 1962.

Burns, Norman, ed. *The Administration of Higher Institutions under Changing Conditions.* Chicago: University of Chicago Press, 1947.

Chabotar, Kent John. "Managing Participative Budgeting in Higher Education." *Change* 27, no. 5 (1995): 21–29.

Chaffee, Ellen Earle, and William G. Tierney. *Collegiate Culture and Leadership Strategies*. New York: American Council on Education and Macmillan, 1988.

Chait, Richard. "The Decade of Trustees." In *An Agenda for the New Decade*. New Directions for Higher Education, ed. Larry W. Jones and Franz A. Nowotny, no. 70. San Francisco: Jossey-Bass, 1990.

———. "The Future of Academic Tenure." *Priorities* [Association of Governing Boards of Universities and Colleges] 3 (1995): 1–12.

Ciompi, K. *How Colleges Choose Students*. New York: College Entrance Examination Board, 1993.

Cleveland, Harlan. "The Dean's Dilemma: Leadership of Equals." *Public Administration Review* 20 (1960): 22–27.

Cohen, Arthur M., and Florence B. Brawer. *Managing Community Colleges*. San Francisco: Jossey-Bass, 1994.

Cole, Elsa Kircher, and Barbara L. Shiels. *Student Legal Issues*. Washington, D.C.: National Association of College and University Attorneys, 1989.

Cole, Johnnetta B., and Roger H. Nozaki. "Out of the Ivory Tower and into the Streets." *Trusteeship* 5 (September/October 1994): 26–29.

Cole, Jonathan R. "Balancing Acts: Dilemmas of Choice Facing Research Universities." *Daedalus* 122 (1993): 1–36.

Collins, Frank, Paul Munter, and Don W. Finn. "The Budgeting Games People Play." *Accounting Review* 62, no. 1 (1987): 29–49.

Collis, John. *Educational Malpractice: Liability of Educators, School Administrators, and School Officials*. Charlottesville, Va.: Michie Company, 1990.

Colloquy for the Year 2000: A Report Submitted by the President, Edward A. Malloy, C.S.C., to the Trustees of the University of Notre Dame. May 7, 1993.

Commission on Institutions of Higher Education. *Standards for Accreditation*. Burlington, Mass.: New England Association of Schools and Colleges, 1992.

Coopers and Lybrand L.L.P. *Reinventing the University: Managing and Financing Institutions of Higher Education*, edited by Sandra L. Johnson and Sean C. Rush. New York: John Wiley and Sons, 1995.

Corson, John J. *Governance of Colleges and Universities*. New York: McGraw-Hill, 1960.

Cross, K. Patricia. "Academic Citizenship." *AAHE* [American Association for Higher Education] *Bulletin* 47, no. 2 (1994): 3–5, 10.

Daane, Roderick. "The Role of University Counsel." *Journal of College and University Law* 12, no. 3 (1985): 399–414.

Dearing, G. Bruce. "The Relation of the Dean to the Faculty." *Journal of General Education* 15 (1963): 191–201. Reprinted in Arthur J. Dibden, ed., *The Academic Deanship in American Colleges and Universities*, Carbondale: Southern Illinois University Press, 1968, 120–32.

Deferrari, Roy J. *The Problems of Administration in the American College*. Washington, D.C.: Catholic University of America Press, 1956.

DeVane, William C. "The Role of the Dean of the College." In *The Academic Deanship in American Colleges and Universities*, edited by Arthur J. Dibden, 241–52. Carbondale: Southern Illinois University Press, 1968.

Dibden, Arthur J., ed. *The Academic Deanship in American Colleges and Universities*. Carbondale: Southern Illinois University Press, 1968.

DiSalvo, David. "Reflections on the Revolution in Telecommunications: An Interview with George Gilder." *Campus* 5, no. 2 (1994): 8–9.

Dupont, Gerald E. "The Dean and His Office." In *The Academic Deanship in American Colleges and Universities*, edited by Arthur J. Dibden, 4–27. Carbondale: Southern Illinois University Press, 1968.

Drucker, Peter F. "Lessons for Successful Nonprofit Governance." *Nonprofit Management and Leadership* 1 (1990): 7–14.

Eames, P., and Thomas P. Hustoles. *Legal Issues in Faculty Employment*. Washington, D.C.: National Association of College and University Attorneys, 1989.

Eble, Kenneth E. *The Art of Administration*. San Francisco: Jossey-Bass, 1981.

Edgerton, Russell. "A National Market for Excellence in Teaching." *Change* 26, no. 5 (1994): 4–5.

Eliot, Charles William. *University Administration*. Boston: Houghton Mifflin, 1908.

El-Khawas, Elaine. *1993 Campus Trends Survey*. Washington, D.C.: American Council on Education, 1993.

Enarson, Harold. "The Academic Vice President or Dean." In *The Academic Deanship in American Colleges and Universities*, edited by Arthur J. Dibden, 57–72. Carbondale: Southern Illinois University Press, 1968.

Entin, David H. "A Second Look: TQM in Ten Boston-Area Colleges, One Year Later." *AAHE* [American Association for Higher Education] *Bulletin* 46, no. 9 (1994): 3–7.

Epstein, Norman L. "The Use and Misuse of College and University Counsel." *Journal of Higher Education* 45 (1974): 635–39.

Fife, Jonathan D., and Lester F. Goodchild, eds. *Administration as a Profession*. New Directions for Higher Education, no. 76. San Francisco: Jossey-Bass, 1991.

Fincher, Cameron. "Administrative Leadership in Higher Education." In *Higher Education: Handbook of Theory and Research*, vol. 3, edited by John C. Smart. New York: Agathon Press, 1987.

Fishbein, Estelle A. "New Strings on the Ivory Tower: The Growth of Accountability in Colleges and Universities." *Journal of College and University Law* 12, no. 3 (1985): 381–98.

Floyd, Carol Everly. *Faculty Participation in Decision Making*. ERIC Clearinghouse on Higher Education. Washington, D.C.: George Washington University, 1986.

Frederick, Peter J. "Student Involvement: Active Learning in Large Classes." In *Teaching Large Classes Well*, edited by Maryellen Gleason Weimer. New Directions for Teaching and Learning, no. 32. San Francisco: Jossey-Bass, 1987.

Fryer, Thomas W., Jr., and John C. Lovas. *Leadership in Governance*. San Francisco: Jossey-Bass, 1990.

Gamson, Zelda F. "Collaborative Learning Comes of Age." *Change* 26, no. 5 (1994): 44–49.

Geoghegan, William. "Stuck at the Barricades." *AAHE* [American Association for Higher Education] *Bulletin* 47, no. 1 (1994): 13–15.

Gibbs, Graham. "Promoting Excellent Teaching Is Harder Than You'd Think: A Note from an Outside Observer of the Roles and Rewards Initiative." *Change* 27, no. 3 (1995): 17–20.

Gibson, Gerald W. *Good Start: A Guidebook for New Faculty in Liberal Arts Colleges*. Bolton, Mass.: Anker, 1992.

Gilmore, Thomas North. *Making a Leadership Change: How Organizations and*

Leaders Can Handle Leadership Transitions Successfully. San Francisco: Jossey-Bass, 1989.

Goodman, Madeleine J. "The Review of Tenured Faculty: A Collegial Model." *Journal of Higher Education* 61, no. 4 (1990): 408–24.

Gould, John W. *The Academic Deanship.* New York: Published for the Institute of Higher Education by the Bureau of Publications, Teachers College, Columbia University, 1964.

———. "The Academic Deanship: A Summary and Perspective." In *The Academic Deanship in American Colleges and Universities,* edited by Arthur J. Dibden, 41–51. Carbondale: Southern Illinois University Press, 1968.

Govindarajan, Vijay. "Impact of Participation in the Budget Process on Managerial Attitudes and Performance: Universalistic and Contingency Perspectives." *Decisions Sciences* 17, no. 4 (1986): 459–516.

Greene, Maxine. "Diversity and Inclusion: Toward a Curriculum for Human Beings." *Teachers College Record* 95, no. 2 (1993): 211–21.

Guskin, Alan E. "Reducing Student Costs and Enhancing Student Learning: Part 1, The University Challenge of the 1990s." *Change* 26, no. 4 (1994): 22–29.

———. "Reducing Student Costs and Enhancing Student Learning: Part 2, Restructuring the Role of the Faculty." *Change* 26, no. 5 (1994): 16–25.

Hahn, Robert. "Getting Serious about Presidential Leadership: Our Collective Responsibility." *Change* 27, no. 5 (1995): 13–19.

Hawkes, Herbert, and Anna Rose. *Through a Dean's Open Door.* New York: McGraw-Hill, 1945.

Hetrick, Robert C., Jr. "Technological Change and Higher Education Policy." *Priorities* [Association of Governing Boards of Universities and Colleges] 1 (1994).

Higgerson, Mary Lou, and Susan S. Rehwaldt. *Complexities of Higher Education Administration: Case Studies and Issues.* Bolton, Mass.: Anker, 1993.

Higgins, Ruth L. "The Functions of the Academic Dean." *Association of American Colleges Bulletin* 33 (1947): 393–99.

Hill, Wayne A., Jr. "Americans with Disabilities Act of 1990: Significant Overlap with Section 504 for Colleges and Universities." *Journal of College and University Law* 18, no. 3 (1992): 389–417.

Hines, Edward R., G. Alan Hickrod, and Gwen B. Pruyne. *State Support for Higher Education: From Expansion to Steady State to Decline, 1969–1989.* MacArthur/Spencer Series, no. 9. Normal, Ill.: Center for Education Finance and Higher Education, 1989.

Hodgkinson, Harold L. *A Demographic Look at Tomorrow.* Washington, D.C.: Institute for Education Leadership, 1992.

Hossler, D. *Enrollment Management: An Integrated Approach.* New York: College Entrance Examination Board, 1984.

Houle, Cyril O. *Governing Boards: Their Nature and Nurture.* San Francisco: Jossey-Bass, 1989.

Hughes, K. Scott. "Transforming Academic Institutions: Colleges and Universities Respond to Change in Society." *NACUBO Business Officer* 29, no. 2 (1995): 21–28.

Institute for Research on Higher Education at the University of Pennsylvania. "Leaving Hats at the Door: Themes from the Pew Campus Roundtables." *Change* 28, no. 3 (1996): 51–52.

Jackson, Thomas H. "The Complicated Balance between Teaching and Research at Universities" (excerpt). *Policy Perspectives* 4, no. 4 (1993): 1B–2B.

Kaplan, William A. *The Law of Higher Education: A Comprehensive Guide to Legal Implications of Administrative Decision Making.* 2d ed. San Francisco: Jossey-Bass, 1985.

———. "Law on the Campus, 1960–85: Years of Growth and Challenge." *Journal of College and University Law* 12, no. 3 (1985): 269–99.

Kaplan, William A., and Barbara A. Lee. *The Law of Higher Education: A Comprehensive Guide to Legal Implications of Administrative Decision Making.* 3d ed. San Francisco: Jossey-Bass, 1995.

Katz, Joseph, and Mildred Henry. *Turning Professors into Teachers: A New Approach to Faculty Development and Student Learning.* American Council on Education Series on Higher Education, 2d ed. Phoenix: Oryx Press, 1993.

Kauffman, Joseph F. "Governing Boards." In *Higher Learning in America: 1980–2000,* edited by Arthur Levine. Baltimore: Johns Hopkins University Press, 1983.

Keller, George. *Academic Strategy: The Management Revolution in American Higher Education.* Baltimore: Johns Hopkins University Press, 1983.

Kendall, Jane. *Combining Service and Learning.* Raleigh, N.C.: National Society for Experiential Education, 1990.

Kennedy, Donald. "Making Choices in the Research University." *Daedalus* 122 (1993): 127–56.

Kerr, Clark, and Marian L. Gade. *The Guardians: Boards of Trustees of American Colleges and Universities.* Washington, D.C.: Association of Governing Boards of Universities and Colleges, 1989.

Knapper, Christopher. "Large Classes and Learning." In *Teaching Large Classes Well,* 5–15. New Directions for Teaching and Learning, ed. Maryellen Gleason Weimer, no. 32. San Francisco: Jossey-Bass, 1987.

Kotler, P., and K. Fox. *Strategic Marketing for Educational Institutions.* Englewood Cliffs, N.J.: Prentice Hall, 1985.

Kuh, George D. "Guiding Principles for Creating Seamless Learning Environments for Undergraduates." *Journal of College Student Development* 37, no. 2 (1996): 135–48.

Kuh, George D., and E. J. Whitt. *The Invisible Tapestry: Culture in American Colleges and Universities.* ASHE-ERIC Higher Education Report, no. 1. Washington, D.C.: Association for the Study of Higher Education, 1988.

Layzell, Daniel T., and Jan W. Lyddon. *Budgeting for Higher Education at the State Level: Enigma, Paradox, and Ritual.* ASHE-ERIC Higher Education Report, no. 4. Washington, D.C.: George Washington University, 1990.

Lederman, Douglas. "Survey of Campus Crime Reports." *Chronicle of Higher Education,* January 20, 1993, A32.

Lee, B. A. *Peer Review Confidentiality: Is It Still Possible?* Washington, D.C.: National Association of College and University Attorneys, 1990.

Leung, Mitzi, and Alan S. Dunkl. "The Effects of Managerial Roles on the Relationship between Budgetary Participation and Job Satisfaction." *Accounting and Finance* 32, no. 1 (1992): 1–10.

Levine, Arthur. "Student Expectations of College." *Change* 25, no. 5 (1993): 4.

Levine, Arthur, and associates. *Shaping Higher Education's Future: Demographic Realities and Opportunities, 1990–2000.* San Francisco: Jossey-Bass, 1989.

Liggett, Lee B. "Issues in Higher Education." Paper presented at the first New England Conference on Higher Education Issues, West Barnstable, Mass., September 18, 1987.

———. "Political Speech in the Dormitory." Paper presented at the annual conference of the National Association of College and University Attorneys, Cincinnati, Ohio, June 1984.

———. "Recommended Procedures for Classifying and Adjudicating Cases Involving Student Academic Dishonesty." Paper presented at the National Association of College and University Attorneys Continuing Legal Education Conference, Washington, D.C., March 1984.

"Lilly Fellows Program in Humanities and the Arts." *Cresset* 59, no. 6 (1996): 42–43.

Litten, L. H. *Ivy Bound: High-Ability Students and College Choice.* New York: College Entrance Examination Board, 1991.

Long, Nicholas T. "May Video Cassettes Be Shown in Dormitory Lounges without Violating Standard License Agreements or the Copyright Laws?" Paper presented at the National Association of College and University Attorneys Continuing Legal Education Conference, Washington, D.C., February 28–March 1, 1986.

———. "Troubled and Aggrieved Students." Paper presented at the annual conference of the National Association of College and University Attorneys, New York, N.Y., June 1982.

Lovett, Clara M. "Breaking through Academic Gridlock." *Chronicle of Higher Education*, April 7, 1995, B1–B2.

Lyle, Edwin L. "Should the Dean Teach?" *Liberal Education* 44 (1963): 379–83.

Mahoney, Richard J. "Chair of the Department of Junkyard Dog: Can Business Redesign Work for the University?" *Business/Higher Education Forum*, February 11, 1994.

Marchese, Theodore. "The Chief Academic Officer: An Interview with Richard J. Miller." *AAHE* (American Association for Higher Education] *Bulletin* 41, no. 6 (1989): 3–6.

Martin, James, James E. Samels, and associates. *Merging Colleges for Mutual Growth: A New Strategy for Academic Managers.* Baltimore: Johns Hopkins University Press, 1994.

Massy, William F., and Andrea K. Wilger. "Improving Productivity: What Faculty Think about It—And Its Effect on Quality." *Change* 27, no. 4 (1995): 10–20.

Massy, William F., Andrea K. Wilger, and Carol Colbeck. "Overcoming 'Hollowed' Collegiality." *Change* 26, no. 4 (1994): 11–20.

McCarthy Jane E., ed. *Resolving Conflict in Higher Education.* New Directions for Higher Education, no. 32. San Francisco: Jossey-Bass, 1980.

McCorkle, Chester O., Jr., and Sandra O. Archibald. *Management and Leadership in Higher Education.* San Francisco: Jossey-Bass, 1982.

McGinnis, F. A. "The Dean and His Duties." *Journal of Higher Education* 4 (1933): 191–96.

Milner, Clyde A. *The Dean of the Small College.* Boston: Christopher Publishing House, 1936.

Mortimer, Kenneth P., and Annette C. Caruse. "The Process of Academic Governance and the Painful Choices of the 1980's." In *Leadership Roles of Chief Aca-*

demic Officers, edited by David G. Brown, 43–47. New Directions for Higher Education, no. 47. San Francisco: Jossey-Bass, 1984.

Mouton, Jane, and Robert Blake. *Synergogy: A New Strategy for Education, Training, and Development.* San Francisco: Jossey-Bass, 1984.

Murphy, Raymond O. "Academic and Student Affairs in Partnership for Freshman Success." In *The Freshman Experience*, edited by John Gardner, 375–88. San Francisco: Jossey-Bass, 1989.

National Association of College and University Attorneys. *Am I Liable? Faculty, Staff, and Institutional Liability in the College and University Setting.* Washington, D.C.: National Association of College and University Attorneys, 1989.

National Association of College and University Business Officers. *Financial Accounting and Reporting Manual for Higher Education.* Washington, D.C.: National Association of College and University Business Officers, 1990.

National Commission on Responsibilities for Financing Postsecondary Education. *Making College Affordable Again, Final Report.* Washington, D.C.: National Commission on Responsibilities for Financing Postsecondary Education, 1993.

Neff, Jeanne. "The New American College." Unpublished position paper developed for "The New American College" study group, August 21, 1992.

Orlikoff, James E. "Trustee Orientation: The Basic Building Block of Board Effectiveness." *Trustee* (1992): 12–13, 22.

Palmer, Parker. *To Know as We Are Known.* New York: Harper and Row, 1983.

Pelikan, Jaroslav. *The Idea of the University: A Reexamination.* New Haven: Yale University Press, 1992.

Perkins, J. A., ed. *The University as an Organization.* New York: McGraw-Hill, 1973.

Pew Higher Education Research Program. "A Call to Meeting." *Policy Perspectives* 6, no. 4 (1993): 1A–12A.

———. "Keeping the Promise." *Policy Perspectives* 4, no. 4 (1992): 1A–8A.

Pew Higher Education Roundtable. "A Calling to Account." *Policy Perspectives* 6, no. 2 (1995): 1A–12A.

———. "Cross Currents." *Policy Perspectives* 5, no. 4 (1995): 1A–12A.

———. "Double Agent." *Policy Perspectives* 6, no. 3 (1996): 1A–12A.

———. "The Lattice and the Ratchet." *Policy Perspectives* 2, no. 4 (1990): 5–8.

———. "To Dance with Change." *Policy Perspectives* 5, no. 3 (1994): 1A–12A.

———. "Twice Imagined." *Policy Perspectives* 6, no. 1 (1995): 1A–12A.

———. "An Uncertain Terrain." *Policy Perspectives* 5, no. 2 (1993): 1A–12A.

Plante, Patricia, and Robert L. Caret. *Myths and Realities of Academic Administration.* New York: American Council on Education and Macmillan, 1990.

Plater, William M. "The Future of Tenure: Rotten with Perfection." Paper presented at the annual meeting of the American Conference of Academic Deans, Washington, D.C., January 13, 1996.

———. "Future Work: Faculty Time in the 21st Century." *Change* 27, no. 3 (1995): 223–33.

"Price of Higher Education Becomes Even Dearer." *New York Times*, September 28, 1994, B8.

Reidhaar, Donald L. "The Assault on the Citadel: Reflections on a Quarter Century of Change in the Relationships between the Student and the University." *Journal of College and University Law* 12 (1985): 343–61.

Rice, R. Eugene. "Making a Place for the New American Scholar." Draft of a discussion paper, American Association for Higher Education Conference on Faculty Roles and Rewards, Atlanta, Ga., January 20, 1992.

Richardson, Richard C., Jr. "Six Ways Universities Can Maintain Quality and Diversity." *Education Digest* 56, no. 5 (1991): 22–25.

Richardson, Richard C., Jr., and Elizabeth Fisk Skinner. *Achieving Quality and Diversity: Universities in a Multicultural Society.* New York: American Council on Education and Macmillan, 1991.

———. "Adapting to Diversity: Organizational Influences on Student Achievement." *Journal of Higher Education* 61, no. 5 (1990): 485–511.

Rosovsky, Henry. *The University: An Owner's Manual.* New York: W. W. Norton, 1990.

"Sacred Landmarks of Cleveland." Special issue of the *Gamut*, February 1991.

Samels, James E. "The Emergence of Proactive University Counsel in the 1990s." *Journal for Higher Education Management* 5, no. 1 (1989): 45–52.

———. "Higher Education Graduates to Preventive Law after Some Resistance." *Preventive Law Reporter* (June 1989).

———. "Legal Audits for Preventive Law Practitioners." Paper presented at a meeting of the Massachusetts Bar Association Business Law Section, Preventive Law Committee, Waltham, Mass., December 14, 1988.

———. "Managing Survival in Higher Education." Paper presented at the sixteenth national assembly of the American Association of University Administrators, Toronto, Ontario, Canada, June 29, 1987.

Samels, James E., and Carol E. Wolff. "Preventive Legal Planning." Paper presented at the annual conference of the American Association of Community and Junior Colleges, Orlando, Fla., April 1986.

Samels, James E., Carol E. Wolff, and Joyce A. Kirby. "The Impact of Federal and State Regulatory Review." Paper presented at the twenty-fifth annual conference of the National Association of College and University Attorneys, Vancouver, B.C., Canada, June 18–25, 1985.

Sanders, Claire. "Search for V-C's Head on a Plate." *Times Higher Education Supplement* [London, England], September 3, 1993, 7.

Scannell, J. J. *The Effect of Financial Aid Policies on Admission and Enrollment.* New York: College Entrance Examination Board, 1992.

Scott, Janny. "Journeys from Ivory Tower: Public Intellectual Is Reborn." *New York Times*, August 9, 1994, 1, B4.

Smith, Daryl G. *The Challenge of Diversity: Involvement or Alienation in the Academy?* ASHE-ERIC Higher Education Report, no. 5. Washington, D.C.: George Washington University, 1989.

Stedry, A. C. "Budgetary Control: A Behavioral Approach." Sloan School of Management Working Paper, no. 43-64. Boston: M.I.T., 1964. Reprinted in M. Alexis and C. J. Wilson, *Organizational Decision Making*, Englewood Cliffs: N.J.: Prentice Hall, 1967, 403–16.

———. *Budget Control and Cost Behavior.* Englewood Cliffs, N.J.: Prentice Hall, 1960.

Taylor, Barbara E. *Working Effectively with Trustees: Building Cooperative Campus*

Leadership. ASHE-ERIC Higher Education Reports, no. 2. Washington, D.C.: Association for the Study of Higher Education, 1987.

Tead, Ordway. *The Art of Administration*. New York: McGraw-Hill, 1951.

Technology and Restructuring Roundtable. *Leveraged Learning: Technology's Role in Restructuring Higher Education*. Stanford, Calif.: Stanford [University] Forum for Higher Education Futures, 1995.

Teitel, Lee. *The Advisory Committee Advantage: Creating an Effective Strategy for Programmatic Improvement*. ASHE-ERIC Higher Education Report, no. 1. Washington, D.C.: George Washington University, 1994.

Thompson, Larry R. "Defining the Roles of the University Attorney." Paper presented at the annual conference of the National Association of College and University Attorneys, Cincinnati, Ohio, June 1984.

———. "Individual and Institutional Liability under Section 1983 for Conduct of Campus Police." Paper presented at the Stetson/National Association of College and University Attorneys Workshop, Clearwater Beach, Fla., 1986.

———. "Section 1983 and the Eleventh Amendment." Paper presented at the annual conference of the National Association of College and University Attorneys, Baltimore, Md., June 1986.

———. "Terminating the At Will Employee—A University Employer's Dilemma." Paper presented at the Stetson/National Association of College and University Attorneys Workshop, Clearwater Beach, Fla., 1985.

Tierney, W. G. "Organizational Culture in Higher Education: Defining the Essentials." *Journal of Higher Education* 59, no. 1 (1988).

Tinto, V. *Leaving College: Rethinking the Causes and Cures of Student Attrition*. Chicago: University of Chicago Press, 1987.

Townsend, Barbara K., and Michael D. Wiese. "The Higher Education Doctorate as a Passport to Higher Education Administration." In *Administration as a Profession*, 5–13. New Directions for Higher Education, ed. Jonathan D. Fife and Lester Goodchild, no. 76. San Francisco: Jossey-Bass, 1991.

Tucker, Allan, and Robert A. Bryan. *The Academic Dean: Dove, Dragon, Diplomat*. 2d ed. New York: American Council on Education and Macmillan, 1991.

Twigg, Carol A. "The Need for a National Learning Infrastructure." *EDUCOM Review* 29, no. 5 (1994): 16–20.

Uchitelle, Louis. "The Rise of the Losing Class." *New York Times*, November 20, 1994, final edition, sec. 4, p. 1, col. 1.

Vaughan, George B. *Pathway to the Presidency: Community College Deans of Instruction*. Washington, D.C.: Community College Press, 1990.

Walker, Donald. *The Effective Administrator: A Practical Approach to Problem Solving, Decision Making, and Campus Leadership*. San Francisco: Jossey-Bass, 1979.

Weeks, Kent B. "Are Private Institutions Still Private?" Paper presented at the twenty-fifth annual conference of the National Association of College and University Attorneys, Vancouver, B.C., Canada, June 18–25, 1985.

———. *Complying with Federal Law: A Reference Manual for College Decision Makers*. Nashville, Tenn.: College Legal Information, 1995.

———. "Emotionally and Psychologically Disturbed Students and Withdrawal Policies." *CLD* 13 (1983): 337.

———. "The Legal Audit." *Lex Collegii* 4, no. 3 (1981).

————. *The Legal Inventory for Independent Colleges and Universities*. Macon, Ga.: Center for Constitutional Studies, Mercer University Press, 1981.

————. "Religion and Higher Education." Paper presented at the annual conference of the National Association of College and University Attorneys, New York, N.Y., June 1982.

Weeks, Kent M., ed., and Mark G. Yudof, ed. of rev. eds. *Legal Deskbook for Independent Colleges and Universities*. Macon, Ga.: Center for Constitutional Studies, Mercer University Press, 1988.

Weimer, Maryellen Gleason. *Teaching Large Classes Well*. New Directions for Teaching and Learning, no. 32. San Francisco: Jossey-Bass, 1987.

Western Interstate Commission for Higher Education. *Reports on Higher Education in the West*. Boulder, Colo.: Western Interstate Commission for Higher Education, 1994.

Whalen, Edward L. *Responsibility Center Budgeting*. Bloomington: Indiana University Press, 1991.

Wilson, Robin. "Professional Peons." *Crosstalk* [Publication of the California Higher Education Policy Center] 2, no. 3 (1994): 10.

Winston, Gordon. "The Decline in Undergraduate Teaching." *Change* 26, no. 5 (1994): 8–15.

Wit, Hans de, ed. *A Comparative Study of Australia, Canada, Europe, and the United States of America*. Amsterdam: European Association for International Education in cooperation with IMHE-OECD and the Association of International Education Administrators, 1995.

Witt, John A. *Building a Better Hospital Board*. Ann Arbor, Mich.: Health Administration Press and the Foundation of the American College of Healthcare Executives, 1987.

Wolotkiewicz, Rita J. *College Administrator's Handbook*. Boston: Allyn and Bacon, 1980.

Woodburne, Lloyd S. *Principles of College and University Administration*. Stanford, Calif.: Stanford University Press, 1958.

Yoshino, Michael Y., and U. Srinivasa Rangan. *Strategic Alliances: An Entrepreneurial Approach to Globalization*. Cambridge: Harvard Business School Press, 1995.

Zemsky, R., and P. Oedel. *The Structure of College Choice*. New York: College Entrance Examination Board, 1983.

Contributors

JAMES MARTIN is the vice president for academic affairs at Mount Ida College in Newton Centre, Massachusetts. He holds a M.Div. and a Ph.D. in English literature, religion, and theology from Boston University, and he is an ordained United Methodist minister. Martin has held fellowships from the National Endowment for the Arts, the National Endowment for the Humanities, and in 1989–90, was in residence at the University of London on a Fulbright Fellowship to research university mergers in England, Ireland, and Wales. In 1989, he and James E. Samels founded the Samels Group, a higher education consulting firm. Martin and Samels authored *Merging Colleges for Mutual Growth: A New Strategy for Academic Managers* (Johns Hopkins University Press, 1994). With Samels, he co-hosts a monthly television program, "Future Shock in Higher Education," on emerging trends in the management of colleges and universities on the Massachusetts Corporation for Educational Telecommunications (MCET) satellite learning network and writes a monthly column, "Higher Ed 101," for the *Boston Business Journal*. He has published numerous articles on higher education management and strategic planning in such journals as the *Chronicle of Higher Education*, *London Times*, *Washington Post*, *Planning for Higher Education*, and *Trusteeship*. He also teaches a course in higher education administration at the Boston College Graduate School of Education.

JAMES E. SAMELS is president of the Samels Group, a higher education consulting firm specializing in long-range academic planning, campus site location/relocation, strategic alliances, enrollment stabilization, degree elevation, and academic program diversification. He has extensive experience in the design and implementation of affiliations and joint ven-

231

tures between institutions of higher education, other nonprofit organizations, and business corporations. He is also the founding partner of Samels Associates, a law firm serving public and private colleges, universities, foundations, educational corporations, nonprofit, and proprietary organizations within and outside Massachusetts. He is a recognized expert in the fields of higher education law, strategic institutional legal planning, government regulations, licensure, and accreditation. Samels has served on the faculties of the University of Massachusetts, Bentley College School of Professional Studies, and the Institute for Educational Management at the Harvard University Graduate School of Education. Prior to his appointment at the University of Massachusetts, he served as the acting and deputy state comptroller in Massachusetts, general counsel special assistant attorney general to the Massachusetts Community College System, and general counsel to the Massachusetts Board of Regents of Higher Education. He holds a master's degree in public administration, a juris doctor degree, and a doctor of education degree. He has published a number of scholarly articles and practical monographs, and he has consulted with and presented research papers at universities, colleges, schools, and ministries of education in the United Kingdom, Sweden, and France.

ROY A. AUSTENSEN is provost and vice president for academic affairs at Valparaiso University. From 1995 to 1997 he also served Valparaiso University as acting chief financial officer. Prior to assuming his present position, he was associate vice president for instruction and dean of undergraduate studies at Illinois State University, where he was a member of the faculty for more than twenty years. He received a Ph.D. in history from the University of Illinois at Urbana-Champaign in 1969 and was a Fulbright Fellow at the University of Vienna. He has held grants and fellowships from the National Endowment for the Humanities, the American Council of Learned Societies, and the United States Department of Education. He has received awards from the German Studies Association and the Conference Group for Central European History for publications in the field of European history. At Illinois State, he received the Outstanding Teaching in the University Award in 1986.

MICHAEL A. BAER is provost and senior vice president of academic affairs at Northeastern University. He also holds an appointment as professor of political science. Prior to 1990, he served as dean of the College of Arts and Sciences, professor of political science, and professor in the Martin School of Public Administration at the University of Kentucky, where he chaired the Department of Political Science from 1977 to 1981. Baer recently completed a term as chair of the executive council of the Inter-University Consortium for Political and Social Research at the University of Michigan, an organization of more than 350 institutions of higher education that archives and disseminates social science data. He has also served as president of the Council of Colleges of Arts and Sciences and as chair of the Commission of the Arts and Sciences of the National Association of State Universities and Land Grant Colleges. Baer has served on the executive council of the Midwest Political Science Association, the board of the British Politics Group, and on several committees of the Southern Political Science Association. Baer earned his M.A. and Ph.D. from the University of Oregon. His major areas of research include interest groups, state and local government, and research methods. He is the co-author of *Lobbying: Interaction and Influence in American State Legislatures* and he recently co-edited *Political Science in America: Oral Histories of a Discipline.* He has consulted with a number of organizations on educational programs, public policy, and the broadcasting of political events, and was instrumental in the establishment of the University of Kentucky's Survey Research Center.

JAMES R. COFFMAN is provost and professor of clinical science at Kansas State University. He has served as a faculty member at the University of Missouri-Columbia and Kansas State University, where he chaired the Department of Clinical Sciences and directed the Veterinary Teaching Hospital. He was dean of the College of Veterinary Medicine before becoming provost. As chief academic officer at Kansas State, his interests include developing new methods of leveraging faculty time and talent, rethinking the academic reward system so that outstanding research *and* teaching are recognized and rewarded, and rethinking general education in order to create a system that provides students with methods and techniques of learning, as well as an understanding of how knowledge grows and changes so that they can be lifelong learners. He has been instrumental in improving shared governance and developing new approaches to planning and the allocation of resources at Kansas State. He has written more than one hundred scientific papers and has served as an editorial board member or as editor of five major journals.

MARK G. EDELSTEIN is president of Diablo Valley College in California. He served for five years as vice president for academic affairs at the College of the Redwoods. From 1987 to 1991, he was the executive director of the Intersegmental Coordinating Council, an organization established by the leaders of California's five educational systems in order to improve coordination among the schools, colleges, and universities of the state and to facilitate the smooth progress of students through the educational systems. Before assuming the duties of executive director, he served two terms as president of the Academic Senate for the California Community Colleges and also served as chair of the Intersegmental Committee of the three academic senates (UC, CSU, and CCC). From 1985 to 1990, Edelstein was extensively involved in the review of the California community colleges and of the state's Master Plan for Higher Education. He has also participated in numerous intersegmental efforts to strengthen the transfer function and to improve the success of under-represented students at all educational levels. He earned his doctorate in English at the State University of New York at Stony Brook and is co-author of a textbook entitled *Inside Writing*.

MICHAEL C. GALLAGHER is president of Mesa State College in Grand Junction, Colorado. He began his career in education at Del Mar College, Corpus Christi, Texas, and has served as director of the Small Business Institute at Southwest Texas State University, as chairman of the Department of Management at the University of Arkansas–Little Rock, and as dean of business and interim chancellor of the University of Houston-Victoria. In 1987, he moved to Idaho State University as dean of the College of Business and in 1989 became vice president for academic affairs at ISU. In addition to spending seven years as a chief academic officer, Gallagher has served on a number of local, regional, and two national governing boards and has held office in a number of professional and civic organizations. He received the M.B.A. and Ph.D. degrees from Texas A&M University. He is the author of two books and more than forty articles and scholarly publications principally in the areas of business management and finance.

ALICE BOURKE HAYES is the president of the University of San Diego. She came to San Diego after serving six years as executive vice president and provost and professor of biology at Saint Louis University. A native of Chicago, she spent twenty-seven years at Loyola University of Chicago, where she served as vice president for academic affairs (1987–89), associate academic vice president (1980–87), dean for the natural sciences (1977–80), and chairperson of the Department of Natural Science (1969–77). She is a member of the boards of trustees of the Pulitzer Publishing Company, the Old Globe Theater, Independent Colleges of Southern California, the San Diego Historical Society, and Catholic Charities. She has been a member of the National Aeronautics and Space Administration's Space Biology Program. Hayes has received awards for leadership and service from the National Multiple Sclerosis Society and the Holocaust Memorial Foundation, among others. A biologist with a Ph.D. in biological sciences from Northwestern University, where she was a National Science Foundation Fellow, she has published numerous books and articles on the natural sciences and on Catholic higher education. She has been awarded a doctor of science, *honoris causa*, by Loyola University of Chicago (1994) and a doctor of humane letters, *honoris causa*, by Fontbonne College (1994).

RUTH LARIMER is dean of the Graduate School of Language and Educational Linguistics and professor at the Monterey Institute of International Studies. Her areas of classroom specialization are teaching methodology, curriculum design, and development of authentic materials. She has worked in several school districts as a resource teacher and consultant and has been a member of the editorial board of *TESOL Quarterly*. Her current research interest is the application of discourse analysis to the development of authentic materials for the classroom. Her master's degree is from the University of California, Los Angeles, and her doctorate is from the University of California, Berkeley. She is the co-author of *Beyond the Classroom*, an intermediate English as a Second Language text, and a listening series, *Real Conversations*.

GEORGIA E. LESH-LAURIE is interim chancellor of the University of Colorado at Denver. Previously, she served as vice chancellor for academic and student affairs on the Denver campus, and prior to that as interim provost and vice president for academic affairs and dean of graduate studies and research at Cleveland State University. She has also been national secretary for the American Society of Zoologists Division of Developmental and Cell Biology, and acted as a reviewer for the Howard Hughes Medical Institute and numerous journals and granting agencies. Lesh-Laurie is a member of Phi Beta Kappa, a fellow of the American Association for the Advancement of Science, a life member of the Corporation for the Bermuda Biological Station for Research. She received her M.S. from the University of Wisconsin and her Ph.D. from Case Western Reserve University; she also received the Carl Wittle Award for Outstanding Undergraduate Teaching from Case Western Reserve University.

PAULA HOOPER MAYHEW is vice president for academic affairs, dean of the faculty, and professor of English at Marymount Manhattan College, where she has led a major restructuring of the curriculum to ensure that it is, and remains, multicultural and woman-focused. She served as the director of the office of New Research on Women at Bryn Mawr College before becoming an academic dean at Empire State University in the State University of New York in 1984. As associate director of the Middle States Commission on Higher Education (1987–92), she had special responsibility for private college and university accreditation within the region and directed services to international programs in member institutions. She helped to revise many of the protocols then used for Middle States accreditation, chaired the group that created "Frameworks for Outcomes Assessment," and wrote and lectured about issues in higher education extensively in this country and abroad. Mayhew received her Ph.D. in English literature from Princeton University; in 1995, she was a Fulbright scholar in the International Education Associates Program in Japan, where she studied the role of women in Japanese higher education. A member of the board of trustees of St. Joseph's College, New York, she also serves on the editorial board of the journal in adult education, *Ocotillo*.

PETER A. STACE is vice president for enrollment at Fordham University in New York. He is responsible for the offices of admissions, institutional research, and financial aid, and he chairs the University Council on Undergraduate Enrollment composed of the university president, selected vice presidents, undergraduate deans, and program directors. Previously, he was vice provost for enrollment management at Northeastern University in Boston where he chaired the strategic planning task force on enrollment and the steering committee for reengineering student administrative services. Stace has served as dean of admission and enrollment planning at Ithaca College in New York. At Syracuse University, he was assistant dean in the College of Arts and Sciences, taught economics in the Maxwell School of Citizenship and Public Affairs, and developed the Lawrinson Hall Living Learning Center. He specializes in using quantitative techniques to focus institutional resources and achieve significant gains in retention, recruitment, quality profile, and net tuition revenue. He is an experienced leader in institutional strategic planning, reengineering of student administrative services, the functional design of student information systems, and building a team approach to managing enrollment.

JON M. STROLLE is associate provost and professor at the Monterey Institute of International Studies. His areas of expertise are language policy, federal language issues, rhetoric of negotiation, and education policy. He is on the executive committee of the Association of International Education Administrators and frequently serves as a consultant to national projects on language and international studies. He has taught at Indiana University and Middlebury College; he was an education policy fellow in the office of the Secretary of the United States Department of Education and a Mellon Fellow at the National Language Center in Washington, D.C. His master's and doctoral degrees are from the University of Wisconsin. He has published studies on the relationship of language and international studies to business and global trade.

Index

Library of Congress Cataloging-in-Publication Data

Martin, James
    First among equals : the role of the chief academic officer /
James Martin, James E. Samels, and associates.
        p.   cm.
Includes bibliographical references and index.
ISBN 0-8018-5612-4 (alk. paper)
1. Deans (Education)—United States.   2. Universities and
colleges—United States—Administration.   I. Samels, James E.
II. Title
LB2341.M2894   1997
378.1'11—dc21   97-11281   CIP

Printed in the United States
30516LVS00010B/75

9 780801 866739